Advanced ECDL

Module 6: Presentation

PAYNE-GALLWAY

Published by Payne-Gallway Publishers Limited
Payne-Gallway is an imprint of Harcourt Education Ltd
Halley Court, Jordan Hill, Oxford, OX2 8EJ

Tel: 01865 888070
Fax: 01865 314029

E-mail: orders@payne-gallway.co.uk
Web: www.payne-gallway.co.uk

Text © Matthew Strawbridge, 2006
First published 2007

09 08 07
10 9 8 7 6 5 4 3 2 1

British Library Cataloguing in Publication Data is available
from the British Library on request

10-digit ISBN: 1 904467 91 1
13-digit ISBN: 978 1 904467 91 5

Designed by Direction Marketing and Communication Ltd

Typeset by Textech India Ltd.

Printed by Scotprint Ltd

Acknowledgements
Microsoft product screen shots reprinted with permission
from Microsoft Corporation.

'Adobe' and 'Photoshop Elements' are either registered
trademarks or trademarks of Adobe Systems Incorporated
in the United States and/or other countries.

Blast FM logo design by gotlogos.com

Binary neutron stars animation provided by NASA.

Music files provided by freeplaymusic.com

The author would like to thank Jon Parish and Richard
Knowles for their invaluable comments on the first draft of
this book.

Ordering Information

You can order from:

Payne-Gallway, FREEPOST (OF1771),
PO Box 381, Oxford OX2 8BR
Tel: 01865 888070
Fax: 01865 314029
E-mail: orders@payne-gallway.co.uk
Web: www.payne-gallway.co.uk

European Computer Driving Licence, ECDL, International
Computer Driving Licence, ICDL, e-Citizen and related logos
are trade marks of The European Computer Driving Licence
Foundation Limited ("ECDL-F") in Ireland and other countries.

Harcourt is an entity independent of ECDL-F and is not
associated with ECDL-F in any manner. This courseware
publication may be used to assist candidates to prepare
for ECDL tests. Neither ECDL-F nor Harcourt Education
warrants that the use of this courseware publication will
ensure passing of ECDL tests. This courseware publication
has been independently reviewed and approved by
ECDL-F as complying with the following standard:

*Technical compliance with the learning objectives of
Advanced Syllabus Version 1.0.*

Confirmation of this approval can be obtained by reviewing
the Courseware Section of the website www.ecdl.com

The material contained in this courseware publication has
not been reviewed for technical accuracy and does not
guarantee that candidates will pass ECDL tests. Any and
all assessment items and/or performance-based exercises
contained in this courseware publication relate solely to this
publication and do not constitute or imply certification by
ECDL-F in respect of ECDL tests or any other ECDL-F test.

For details on sitting ECDL tests and other ECDL-F tests
in your country, please contact your country's National
ECDL/ICDL designated Licensee or visit ECDL-F's web
site at www.ecdl.com.

Candidates using this courseware publication must be
registered with the National Licensee, before undertaking
ECDL tests. Without a valid registration, ECDL tests
cannot be undertaken and no ECDL certificate, nor any
other form of recognition, can be given to a candidate.
Registration should be undertaken with your country's
National ECDL/ICDL designated Licensee at any
Approved ECDL Test Centre.

ECDL Advanced Syllabus version 1.0 is the official
syllabus of the ECDL certification programme at the date
of approval of this courseware publication.

Contents

Introduction

Who is this book for?

This book is suitable for anyone studying for **ECDL Advanced Module 6: Presentations**, whether at school, in an adult class or at home. Students are expected to have a level of knowledge of **Microsoft PowerPoint** equivalent to the basic-level ECDL Presentation module.

The approach

The approach is very much one of 'learning by doing'. Students are guided step by step through creating real presentations, with numerous screenshots showing exactly what should appear on the screen at each stage.

Syllabus topics are introduced naturally whenever they are needed during the development of the presentations. This helps to demonstrate **why**, as well as **how**, to use these advanced features. Each of these chapters ends with a **Test yourself** section, which contains exercises that consolidate the skills learnt in that chapter.

Software used

For this module you will be using **Microsoft PowerPoint**, one of many presentation packages. **PowerPoint 2003** has been used in this book, but you should still be able to follow the steps (with a little common sense) if you are using a different version.

Chapter 4 requires **Photoshop Elements** but, again, you should be able to follow the instructions using alternative graphics-editing software if you prefer. Similarly, Chapter 8 requires **Microsoft Word** and **Microsoft Excel**, but only a very basic level of competence is required.

If you are learning with other people, you may find it useful to have a pair of **headphones** to plug into your PC when working through the last part of the book (Chapter 6 onwards).

Extra resources

The exercises have been designed so that you do not need to load documents from a CD or the Internet – you create the documents as you go along. However, there are some media files that you will need to download from the publisher's website: www.payne-gallway.co.uk. This site also contains lots of other useful supporting material.

About this book

As well as the main text, you will find useful information in shaded boxes throughout this book. Two types of information are presented in this way. The first references the ECDL topic that is being covered.

SYLLABUS

Ref: AM6.x.x.x
Boxes like this show which topic from the ECDL syllabus you are covering.

The second, more general, box is home to occasional tips, notes and warnings. These provide extra information (for example, about why PowerPoint does something a certain way), and you should make sure you read them all.

TIP

Tips, notes and warnings appear in boxes like this one. Make sure you read these – they are usually important.

You will also find two types of list:

This is an **information list** item.

This is an **action list** item. You should perform the actions given in every action list item you come to. It is a good idea to read the whole action before starting to do it, because long actions often contain hints that clarify what you should be doing.

Make sure you save the files you create somewhere safe – you will usually need them again in later chapters (you can also download them from the publisher's website – www.payne-gallway.co.uk/ecdl).

1 Getting your message across

Introduction

This chapter considers some of the 'soft skills' that you will need to master in order to create and deliver effective presentations. There are no practical steps for you to work through in PowerPoint, but the information you learn here is important and is likely to form part of the exam.

In this chapter, you will

- learn how to adapt your presentation's design and delivery to suit the **environment**

- think about how to tailor your presentations to suit the **demographics** of your audience

- learn about the importance of **graphical presentation** in helping you to get your message across

- find out why you should always **keep it simple, stupid**!

- learn how your use of **colour** can affect people's moods, or simply distract them from your message

- consider a sample **presentation structure**

- learn how to tailor your content to the time available and adjust your **pace** to suit the needs of your audience.

Environment

SYLLABUS

Ref: AM6.1.1.1
Understand how audience size, room size, room lighting impacts on planning of a presentation such as: need for a microphone, need for a projector, need to adjust contrast between background and data for legibility.

Audience and room size

The environment in which you are to make a presentation should affect how you prepare that presentation. If you use the same design and presentation techniques irrespective of the environment, you may not be able to put your message across as clearly as you would if you gave some thought in advance to the logistics of the presentation.

If you are presenting to only a handful of people, it may be acceptable to run your presentation from a monitor connected to your laptop. If your audience is larger, filling a small room, then you will need to project your presentation on to a large screen. If your audience is larger still, you may need to use a microphone to make yourself audible at the back of the room, although this may strip out some of the character from your voice and make your presentation less personal.

TIP

If you are presenting to a large audience, whether or not you are using a microphone, it is worth asking at the outset whether people at the back of the room can hear you clearly. If they can't, you will need to speak more loudly or turn up the volume of the microphone. Imagine that you are talking to someone just beyond the back wall of the room and project your voice accordingly, even when you are looking at someone in the front row.

TIP

If you find your audience's attention is wandering, a good way to get it back is suddenly to start talking more quietly. Just make sure it's deliberate!

The size of the audience will probably also change the interactive element of your presentation: whereas you might encourage a small audience to chip in with questions as they occur to them, it may be more convenient to ask a larger audience to reserve their questions until the end of the presentation. If you are comfortable taking questions throughout your presentation, this will help to put your audience at ease and let you build up rapport with them. This, in turn, will make them more receptive to your message. Remember, however, that it is *your* presentation – don't let one or two 'experts' in the audience take over with persistent cross-examination.

When someone asks a question, always repeat it out loud to everybody else. This ensures you have heard the question correctly and that everyone can hear the question. It also gives you a little thinking time for your answer.

Finally, remember that some people in a large audience will be a long way from the screen. It is good practice to use large, clear fonts and uncluttered slides in all your presentations, but this is particularly important when presenting to large audiences.

Room layout

There are lots of different types of room layout (see Figure 1.1), and choosing a suitable one can improve dramatically the impact of your presentation.

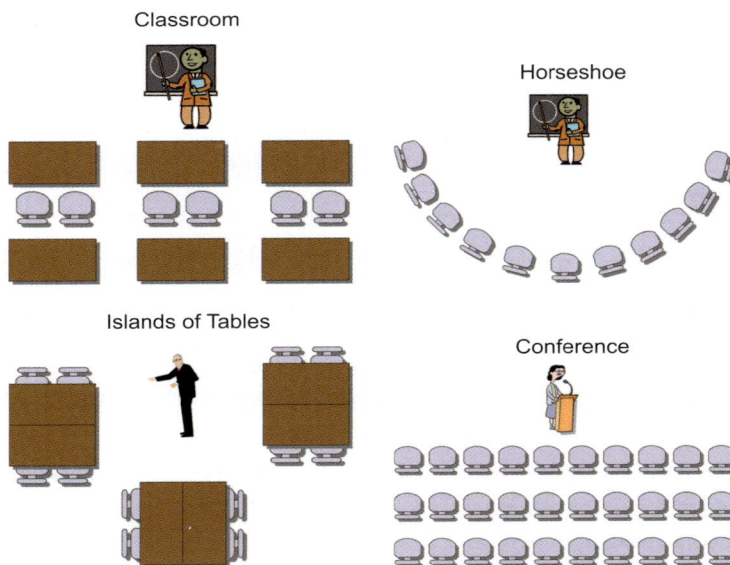

Classroom

Horseshoe

Islands of Tables

Conference

Figure 1.1: Table arrangements

Many rooms, by default, are set up in the **classroom** style, which may have subconscious negative associations for some members of your audience.

A **horseshoe** arrangement is good for groups of up to a dozen. This encourages participation and gives you, as the presenter, room to move around.

For a presentation that includes group activities for the audience (for example, a training course), **islands of tables** may be appropriate. However, this arrangement makes it more difficult for you to regain the audience's attention between their activities.

A **conference** layout is often mandatory when the audience is large.

Lighting

The lighting in the room will also affect how clear your presentation is. This may, however, not be something you can easily check in advance. If you are projecting your presentation, then strong sunlight will tend to brighten the whole of the projected image and will reduce the contrast between the background and the text, making it more difficult to read.

> **TIP**
>
> Use a light background for presentations that will be projected on to a screen and a dark background for presentations that will be viewed onscreen.

You will see later in this chapter (page 12) that PowerPoint's built-in colour schemes have a deliberate high contrast between the background and text colours. If you have created your own colour scheme and find that it is not clear because of the lighting conditions, you can quickly change it to one of the default schemes (see page 20).

Audience

> **SYLLABUS**
>
> **Ref: AM6.1.1.2**
> Understand how audience demography and knowledge of subject impacts on planning of a presentation such as: need to present message differently based on age, educational level, occupation, cultural background, need for elementary explanations or otherwise.

Demographics is just a technical term for population characteristics. The following sections list some of the characteristics audiences may have, and the way these characteristics can affect the design or delivery of your presentation.

Age

Teenagers	May get bored easily.
Young adults	How does your topic match their aspirations?
Middle-aged	May have seen lots of other presentations on this topic.
Senior citizens	Impaired hearing/eyesight likely. Perhaps quite conservative.

Educational level

Moderate education	Use simple terms and logical arguments. Slow pace.
Average	Avoid unnecessary complexity. Medium pace.
Academic	Be prepared for tricky questions. Quicker pace.

Occupation

Manufacturing	May respond better to practical examples rather than theory.
Service industries	How will what you are telling them affect their clients?
Education	May respond well to abstract ideas.
Professions	Well educated. May prefer shorter presentations.

Cultural background

The culture of an audience is their shared experiences that have formed their personalities. As well as the obvious categories of ethnicity, nationality and religion, there are more subtle cultural groupings towards whom you may wish to target your presentation. For example, the employees of a small start-up business will have a different culture from those who have spent years working for a large corporation.

Take particular care when using humour. Jokes are notorious for not travelling well between cultures.

Level of knowledge

It is important that you gauge the level of knowledge the audience have about your topic before you start presenting, because this will help you to judge the pace. Sometimes it is only possible to do this once you start giving the presentation. If an audience is more knowledgeable than you expected, you may be able to skip some of your slides.

The key here is to communicate in broadly the same terms that the audience would use to discuss the subject among themselves; in other words, to **pitch** your presentation at the right level. If you get this wrong, you will notice a sea of bored faces in front of you! If you pitch the presentation at too low a level, you will be telling the audience lots of things they already know, and they will switch off. If you go into too much detail and use **jargon** the audience don't understand, then they, too, will switch off; instead they need explanations of the basic points of the topic.

As a presenter, you have to work very hard to keep people interested in what you have to say! The next section has some practical advice on this topic.

Graphical presentation

SYLLABUS

Ref: AM6.1.2.1
Understand that an audience may learn most from pictures, images, charts. Understand that text in a presentation should support graphical information. Understand the importance of limiting the level of detail in graphical and text information and using a consistent design scheme to enhance clarity.

Words or pictures?

It may be a cliché, but it's true: 'a picture speaks a thousand words.' Your presentations will have no shortage of words, but consider using graphics wherever you can – they grab people's attention better than words and help to break up the words you do use.

People have different styles of learning: some learn best by **hearing**, some by **doing** and some by **seeing**. Your dialogue will accommodate the hearing-learners. If you add some interactive components to your presentation, you will engage the doing-learners. Finally, adding plenty of graphics will get your point across to the seeing-learners.

Figure 1.2 shows some sales figures presented as text. Figure 1.3 shows how much better it is to present this type of information graphically – you can see at a glance that sales have increased

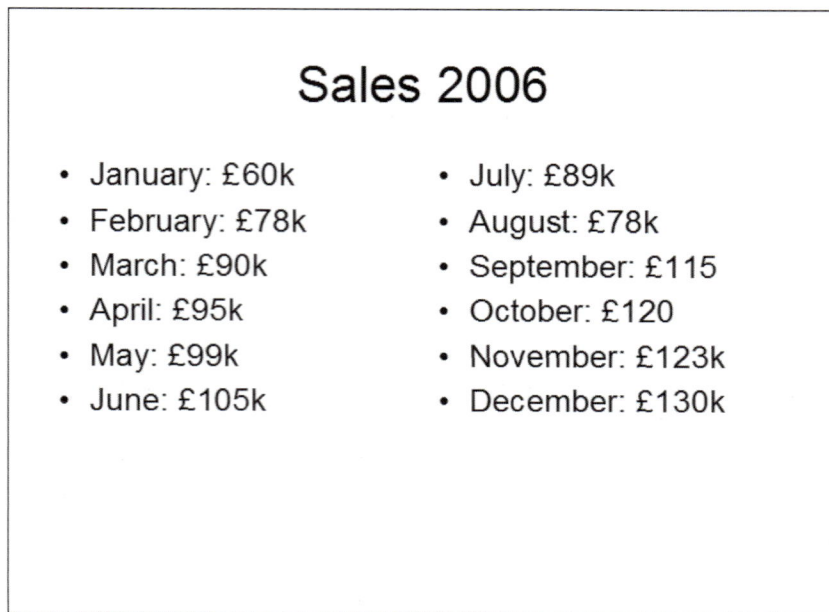

Sales 2006

- January: £60k
- February: £78k
- March: £90k
- April: £95k
- May: £99k
- June: £105k

- July: £89k
- August: £78k
- September: £115
- October: £120
- November: £123k
- December: £130k

Figure 1.2: A text-heavy slide

over the year – apart from poor sales over the summer. If the sales figures were for a company that makes hot-water bottles, then the clip art adds a touch of humour and explains why sales fell off during the summer.

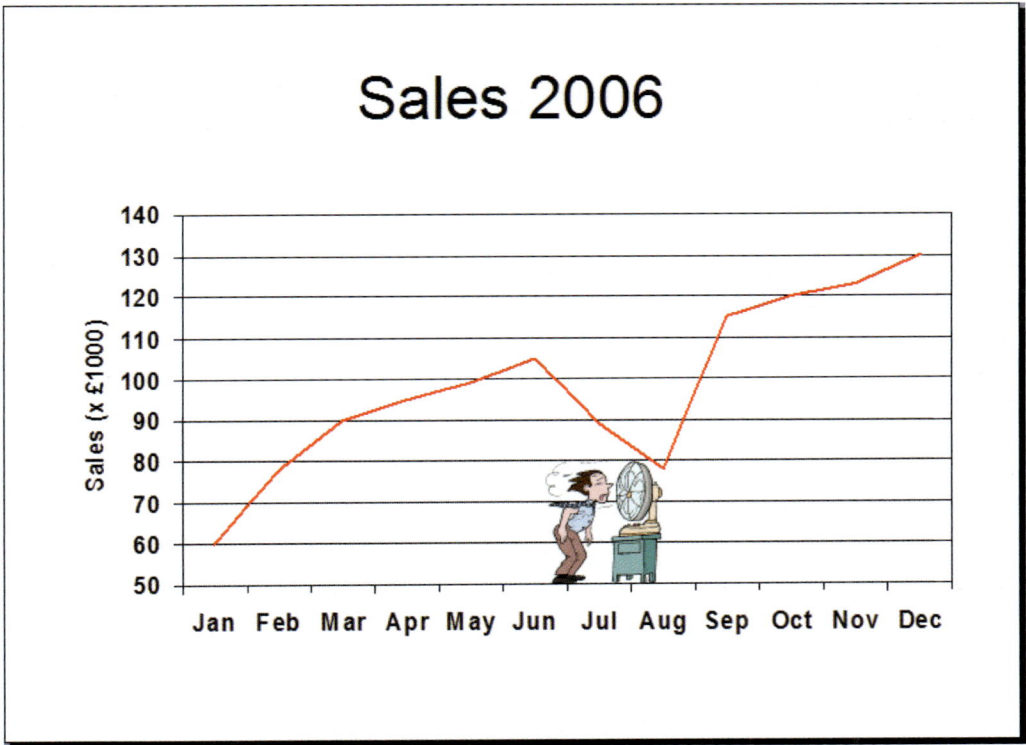

Figure 1.3: The same information presented graphically

If you make your main points using pictures and use text to expand on these central themes only, then you stand the best chance of your presentation sticking in your audience's minds.

Level of detail

There is a well-known design principle called **KISS**, which stands for **Keep It Simple, Stupid**! The idea here is to resist the temptation to make things more complicated than they really need to be. It's a good idea to bear this maxim in mind when designing presentations. If you want people to remember your presentation, keep your points simple and repeat them several times. If you blast your audience with information, they are likely to remember less than if you keep it simple.

TIP

As a rule of thumb, use about five bullet points on each slide. You don't have to write these as complete sentences.

Remember that you understand your subject well, but your audience are playing catch-up. Things that seem plain to you could be complicated or surprising to your audience, who may need time to absorb this information. If you go into too much detail before your audience understand the higher-level concepts, they will not be able to keep up.

TIP

You can still create slides containing detailed content that you think you may be asked about. If you put them at the end of the presentation, after a blank slide, then you can display them if you need to when you are taking questions from the audience.

Consistency of design

Although it's a good idea to use a range of presentation methods – text, charts, cartoons and so on – to get your points across and to keep the audience's attention, make sure that the overall package has a consistent design. For example, avoid mixing different types of chart when illustrating the same type of information, as people may want to compare them.

One useful design technique is to use **breadcrumbs**: components that show the audience where they are in the structure of the presentation. As you might have guessed, these navigation aids are named after the trail left by Hansel and Gretel in the fairy tale. A good way to implement breadcrumbs is to create a slide that lists the main parts of your presentation, and then to repeat that slide as you begin each new part, indicating where you are (see Figure 1.4).

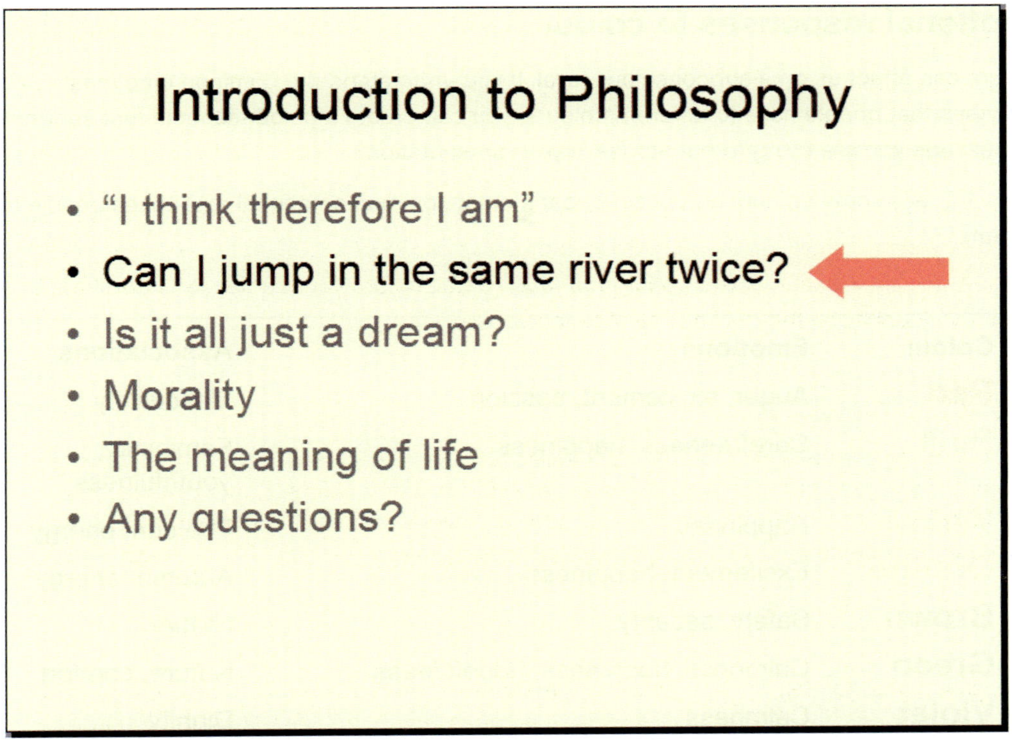

Introduction to Philosophy

- "I think therefore I am"
- Can I jump in the same river twice?
- Is it all just a dream?
- Morality
- The meaning of life
- Any questions?

Figure 1.4: Example of using breadcrumbs to show the audience how far through the presentation you are

Use of colour

SYLLABUS

Ref: AM6.1.2.2
Understand how choice of font colours, number of colours used may elicit different responses from members of an audience such as: varying emotional responses, possible distraction from key points by excess use of colour. Be aware of colour blindness problems.

Emotional responses to colour

Colours can affect us on a subconscious level. If you understand the common emotional responses that people have to different colours, you can create a colour scheme that supports the message you are trying to put across in your presentation.

Figure 1.5 lists some colours and describes the most common emotional responses people have to them.

Colour	Emotions	Associations
Red	Anger, excitement, passion	Masculinity
Pink	Carefreeness, happiness	Femininity, youthfulness
Yellow	Happiness	The sun, energy
Orange	Excitement, happiness	Autumn, energy
Brown	Safety, security	Nature
Green	Calmness, happiness, hopefulness	Nature, comfort
Violet	Calmness	Dignity
Blue	Calmness, tranquillity, security, sadness	Sea, sky
Grey	Sadness, tiredness	Neutrality
White	Emptiness, sadness	Purity, cleanliness
Black	Sadness, seriousness	Death, night

Figure 1.5: Common emotional responses to colours

The term **warmth** is often applied to colours. Red, yellow and orange are warm colours; blue, green and white are cold colours. In general, the warm colours tend to have more positive emotional responses and the cold colours have more negative ones, but there is a lot of overlap.

Throughout this book, you will be using the example of Blast FM, a radio station that is investigating whether to broadcast its music online as well as over the airwaves. Blast FM have deliberately chosen warm reds and oranges for their logo (see Figure 1.6). This gives it a passionate, energetic feel. Compare this with the effect you get by swapping red for blue (Figure 1.7). This alternative logo has the opposite feel – it is cool and sharp.

Figure 1.6: The Blast FM logo

Figure 1.7: The Blast FM logo in blue

11

Colour as a distraction

PowerPoint allows you to set up colour schemes, with a different colour for each of eight components. Figure 1.8 shows the breakdown of the 12 standard colour schemes in PowerPoint, one per column.

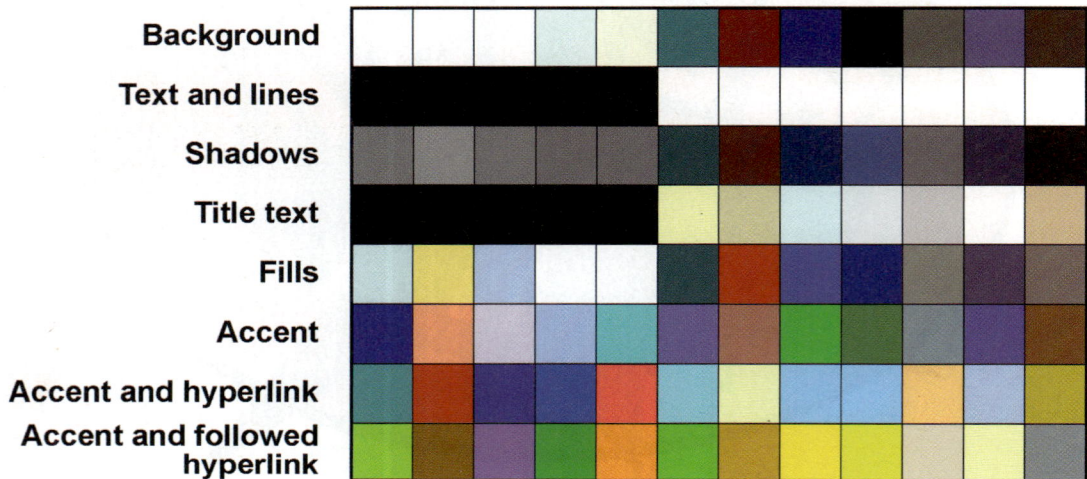

Figure 1.8: Standard colour schemes in PowerPoint

You can pick up some useful tips from these standard colour schemes.

- Use either light backgrounds with black text or dark backgrounds with white text.

- Shadows should either be a shade of grey or a darker version of the background colour.

- You can use a different colour to distinguish the title from the main text. This reinforces the logic of your structure.

- The fill colour should be similar to the background.

- Blue is a good colour for hyperlinks unless you have a particularly warm colour scheme.

The PowerPoint colour schemes are useful because they limit the palette of colours you are tempted to use in a presentation. Using too many colours, or colours that clash, will distract your audience from the message you are trying to put across. Figure 1.9 demonstrates this, and gives some other advice about slide design.

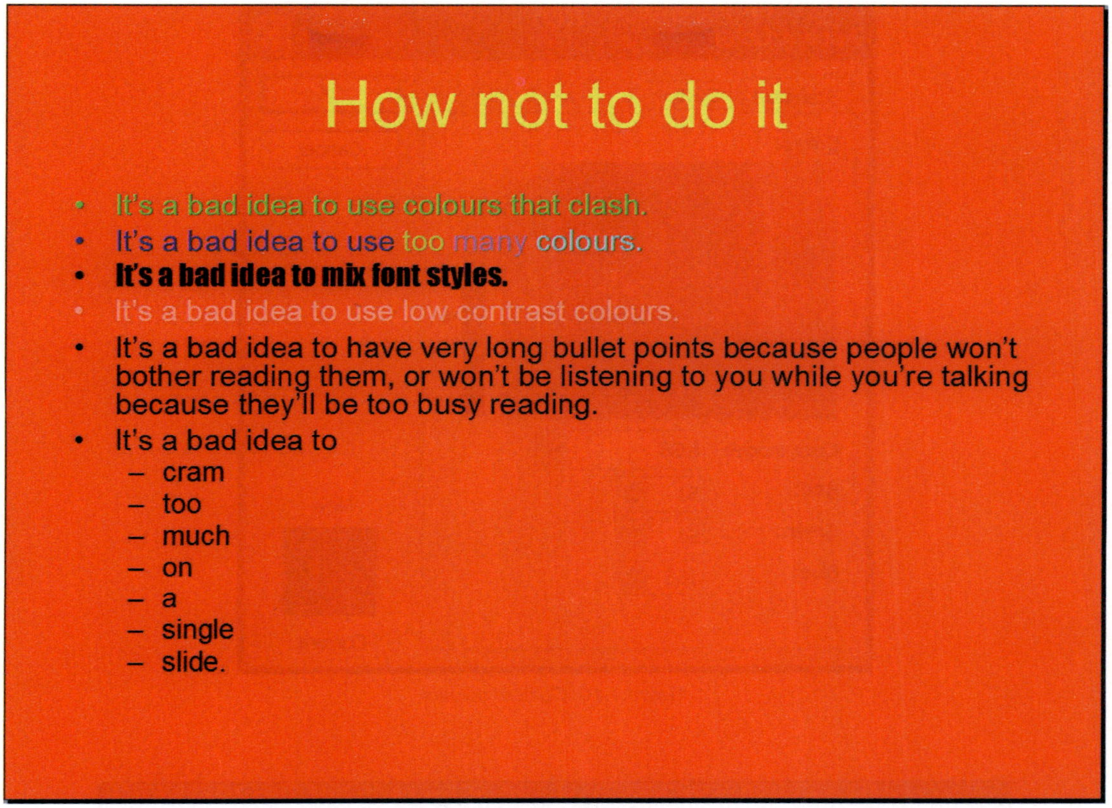

Figure 1.9: How not to do it

Colour blindness

Around one in twelve men and one in twenty women have some form of colour blindness. The most common form of colour blindness is a reduced sensitivity to the colour green; other forms consist of reduced or zero sensitivity to red, green or blue. In very rare cases, people can see only in shades of a single colour.

You can view the **Red**, **Green** and **Blue** components of the colours in your colour scheme using the **Custom** tab in the dialogue box that appears when you change one of the colours (see Figure 1.10). Each of these components is given as a number between 0 and 255. Make sure that you are not using any two colours that differ only in one of the three components. For example, if you have a text colour of pure blue (Red = 0, Green = 0, Blue = 255) and a background of cyan (Red = 0, Green = 255, Blue = 255), as shown in Figure 1.11, then people with reduced sensitivity to the colour green may not be able to read the text.

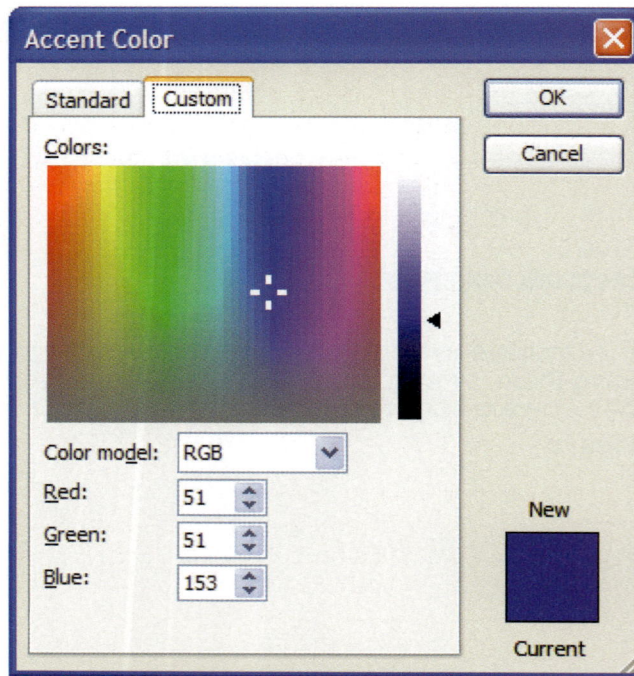

Figure 1.10: Custom colours

Figure 1.11: A poor choice of colour scheme – not everyone will be able to read the text

Planning and design

Structure of the presentation

It is important that you structure your presentations in a logical way. This will help you because there will then be a clear place to put each piece of information, and it will help your audience to understand what you are trying to say.

Here is a possible structure for a presentation, which follows a logical order.

- Presentation **title**, including your name and contact details.

- An **outline** of your presentation (perhaps as a breadcrumb feature).

- The **body** of the presentation. This part will have most of the slides, so it is important that its internal structure is logical too. If you are trying to persuade people, build your case in small, logical steps. If you are simply delivering information, try to arrange it in a sensible order.

- Your **conclusion**. Summarise the main points you have made – what is the minimum information you would like the audience to remember from your presentation?

- A final slide, inviting the audience to ask you **questions**.

- A **blank slide**, marking the end of the presentation.

- Any **detailed slides** that you may wish to display to make specific points during the question-and-answer session, but which you otherwise won't show at all.

You should also use correct spelling and grammar, and make sure that you use grammar consistently. For example, pick a tense – past, present or future – and stick to it throughout. Similarly, you may choose to use **ing** words for all of your bullets, such as **starting a business**, **raising finance** and **marketing** on a slide show about small businesses.

Practising

This book teaches you how to use PowerPoint to create smart and interesting presentation files. However, all your hard work will be wasted if your presentation style is dull and stilted. There is only one remedy: **you must practise**.

> **TIP**
>
> You might even go so far as to record yourself on video or tape, or practise in front of a live audience.

If your presentation is fairly short (say, up to half an hour), run through it as if it were 'live' – in an empty room, preferably the actual venue, talk as if there were people in the room, use gestures and make eye contact with your imaginary audience – **at least** half a dozen times. Over-practising is unlikely to take the edge off your presentation; in fact, you should practise until you are thoroughly bored with the presentation!

If the presentation is longer and you cannot trim it back, then make sure that you rehearse the first twenty minutes. Delivering this well will set the tone for the rest of your presentation.

Time constraints

You may find that you have to give the same presentation many times, and that the time you have to fill is not always the same. One of the advantages of keeping your slides simple is that this gives you much more flexibility in how much you say about each of the points. If you have more time than usual then you can give the audience more background information, being careful to pitch this at the correct level.

> **TIP**
>
> Have you ever attended a presentation or a meeting where the presenter or chairperson says **We've got a lot to get through**? Everyone immediately switches into a negative mood! If you find yourself saying something like this, it shows that you need to be more ruthless in cutting extraneous material from your presentation.

Sometimes the length of the presentation is up to you. In this case, you can tailor your delivery according to the audience's needs, and in particular their attention span. It may be difficult to judge how long the whole presentation will take to deliver, but you should be able to pace yourself slide by slide. If you spend too long on each one, then the audience will get bored; if you move through the slides too quickly, then the audience won't have time to assimilate the information you are giving them.

The longer your presentation is, the harder you will find it to keep your audience's attention. However good your presentation style, and however interesting your topic, you can bet that nobody is sitting there thinking **I could listen to this all day**; there will, however, be people there who didn't really want to hear your presentation in the first place, or who have an important call to make, or who need to go to the toilet. The pleasant surprise people get from a concise, punchy presentation puts them in a receptive frame of mind. This is an example of the KISS principle.

> **TIP**
>
> As a rule of thumb, try to go through about one or two slides per minute of your presentation.

Conclusions

This chapter has demonstrated the following points.

- You should adapt your presentation to take account of the environment (audience and room size, lighting conditions) in which you will deliver it.

- Use a light background for presentations that will be projected on to a screen and a dark background for presentations that will be viewed onscreen.

- Tailor your presentation to suit the demographics (age, education level, occupation, cultural background and level of knowledge) of your audience.

- Present your information graphically whenever possible.

- Keep it simple, stupid!

- You can use breadcrumbs to keep the audience oriented.

- Use a colour scheme that is suitable to the emotional response you want your audience to experience, and avoid distracting them with colour.

- Structure your presentations logically.

- Tailor your content to the time available and adjust your pace to suit the needs of your audience.

Test yourself

1. Name three things you would do differently when presenting to an audience of 100 compared with an audience of 5.

2. Suppose you work for a pharmaceutical company that has just made a major breakthrough. Everyone is interested in this new discovery, and you have been asked to give talks in a local school, at a medical convention and to the local branch of the Women's Institute. How would you tailor your presentation for these three different audiences?

3. Which of the demographic groups discussed in this chapter do you think it is most important to consider when preparing your presentation? Which is the least important?

4. What are the three different ways in which people learn? How can you make sure that your presentations appeal to all three groups of learners?

5. Search the Web for information about **pictograms**. What do these tell you about visual communication?

6. Name two colours associated with energy, two colours associated with nature and two colours associated with calmness.

7. Reduced sensitivity to which colour is the most common form of colour blindness?

2 Designing a presentation template

Introduction

In this chapter, you will go through the process of setting up templates with a **slide master**, **title master** and **colour scheme**. You will then create presentations based on these templates, and will learn how to generate slides from a word-processed outline and how to import slides from other presentations.

In this chapter, you will

- set up the **slide master** and **title master** for a presentation

- customise the **bullet style** used in a presentation

- learn how to **fill a slide's background** with a gradient fill, texture, pattern or picture

- discover how to **omit background graphics** from slides

- create slides based on an **outline** created in Word

- **merge in slides** from another presentation.

Creating a new template

We will start by creating the templates that will form the basis of the presentations that the radio station Blast FM will be making as they move into Internet radio.

SYLLABUS

Ref: AM6.2.1.1
Create and save a new presentation template with features such as: custom background fill effects, logo, spacing between bullet points.

Open PowerPoint. It should start with a new blank presentation, as shown in Figure 2.1.

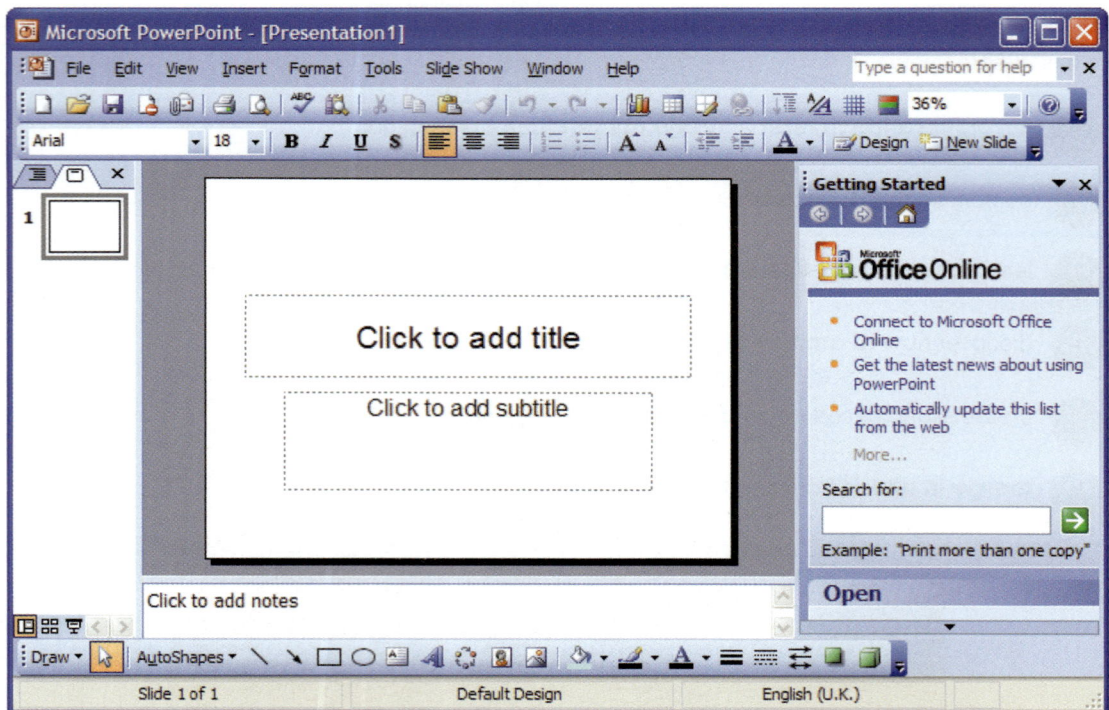

Figure 2.1: PowerPoint with a new blank presentation

First, set the colour scheme. The Blast FM logo has reds and yellows in it, so choose a compatible colour scheme.

From the menu, select **Format**, **Slide Design**. The **Slide Design** task pane appears. Click the **Color Schemes** link to show a list of defined colour schemes. Click the one with the red-brown background, as shown in Figure 2.2.

Your colour scheme previews may be smaller than the one shown in Figure 2.2. You can change between large and small previews by hovering your mouse pointer over any of the previews, clicking the arrow that appears on its right-hand side and selecting **Show Large Previews** from the menu that appears.

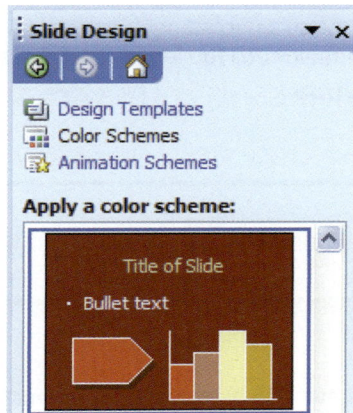

Figure 2.2: Choosing a colour scheme

From the menu, select **View**, **Master**, **Slide Master**. The slide master appears, as shown in Figure 2.3.

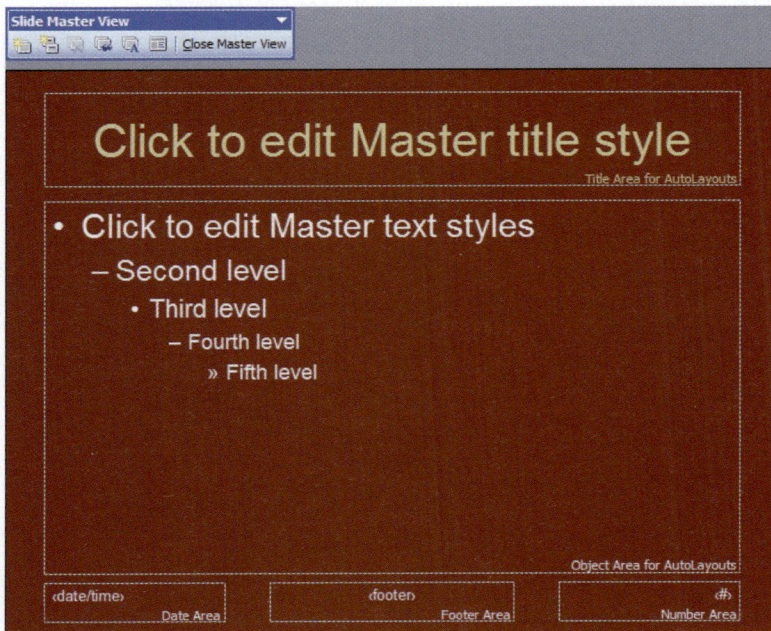

Figure 2.3: The slide master

Adding the Blast FM logo

We want the Blast FM logo on every slide, since this is useful for brand recognition. However, we don't want it to overpower the slide's contents, so make it quite small and put it in the bottom right corner. At the moment, the page number placeholder lives there, so you should rearrange these placeholders to make room for the logo.

Drag the **Date Area** placeholder up to the top right of the slide master.

Move the **Footer Area** placeholder to the left so that it is aligned with the left-hand side of the **Title Area** and **Object Area**.

> **TIP**
>
> You can constrain a move to a single dimension by holding down the **Shift** key while you drag the object.

Center

Move the **Number Area** so that it is horizontally in the middle of the slide master. Click on the **Number Area** and press the **Center** button on the **Formatting** toolbar so that the page number becomes centred within the **Number Area** (you will see the **<#>** move from the right to the centre, as shown in Figure 2.4).

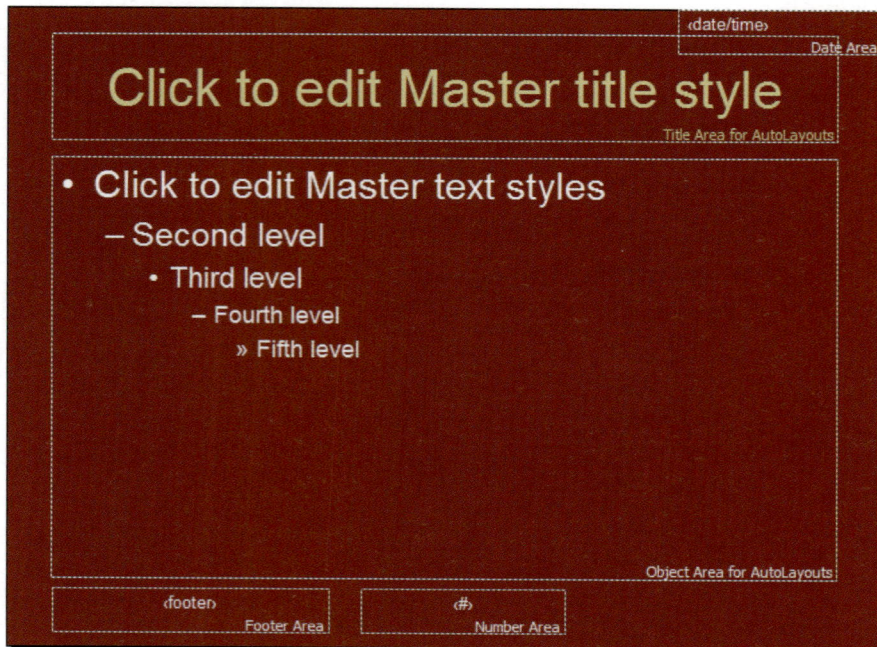

Click to edit Master title style

- Click to edit Master text styles
  - Second level
    - Third level
      - Fourth level
        » Fifth level

‹date/time›
Date Area

Title Area for AutoLayouts

Object Area for AutoLayouts

‹footer›
Footer Area

‹#›
Number Area

Figure 2.4: Moving the placeholders to make room for the logo

You now need the Blast FM logo. You can download this from the publisher's website (http://www.payne-gallway.co.uk/ecdl) if you haven't already done so.

From the menu, select **Insert**, **Picture**, **From File**. The **Insert Picture** dialogue box appears. Navigate to your saved **logo.tif** file and press **Insert**.

Use a corner handle to reduce the image's size, and drag it to the bottom right of the slide master.

Next, get rid of the white border round the logo so that it blends in with the coloured background.

The **Picture** toolbar should be on display because you have a picture selected. If not, you can open it by selecting **View**, **Toolbars**, **Picture** from the main menu. Select the **Set Transparent Color** tool on the **Picture** toolbar and then click in the white border around the edge of the logo. This should become transparent, as shown in Figure 2.5.

Set Transparent Color

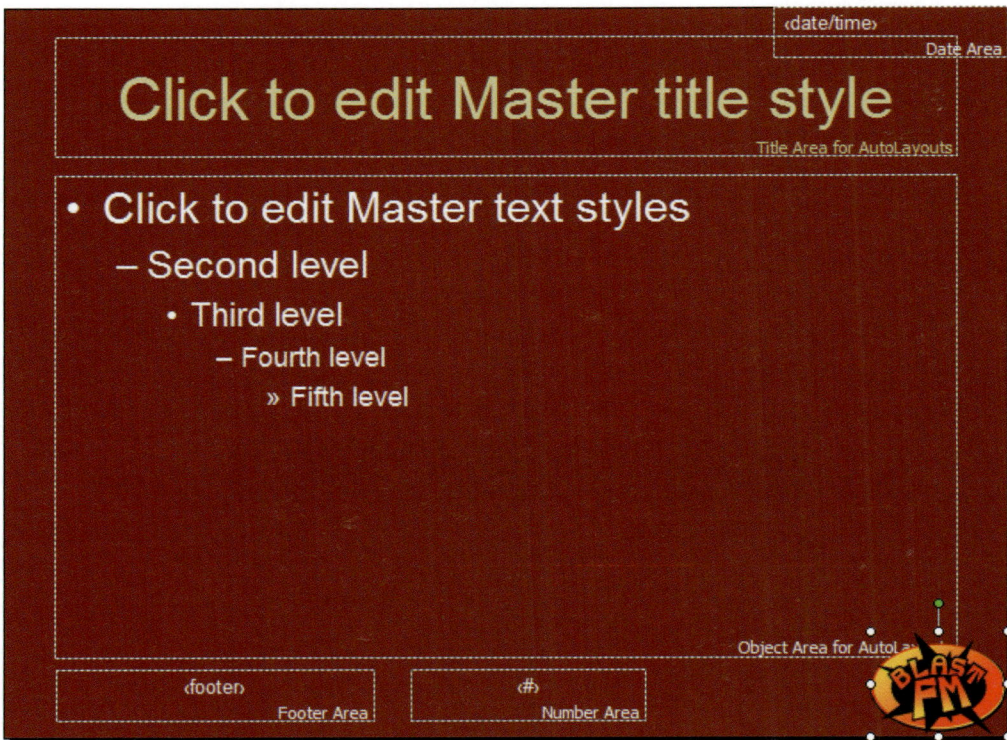

Figure 2.5: The logo in position in the bottom right corner of the slide master

Customising the bullets

Change the bullet style to reflect the dynamic nature of the Blast FM brand.

- Click anywhere in the first bullet point, then, from the menu, select **Format**, **Bullets and Numbering**. The **Bullets and Numbering** dialogue box appears.

- Click on the **Customize** button. The **Symbol** dialogue box appears. Choose the **Wingdings** font from the top drop-down list. Click the **bomb** icon and then press **OK**.

- In the **Bullets and Numbering** dialogue box, set the **Size** to **75% of text**. From the **Color** drop-down list, select the title colour (tan). Press **OK** to confirm the change.

- Repeat these steps for the second-level bullet, choosing the **explosion** symbol from the **Webdings** font.

- Delete the bullets for level three and beyond – you won't be using these.

- Select the second-level bullet and choose **Format**, **Line Spacing** from the menu. The **Line Spacing** dialogue box appears.

The default line settings have **0.2 Lines** before the paragraph and **0 Lines** after it. Change this so that the second-level bullets are displayed slightly closer to their first-level (parent) bullet than they are to the bullet that follows.

- Change the **Before paragraph** setting to **0 Lines** and the **After paragraph** setting to **0.1 Lines**, as shown in Figure 2.6. Press **OK** to make the change.

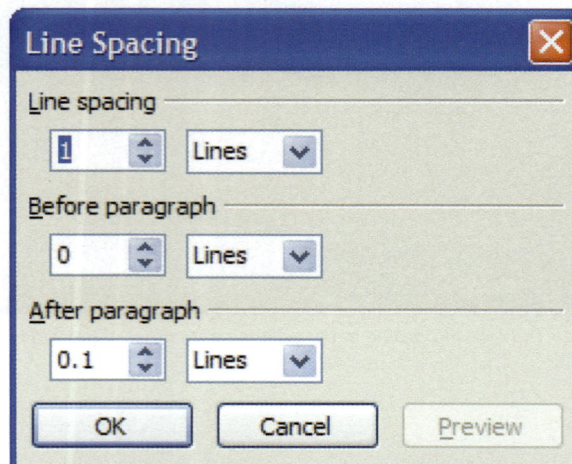

Figure 2.6: Changing the line spacing between bullet points

Your bullets should now look something like Figure 2.7 (some extra entries have been added so that you can see that the second-level bullets are indeed grouped closer to their parent).

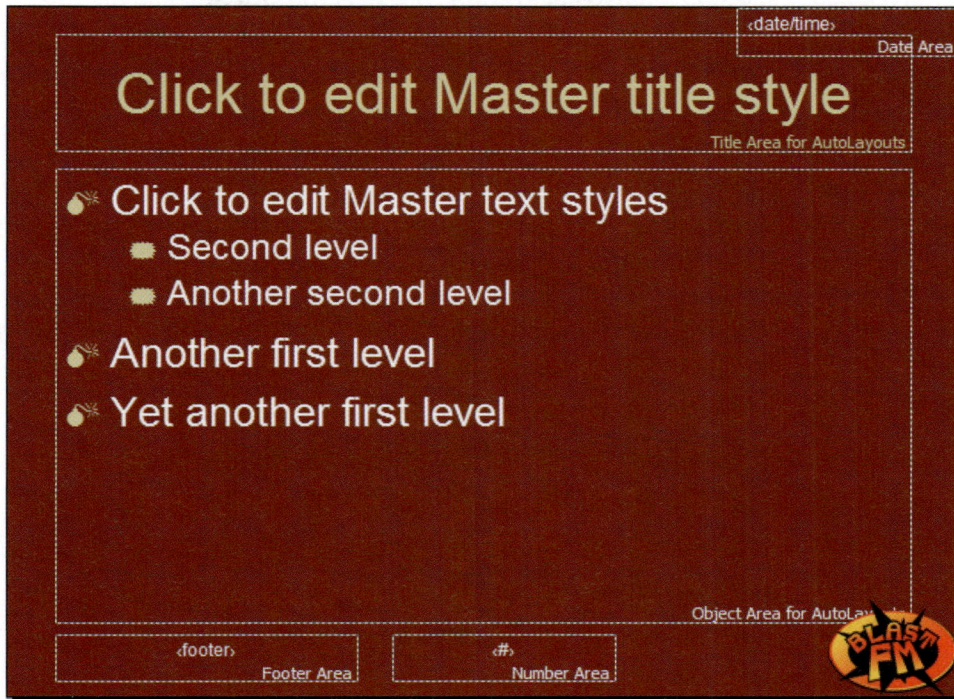

Figure 2.7: Customised bullets

> **TIP**
>
> If you want to adjust the spacing between the bullet symbol and the text, make sure that the ruler is displayed (**View, Ruler**) and drag the indent markers slightly.

Adding a title master

You will also add a title master, which will take over from the template master for the title slides in your presentations (usually at the start of the presentation and at the start of any parts you decide to split the presentation into). You can be a bit more daring with the colour of the title master, since you want these slides to stand out.

From the menu, select **Insert**, **New Title Master**. A new slide appears, picking up its formatting from the slide master.

Notice how the Blast FM logo changes from yellow in the top left to red in the bottom right. You can reflect this in the background of the title master.

➤ From the menu, select **Format**, **Background**. The **Background** dialogue box appears.

➤ Click the arrow to the right of the current background colour and select **Fill Effects** from the menu that appears. The **Fill Effects** dialogue box opens.

➤ Take a quick look at the **Texture**, **Pattern** and **Picture** dialogue boxes. These are fairly self-explanatory. You won't be using them here, but it's handy to know that they're there.

➤ On the **Gradient** tab, select the **Two colors** option (Figure 2.8). Change **Color 1** to a bright yellow and **Color 2** to a bright red. From the list of **Shading styles**, select **Diagonal up**.

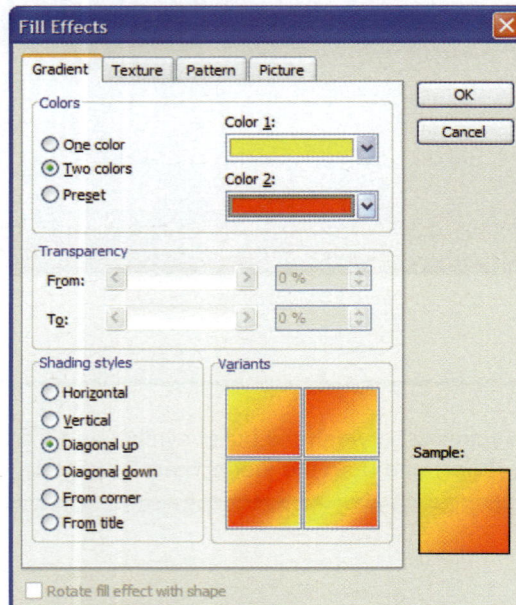

Figure 2.8: Setting a two-colour gradient fill for the background

➤ Press **OK** to close the **Fill Effects** dialogue box.

➤ In the **Background** dialogue box, press **Preview**. This shows what the slide will look like if you choose to make the effect permanent.

This looks OK, but we can do better by using one of PowerPoint's preset fill styles.

➤ Click the arrow to the right of the new graduated fill colour in the **Background** dialogue box, and choose **Fill Effects**. The **Fill Effects** dialogue box appears again.

This time, select **Preset** and then pick **Fire** from the list of **Preset colors**. From the list of **Shading** styles, select **Diagonal up** again.

Press **OK** to close the **Fill Effects** dialogue box. Press **Apply** on the **Background** dialogue box.

The title text doesn't show up very well, so click in it and then use the **Font Color** control on the **Formatting** toolbar to select the shadow colour, as shown in Figure 2.9.

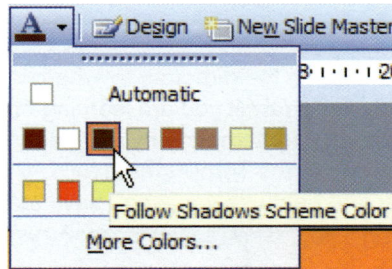

Figure 2.9: Changing the colour of the title text

Your title master should now look like Figure 2.10.

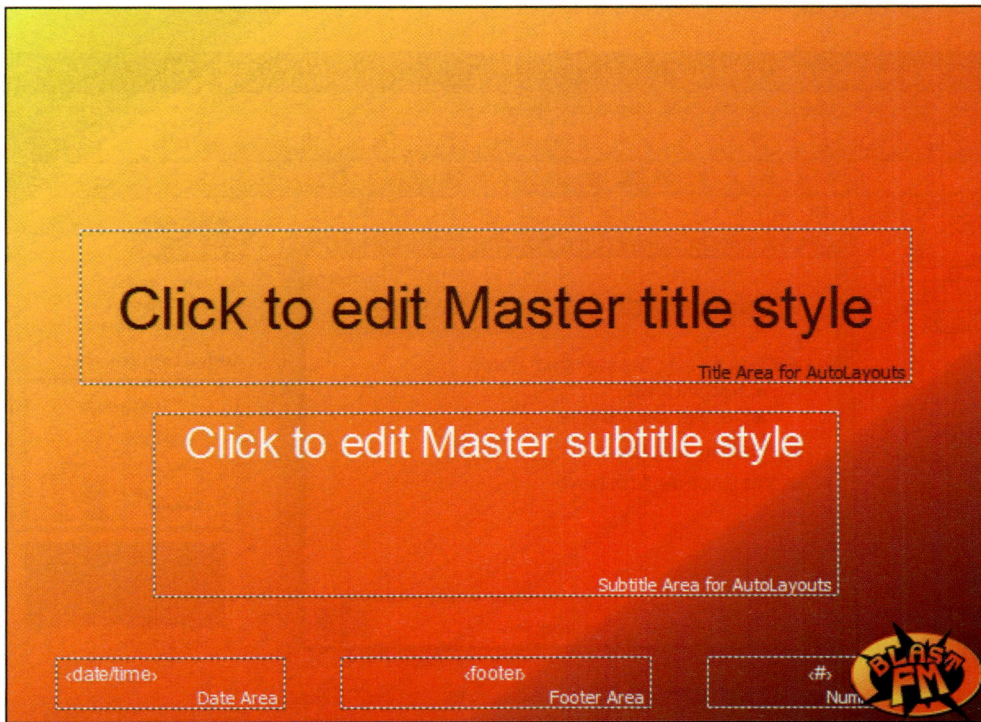

Figure 2.10: Funky design for the title master

Saving the template

Save two copies of this template: the template as it currently stands, and a version with a lighter background suitable for use with a projector.

From the menu, select **File**, **Save As**. The **Save As** dialogue box appears.

Change the **Save as type** drop-down list to **Design Template (*.pot)**. PowerPoint automatically changes to your **Templates** directory.

TIP

At this stage, you may wish to change the directory to wherever you plan to save the rest of your work. This is particularly important if you are learning on a shared computer – you don't want someone else to delete your template by accident or to overwrite it with one of his or her own. However, saving in the **Templates** directory will make it easier to create documents based on the template because you won't have to browse for it each time.

Save the template as **Blast FM.pot**.

Change the colour scheme of your template to the standard scheme with a light yellow background, as shown in Figure 2.11.

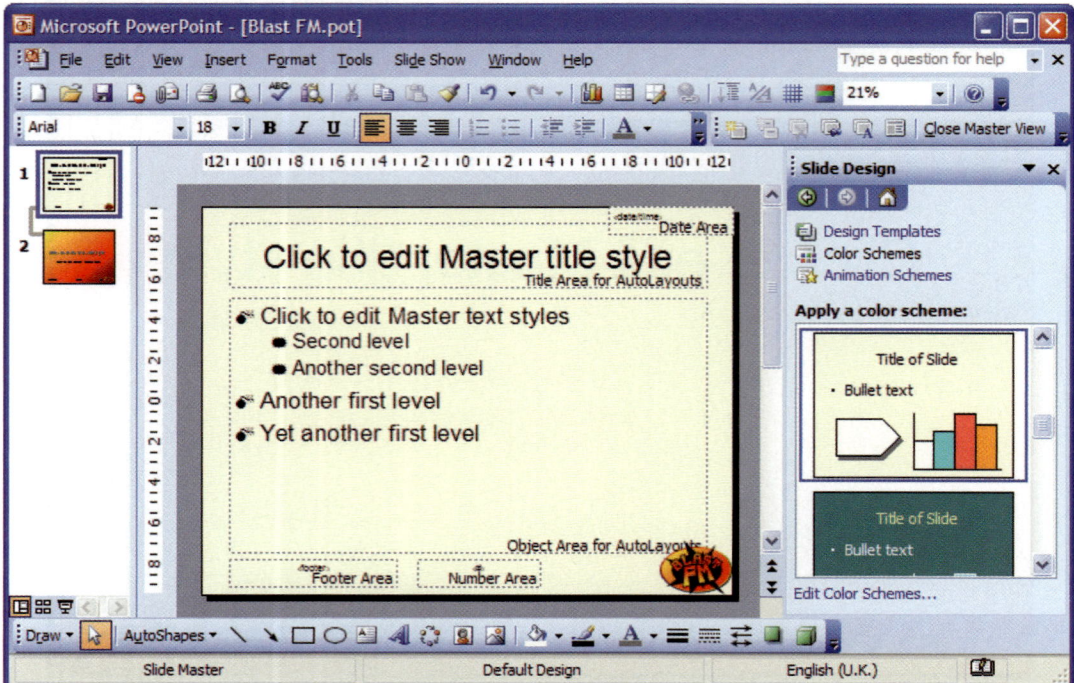

Figure 2.11: Changing the colour scheme

> **Note!**
>
> Changing the colour scheme has not changed our custom background on the title master. You may need to lighten this manually if it turns out that the title slides are difficult to read from a projection screen.

➡ Use **File**, **Save As** to save the modified template as **Blast FM Light.pot** in the same folder as you saved the darker template.

➡ From the menu, select **File**, **Close**.

Merging information into a presentation

Creating a presentation

Shortly, we'll be looking at some ways to merge information into a presentation. Before we can do this, we need a simple presentation containing some information that we may wish to use elsewhere.

Create a few slides that give some background information about Blast FM.

➡ From the menu, select **File**, **New**. Click on the **From design template** link. A blank document appears, using the default template. Click on the **Browse** link at the bottom of the **Slide Design** task pane. The **Apply Design Template** dialogue box appears. Navigate to your **Blast FM.pot** template and press **Apply**.

You should now have a single slide in your presentation, with the title master style (the gradient fill from yellow to red) applied to it.

➡ Change the title to **About Blast FM**. Leave the subtitle as it is – this won't be displayed when you run the presentation.

➡ Create a new slide (see the following tip).

TIP

There are several ways to create a new slide:

• You can right-click anywhere in the slide thumbnails on the left of the PowerPoint window and choose **New Slide** from the menu that appears.

• You can select **Insert**, **New Slide** from the main menu.

• You can use the keyboard shortcut **Ctrl + M**.

Fill in the slide as shown in Figure 2.12.

TIP

To get the dashes, just type a **space** followed by **two hyphens** and then another **space**. PowerPoint will automatically convert the hyphens to a dash after you finish typing the next word.

TIP

You can use **Tab** and **Shift + Tab** to change the level of a bullet when your cursor is on the far left of the bullet text.

Figure 2.12: The history of Blast FM

Create another slide. Choose the title and two bulleted lists layout. Fill in the text shown in Figure 2.13 and then use **AutoShapes** (from the **Drawing** toolbar) to make the slide a bit more interesting.

Figure 2.13: 'Our kind of music' slide

Create two more slides, as shown in Figure 2.14.

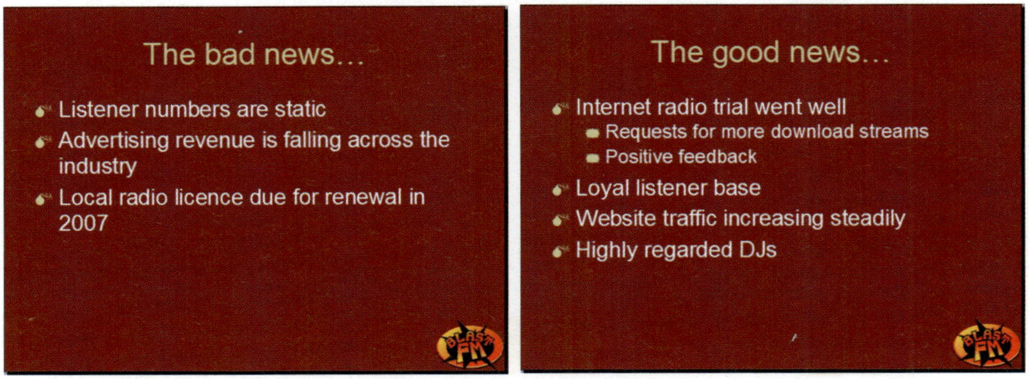

Figure 2.14: There's some bad news and some good news

Create a final slide to use as the first slide in the presentation. This will give you a chance to see how to add a picture fill effect to a slide.

SYLLABUS

Ref: AM6.2.1.4
Apply graduated background fill colours, texture, patterns, picture fill effect to a slide, slides in a presentation.

Create a new slide and drag it up in the list of slides on the left of the PowerPoint window so that it becomes the new first slide.

Select the **Blank** content layout for this slide.

From the menu, select **Format**, **Background**. The **Background** dialogue box appears.

Click on the arrow to the right of the current background colour and then select **Fill Effects** from the menu that appears. The **Fill Effects** dialogue box appears.

Switch to the **Picture** tab and press the **Select Picture** button. Navigate to your **logo.tif** file and add it.

Press **OK** on the **Fill Effects** dialogue box.

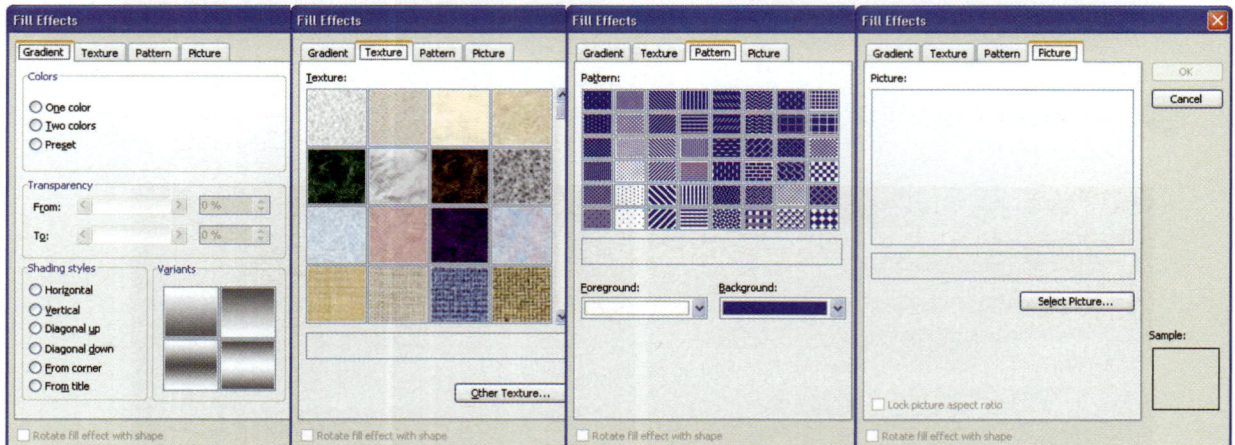

Figure 2.15: The four tabs of the Fill Effects dialogue box

Ref: AM6.3.1.6
Omit background graphics from a slide(s).

➡ In the **Background** dialogue box, tick the **Omit background graphics from master** button. This prevents this slide from inheriting background graphics from the slide master.

➡ Press the **Apply** button (not **Apply to All**).

Your presentation should now look like Figure 2.16.

Figure 2.16: A splash screen to start the presentation

TIP

You've already seen, when preparing the templates, how to apply graduated backgrounds to a slide. You now know how to apply a picture fill effect. To apply a texture or a pattern instead, simply select the one you want from the appropriate tab in the **Fill Effects** dialogue box.

TIP

To apply the new effect to every slide in your presentation, you would press the **Apply to All** button instead of the **Apply** button on the **Background** dialogue box. If you wish to apply a background effect to some slides but not to others, select all the slides you want to change before you apply the new background (hold down the **Ctrl** key and click the slide thumbnails in the area on the left of the PowerPoint window). This technique also allows you to omit the background graphics from your selected slides.

Merging in a word-processed outline

SYLLABUS

Ref: AM6.2.1.3
Merge a word-processed outline into a presentation.

Save your presentation as **About Blast FM.ppt** and then close it.

Note!

¶
Show/Hide ¶

All the Word screenshots in this book assume that you have got the **Show/Hide ¶** button selected on the **Standard** toolbar to show the non-printing characters.

Blast FM needs to raise some money to fund their expansion into Internet radio. Create a presentation they can show to potential investors. Start by creating an outline of the presentation in Word.

Load Microsoft Word. A blank document will be created automatically.

From the menu, select **View**, **Outline**. This switches Word into **Outline** view.

Create the outline shown in Figure 2.17. There are three levels to the outline. Each of the lines at the top level will become a new slide, and the second and third levels will become bullets and nested bullets on those slides. Use the **Promote** and **Demote** buttons on the **Outlining** toolbar to change the levels.

- **Logo slide**
- *** Overview**
- **History**
- **Our kind of music**
- *** Current position**
- **Listener demographics**
    - *20 000 regular listeners*
    - *Listener age*
        - **25% aged under 18**
        - **60% aged 18–29**
        - **15% aged 30 or over**
    - *95% would recommend Blast FM to friends*
- **Advertising**
    - *Add graph here*
- **Listeners**
    - *Add graph here*
- *** Planned development**
- **Internet radio pilot study**
    - *50 live streams*
        - **Minimal advertising so far**
        - **Estimate could have filled 250 at peak times**
    - *98% uptime*
    - *Over 200 requests for more information*
- **Funding requirements**
- **BLANK PAGE**
- **Accounts 2005–2006**
- **Website stats**

Figure 2.17: Outline for a new presentation

Note

The names of the slides that will become title slides have all been started with a * character. This has no meaning in Word or PowerPoint; it is just for convenience.

Save your document as **Investment outline.doc**.

Close your document. (If you try to import a document into PowerPoint when it is still open in Word, you get a rather cryptic error message and the import fails.)

Switch back to PowerPoint (or open PowerPoint again if you closed it).

If you haven't already got a new blank presentation on display, select **File**, **New** from the menu and then click **Blank Presentation** in the task pane.

From the menu, select **Insert**, **Slides from Outline**. The **Insert Outline** dialogue box appears.

Navigate to your saved **Investment outline.doc**, select it and then press the **Insert** button. Lots of new slides are added to your document, based on the outline (you should have 15 in total, including the original blank title page).

Note!

The imported outline slides are created after the currently selected slide; this process does not delete any slides you already have.

TIP

If you want to create a new presentation, instead of merging into an existing one, in Word you can do **File**, **Send To**, **Microsoft Office PowerPoint**.

From the menu, select **Format**, **Slide Design**. The **Slide Design** task pane appears. Select **Browse** from the bottom of this, and choose your saved **Blast FM Light.pot** template. Press **Apply**.

View Slide 7, which is a good example of how the outline plan has been transformed. It should look like Figure 2.18. Compare this with the relevant section of the outline shown in Figure 2.17.

Listener demographics

- *20 000 regular listeners*
- *Listener age*
  - *25% aged under 18*
  - *60% aged 18–29*
  - *15% aged 30 or over*
- *95% would recommend Blast FM to friends*

Figure 2.18: Example of a slide imported from an outline

Right-click the first slide in the **Slides** list on the left-hand side of the PowerPoint window, as shown in Figure 2.19, and select **Delete Slide** from the menu that appears.

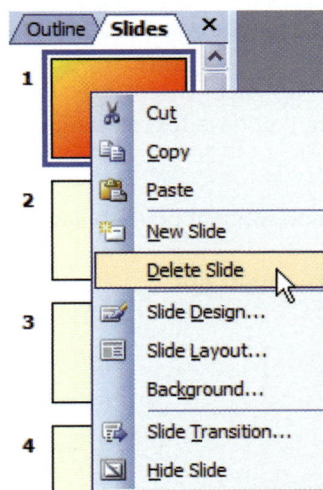

Figure 2.19: Deleting a slide

Move to what is now Slide 2: **Overview**. From the menu, select **Format**, **Slide Layout**. Select the **Title Slide** layout from the task pane. The slide's background should change to orange, as it now gets its style from the title master instead of the slide master. Delete the * character from the title text. Your slide should now look like Figure 2.20.

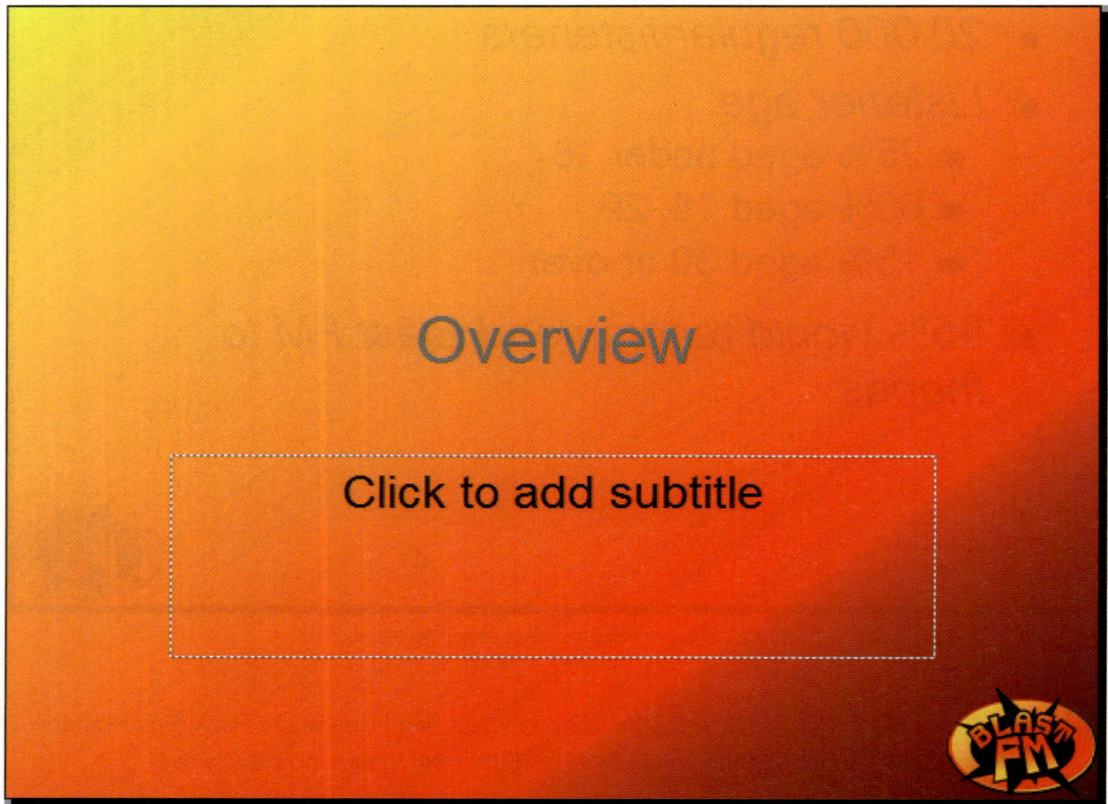

Figure 2.20: Changing a slide to a title slide

Go through all the other slides that have text starting with a * character, changing them to title slides.

We haven't finished yet, but this is a convenient point to save the presentation.

Save the presentation as **Investment.ppt**.

Merging in slides from another presentation

SYLLABUS

Ref: AM6.2.1.2
Merge slides, a complete presentation, with an existing presentation.

You may have noticed that the outline contained references to slides that you already created in the **About Blast FM.ppt** presentation. This was deliberate – you can import these slides to reuse them in the current presentation.

➡ From the menu, select **Insert**, **Slides from Files**. The **Slide Finder** dialogue box appears.

Note!

The **Slide Finder** dialogue box is unusual because it does not stop you from interacting with the rest of PowerPoint.

➡ Press the **Browse** button and find your **About Blast FM.ppt** presentation.

Your **Slide Finder** dialogue box should now look like Figure 2.21.

You can switch to a list view, if you prefer, by clicking here

Figure 2.21: The Slide Finder dialogue box

Start by importing the logo slide.

Select the first slide in the main PowerPoint window. Click once on the first slide in the **Slide Finder** dialogue box – it will get a blue outline to show that it is selected. Make sure that the **Keep source formatting** box is ticked and then press the **Insert** button.

Note!

If you don't tick the **Keep source formatting** box then you'll just get a blank slide. Remember that the Blast FM logo is on the slide's background, so you don't want it to be overridden with the default background of your new presentation. In general, tick **Keep source formatting** when you want to copy formatting information with the slide, and untick it to change the formatting to match the destination.

The new logo appears as a new slide after Slide 1. You can delete the placeholder slide that was created from the outline.

Delete Slide 1 from the presentation so that the imported logo slide becomes the new Slide 1.

Now you can try importing two slides at once.

TIP

In the **Slide Finder** dialogue box, clicking a selected slide deselects it again. You can click as many slides as you want to add them to the selection – you don't need to hold down the **Ctrl** key.

Select Slide 3 (**History**) in the main PowerPoint window. Click on Slide 1 in the **Slide Finder** dialogue box to deselect it. Still in the dialogue box, click on Slide 3 and then on Slide 4. Both these slides should gain blue selection boxes. Untick the box for **Keep source formatting** because you want the imported slides to use the lighter colour scheme. Press **Insert**.

The two imported slides appear as Slides 4 and 5 in the new presentation.

Delete the two placeholder slides either side of these new imported slides.

Press the **Close** button to close the **Slide Finder** dialogue box.

Now make the blank page truly blank. This will indicate the end of the presentation. The pages that come after this will only be displayed if the presenter needs them in order to answer questions from the audience.

- Select Slide 12 (**BLANK PAGE**). Change its **Slide Layout** to **Blank**. Click in the text **BLANK PAGE**, then click on the outline of the rectangle that appears around it (thereby selecting the text area). Press the **Delete** key to delete the text.

- From the menu, select **Format**, **Background**. The **Background** dialogue box appears. Click on the arrow to the right of the current background colour and use **More Colors** to select black. Tick the box for **Omit background graphics from master**. Press **Apply**. The slide changes to pure black.

- Save the file and then try running the slide show. You will fill in more of the pages in later chapters.

Conclusions

This exercise has demonstrated the following points.

- If you edit the bullet styles on the slide master, these styles will apply to all the slides in your presentation. You can change the bullet styles, the line spacing and the gap between the bullets and the text.

- If you create a title master then it will apply to all those slides that have a **Title** layout.

- The menu option **Format**, **Background** allows you to set the background of slides to a gradient fill, texture, pattern or picture. You can choose whether or not to include the background graphics from the master slide.

- You can use **Insert**, **Slides from Outline** to merge in a word-processed outline. PowerPoint will generate a new slide for each level-one heading in the outline, with lower-level headings becoming bullets and nested bullets on the new slides.

- You can use **Insert**, **Slides from Files** to merge in slides from an existing presentation. You can choose to keep the source formatting or to apply the new presentation's standard formatting to the imported slides.

Test yourself

1. Create a PowerPoint template suitable for Smith & Smith Ltd (a company in the building trade), as shown in Figure 2.22. Use a brick design for the background fill and add some suitable clip art (e.g. search for **builder**). Increase the line spacing of the bullets and change the top-level bullets to use a house icon (from the **Webdings** font). Save your template as **Builders.pot**.

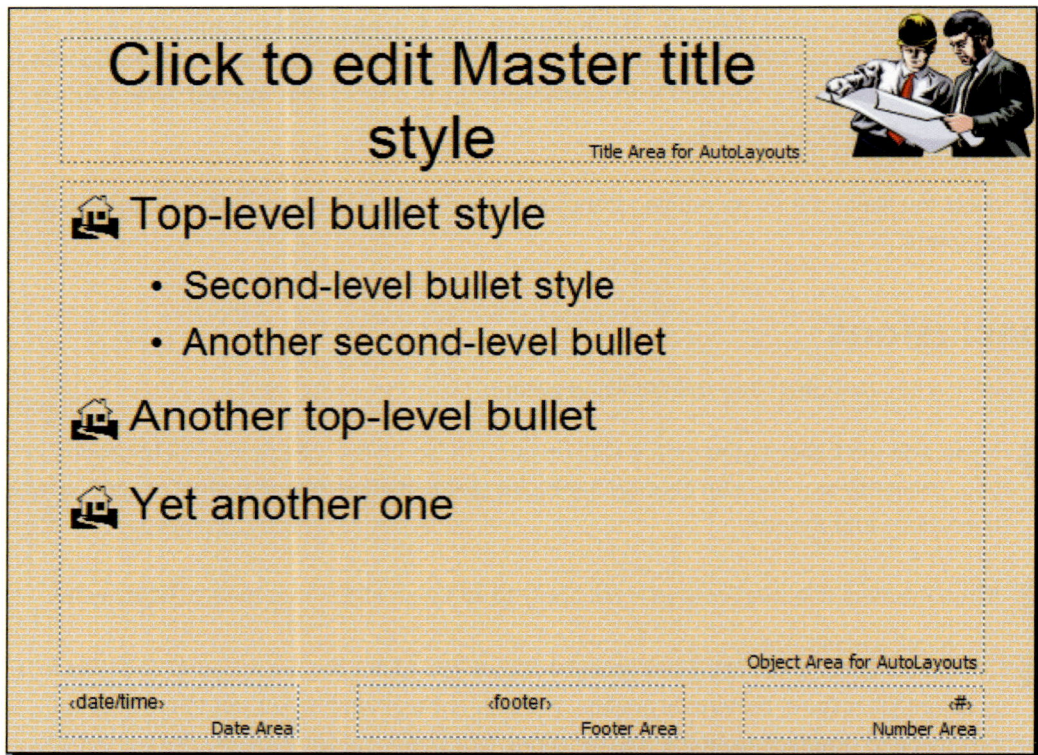

Figure 2.22: Presentation design for a building company

2. Use Word to create the presentation outline shown in Figure 2.23. Save this document as **Smith and Smith.doc**. Use this outline to create a presentation based on the template you created in Exercise 1. Delete any blank slides from your presentation and change the first slide to have a **Title Slide** layout. Omit the background graphic (the clip art) from the first slide. Your presentation should look like Figure 2.24. Save it as **Smith and Smith.ppt**.

- **Smith & Smith Ltd**
- **About us**
  - *Professional*
  - *Reliable*
  - *Good value*
- **Current developments**
  - *King's Road*
    - **3 detached houses**
    - **1 bungalow**
  - *Queen's Avenue*
    - **Converting the manor house into flats**
- **More information**
  - *Call in to our office*
  - *Phone us*
  - *Email us*

Figure 2.23: Overview for a presentation

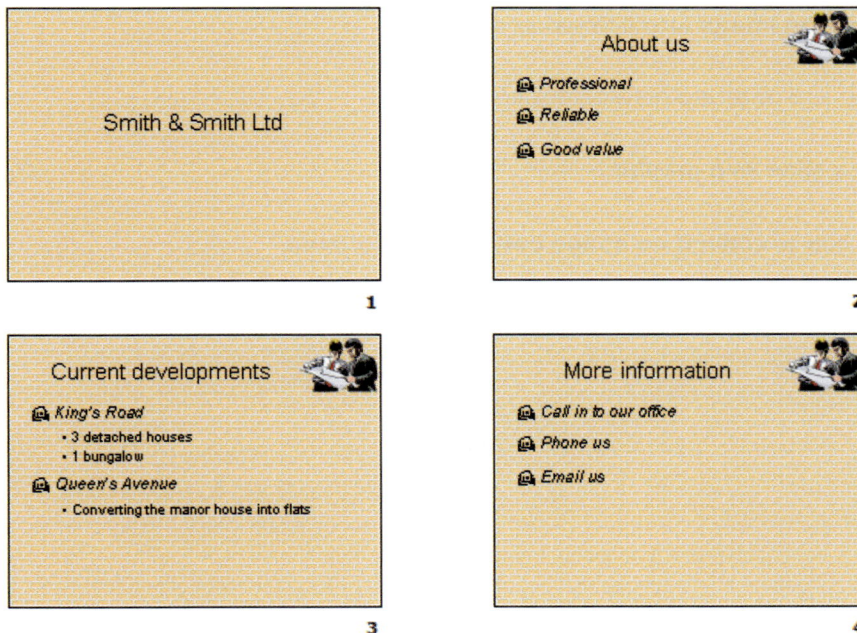

Smith & Smith Ltd

1

About us

🔊 *Professional*

🔊 *Reliable*

🔊 *Good value*

2

Current developments

🔊 *King's Road*
  - 3 detached houses
  - 1 bungalow

🔊 *Queen's Avenue*
  - Converting the manor house into flats

3

More information

🔊 *Call in to our office*

🔊 *Phone us*

🔊 *Email us*

4

Figure 2.24: Slides created from a word-processed outline

3. Import the slide titled **The good news…** from **About Blast FM.ppt** into **Investment.ppt** after the slide **Listeners**. Make sure it doesn't override the **Investment.ppt** colour scheme. Rename this slide **Platform for growth**.

3 Editing images I

Introduction

In this chapter, you will use PowerPoint's built-in drawing tools to create a copy of the Blast FM logo. It won't be an exact match, but it will allow you to explore the different tools that are available to you.

In this chapter, you will

- learn how to apply **advanced fill effects**, such as graduated background colours, textures, patterns and pictures

- use **flip**, **rotate** and **resize** techniques to manipulate drawing objects

- apply **shadow** and **3-D** effects to drawing objects

- **change an image into a drawing object**

- **group** and **ungroup** drawing objects

- **save a slide as a graphic**

- learn how to **convert an image between file formats**.

Recreating the Blast FM logo

In order to test-drive PowerPoint's graphics capabilities, try to recreate the Blast FM logo (Figure 3.1) using PowerPoint's drawing tools.

Figure 3.1: The Blast FM logo

Creating the logo oval

Start by drawing the various ovals that make up the logo's background.

- Open a new blank PowerPoint presentation.

- The presentation will have a single slide. Change its **Layout** to **Blank**.

- If the **Drawing** toolbar isn't displayed, select **View**, **Toolbars**, **Drawing** from the main menu.

- Use the **Oval** tool from the **Drawing** toolbar to draw an oval that completely fills the slide (click on the top left corner and then drag to the bottom right corner). The colour doesn't matter since we're going to change it anyway. Your slide should look something like Figure 3.2.

Oval

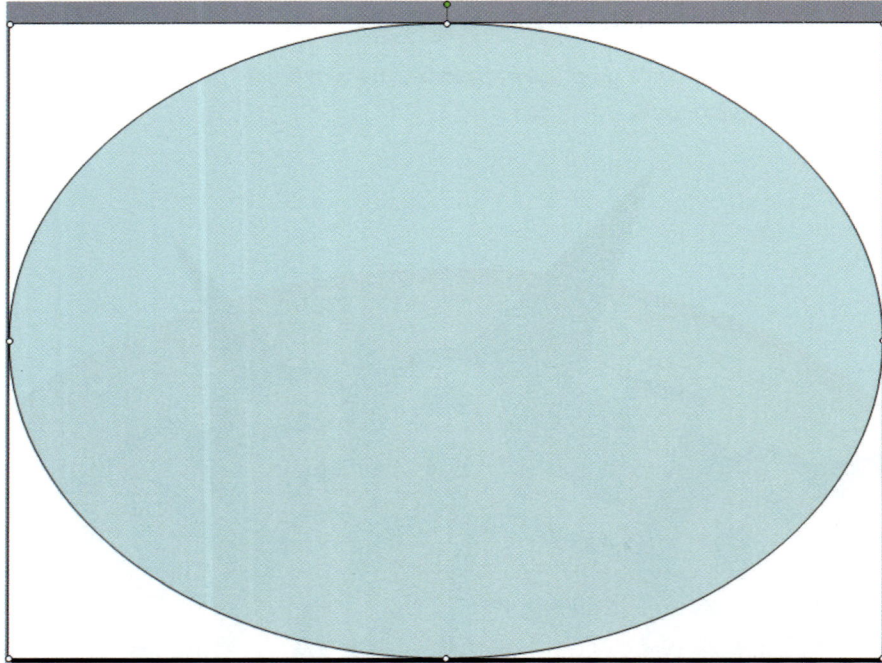

Figure 3.2: The first oval

SYLLABUS

Ref: AM6.3.2.4
Apply graduated background fill colours, texture, patterns, picture fill effect to a drawn object in a presentation.

Double-click in the oval. The **Format AutoShape** dialogue box appears. Click on the arrow to the right of the fill colour and select **Fill Effects** from the menu that appears. The **Fill Effects** dialogue box appears.

Note!

You have already used the **Fill Effects** dialogue box in Chapter 2. The technique for adding fill effects to a drawn object is exactly the same as for adding fill effects to the background of a slide. You will only be adding a graduated background fill here, but you can add a texture, pattern or picture by using the other tabs.

Select the **Fire** preset colour scheme (click **Preset** and then select **Fire** from the drop down list). From the list of **Shading styles**, select **Diagonal up**, and click on the top-right variant, as shown in Figure 3.3. Make sure that the **Rotate fill effect with shape** box is ticked. Press **OK**.

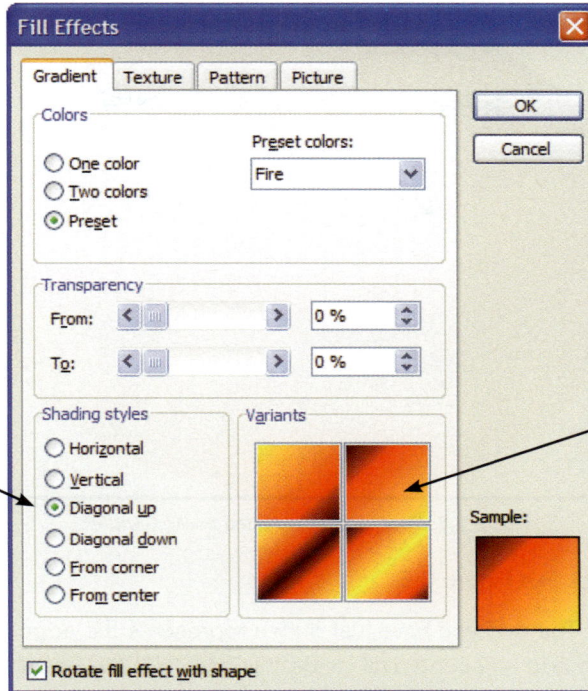

Select this shading style

Select this variant

Figure 3.3: Setting a graduated fill effect

In the **Format AutoShape** dialogue box, make sure that the **Transparency** is set to **0%** and change the **Line Color** to **No Line**, as shown in Figure 3.4. Press **OK**.

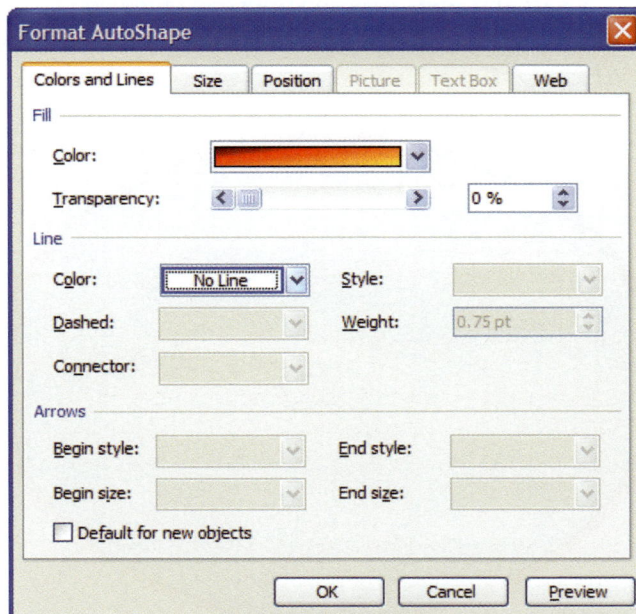

Figure 3.4: Removing the outline

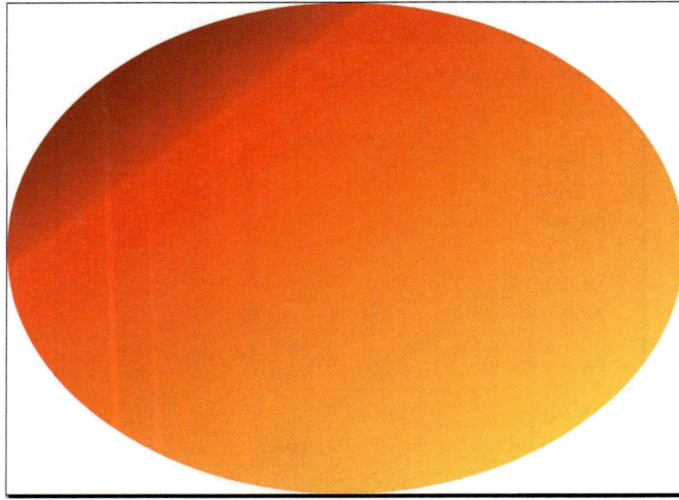

Figure 3.5: Oval with a graduated background fill

Your oval should now look like Figure 3.5.

Look back at Figure 3.1. The oval you have just drawn represents the edge of the logo's oval background. You need to add a second oval inside this one, with the colour flowing in the opposite direction.

Use the **Oval** tool again, and draw another oval to cover the slide. It should completely obscure the colour-graduated oval, so that your slide looks again as it did in Figure 3.2.

Hold down both the **Ctrl** and **Shift** keys and drag one of the corner selection handles of your new oval. Leave a thin strip of the lower oval showing around the edge of the new oval, as shown in Figure 3.6.

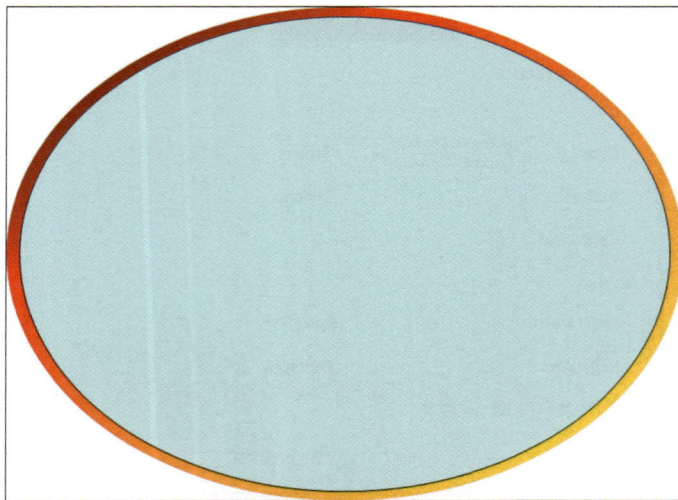

Figure 3.6: Creating the second oval

The **Ctrl** key anchors the centre of the shape as you resize it. The **Shift** key fixes the width-to-height ratio so that the resized shape is not skewed.

You can use the style you set for the first oval to set the style for the new one.

Ref: AM6.3.2.5
Pick up a style from an object and apply it to another object.

Click on the outer oval to select it. Click the **Format Painter** button in the **Standard** toolbar. Now click on the inner oval.

Format Painter

The inner oval picks up the style copied from the outer oval. In this instance, it becomes invisible! Because the **Rotate fill effect with shape** box was ticked when you created the outer oval, you can easily change the direction of the graduated fill for the inner oval by rotating it through 180 degrees.

Ref: AM6.3.3.3
Rotate, flip, mirror an image.

With the inner oval selected (as it will be, following the previous step), try dragging its green handle. This rotates the shape. Hold down the **Shift** key (which makes the angle jump in fixed steps) and drag the inner rectangle through 180 degrees so that it looks like Figure 3.7.

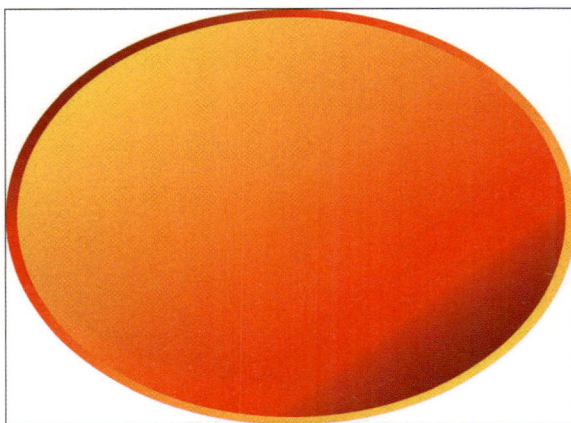

Figure 3.7: Flipping the inner oval (and its graduated fill)

There is an alternative way to achieve the same effect (this will put it back the way it was before).

> With the inner oval selected, click the **Draw** button on the left of the **Drawing** toolbar. From this menu, select **Rotate or Flip**, **Flip Horizontal**. Repeat this with **Flip Vertical**. Your inner oval should be hidden again.

> **TIP**
>
> You can flip and rotate imported images as well as drawing objects. You can create a mirrored effect by duplicating an image (use cut and paste or press **Ctrl + D**) and then flipping it.

> Use whichever technique you prefer so that your slide looks like Figure 3.7 again.

Shadow

If you look back at Figure 3.1, you will notice that the logo has a black shadow below it. You could recreate this effect by drawing a black oval, but a more sophisticated technique is to use PowerPoint's built-in shadow tool.

First, shrink the ovals slightly to make room.

> Press **Ctrl + A** to select everything on the slide. Hold down **Ctrl + Shift** and drag any of the corner handles towards the centre of your slide. Release the mouse button (followed by the keys) when you have created a small border, as shown in Figure 3.8.

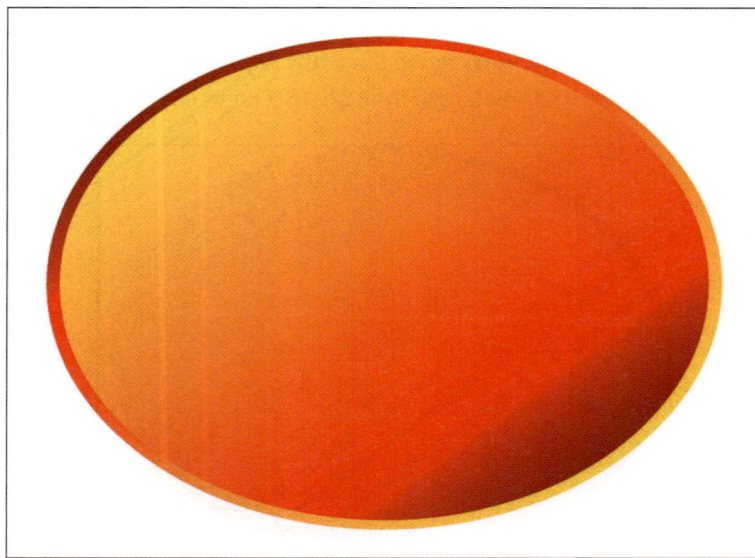

Figure 3.8: Adding a border

Ref: AM6.3.2.3
Apply, reposition a shadow of a specified colour on a picture, image, drawn object.

Click on the grey area outside the slide to clear the selection, then click just on the outer oval to select it.

Use the **Shadow Style** tool in the **Drawing** toolbar to assign **Shadow Style 6** to the outer oval, as shown in Figure 3.9.

Shadow Style

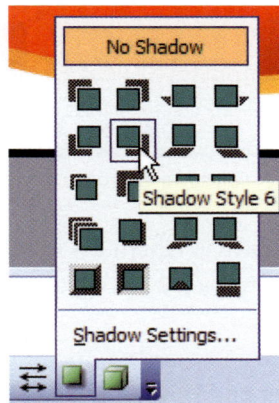

Figure 3.9: Adding a shadow

The shadow appears. It will use the **Shadows** colour from the default colour scheme. Override the colour of this particular shadow to black.

Click the **Shadow Style** tool again, but this time select **Shadow Settings** from the bottom of the menu that appears. The **Shadow Settings** toolbar appears.

Press the arrow to the right of the **Shadow Color** icon and then select **More Shadow Colors** from the menu that appears, as shown in Figure 3.10. The **Colors** dialogue box appears.

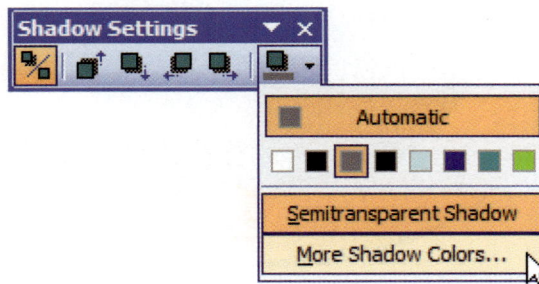

Figure 3.10: Changing the shadow settings

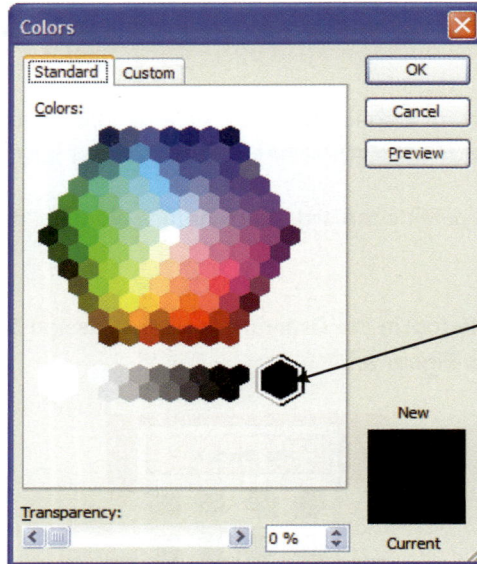

Figure 3.11: Changing the colour of the shadow

Select the black hexagon, as shown in Figure 3.11. Set the **Transparency** to **0%**, otherwise you will get a shade of grey (as the white slide background will show through). Press **OK**.

Use the **Nudge Shadow Down** and **Nudge Shadow Right** controls on the **Shadow Settings** toolbar to increase the size of the shadow.

Draw a black oval over the top to form the centre of the logo, which should then look like Figure 3.12.

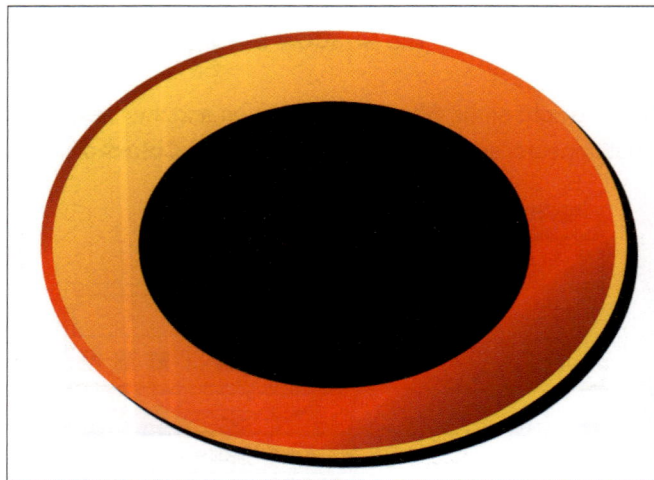

Figure 3.12: Oval background with a big black shadow

Adding the explosion

Look back at Figure 3.1. The next stage is to add the black explosion. You could draw this as a series of black triangles, but instead we will adapt some existing clip art of an explosion – it won't exactly match the original logo, but it is an interesting technique.

Press **Ctrl + M** to add a second slide to the presentation. Set its **Layout** to **Blank**.

From the menu, select **Insert**, **Picture**, **Clip Art**. The **Clip Art** task pane appears.

In the **Search for** box, type **explosion** and press the **Go** button.

> **Note!**
>
> This step assumes that you are using a computer connected to the Internet, or that this particular piece of clip art has been installed to your PC. If you don't get any results from your search, search again without anything in the **Search for** box, and pick any piece of clip art. You can still practise the technique; you just won't get an explosion effect.

Select the style of explosion shown in Figure 3.13. It should appear in your slide.

Figure 3.13: Explosion clip art

Converting clip art to a drawing

We want to break this image up and copy just the basic shape to the other slide. At the moment, PowerPoint is treating the clip art as a picture rather than a collection of objects. However, it's easy to perform the conversion.

SYLLABUS

Ref: AM6.3.1.1
Convert a picture to a drawn object.

Right-click the explosion on the slide and select **Grouping**, **Ungroup** from the menu. The warning dialogue shown in Figure 3.14 appears. Press **Yes**.

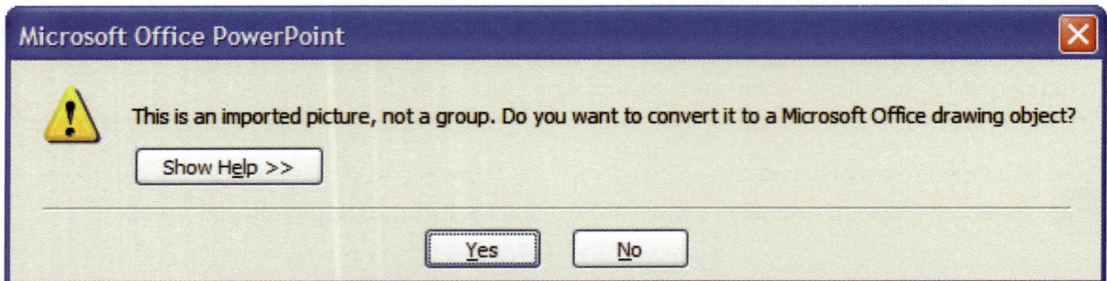

Microsoft Office PowerPoint

⚠ This is an imported picture, not a group. Do you want to convert it to a Microsoft Office drawing object?

Show Help >>

Yes   No

Figure 3.14: Warning about the imminent conversion

Ungrouping

Try clicking different parts of the explosion shape. You should see grey selection handles appear around the part you clicked, as well as white selection handles around the whole shape (see Figure 3.15(a)). This is because the picture has been converted to a group of objects. You can ungroup it to enable you to edit the objects individually.

SYLLABUS

Ref: AM6.3.1.2
Group, ungroup drawn objects in a slide.

Right-click on the explosion and select **Grouping**, **Ungroup** from the menu that appears. Each of the shapes now gets its own white selection handles, as shown in Figure 3.15(b).

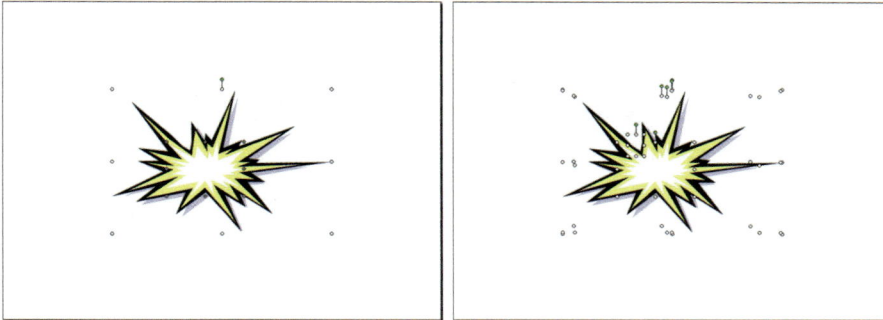

Figure 3.15: The explosion object (a) grouped and (b) ungrouped

TIP

Having ungrouped an object, you can later select any of its subcomponents and use **Grouping**, **Regroup** to regroup it with all the other subcomponents that made up the original object. This is particularly useful if you have several composite objects close to one another. Alternatively, you can use **Grouping**, **Group** to group together whichever objects you have selected at the time.

Change the background of this slide only to any colour that is not in the explosion (refer back to Chapter 2 if you cannot remember how to do this).

Drag each of the components of the explosion out on to the slide so that you can see what they look like. (One of them is a transparent rectangle – just press **Delete** when you have this selected.)

Your slide should look something like Figure 3.16.

Figure 3.16: Examining the components of the explosion

Use the white shape as your explosion in the logo – this is the chunkiest one.

Copy the white shape and paste it on to the first slide. Double-click on the new explosion shape and change its fill colour to black. Rotate and resize it to echo the explosion effect from the real logo. You may also need to adjust the size of your black oval slightly to get the best effect and to avoid any very small spikes from sticking out.

Note!

Remember that the purpose of this exercise is to learn the techniques, not to create an exact replica of the logo.

Your logo should look something like Figure 3.17.

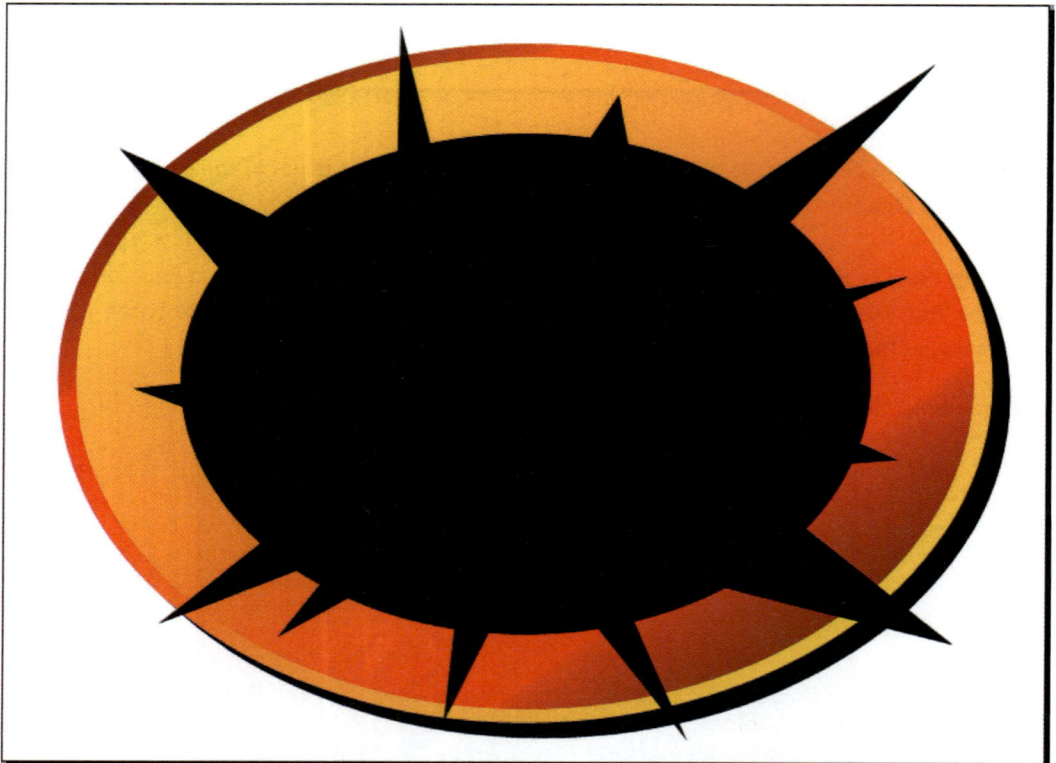

Figure 3.17: Adding the explosion shape to the logo

Adding the text

The final component to add is the **BLAST FM** text. We will use WordArt for this.

➡ Press the **Insert WordArt** button on the **Drawing** toolbar. The **WordArt Gallery** dialogue box appears. Select the arced text style shown in Figure 3.18 and press **OK**.

Insert WordArt

Use this style for the first line of text

Use this style for the second line of text

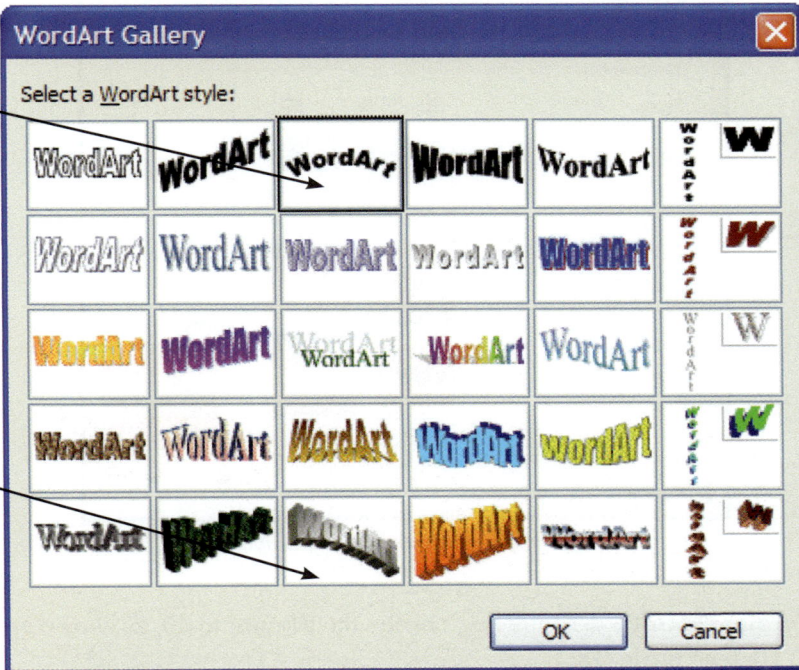

Figure 3.18: Adding WordArt

➡ Change the text to **BLAST** and pick a suitable font (you won't be able to match the real logo's font exactly). The size doesn't matter because you will be resizing the text manually. Press **OK**.

The text will probably appear in black because this was the last colour you used. This doesn't show up against the black explosion. Change the text colour.

➡ From the menu, select **Format**, **WordArt**. The **Format WordArt** dialogue box appears. On the **Colors and Lines** tab, in the **Fill** pane, click on the arrow to the right of the **Color** box. Select **Fill Effects**. The **Fill Effects** dialogue box appears.

➡ Set the fill to the effect shown in Figure 3.19.

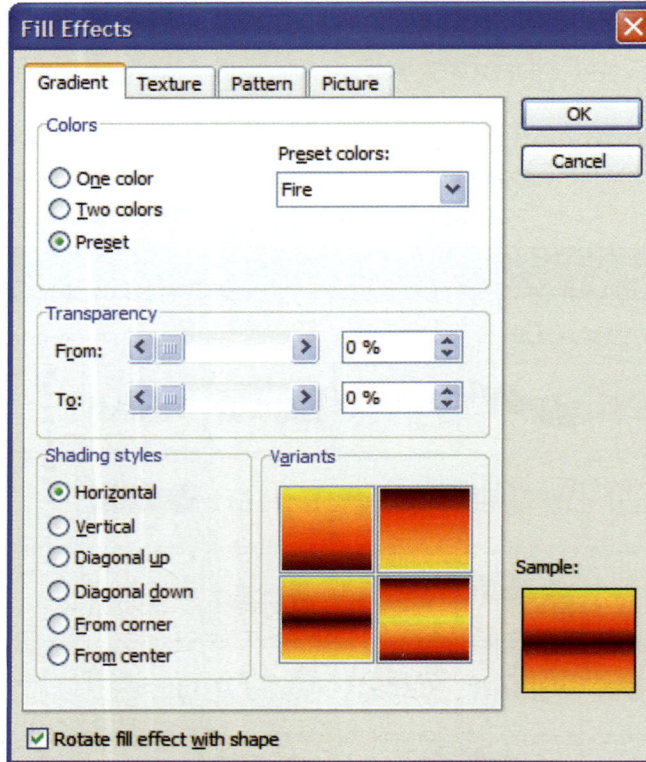

Figure 3.19: Setting the fill effect for the text

In the **Format WordArt** dialogue box, change the **Weight** to **10**, as shown in Figure 3.20, then press **OK**.

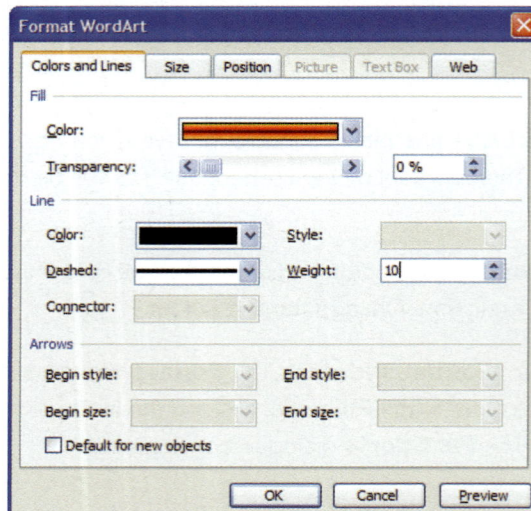

Figure 3.20: Setting the format for the text

Resize your text so that it is big and chunky and overlaps the orange border.

TIP

You can use the yellow selection handle to adjust the curvature of the text path.

Use the **Insert WordArt** button to add the text **FM**, this time using a different style from the **WordArt Gallery** (see Figure 3.18) so that the second line tapers off to the right.

Your logo should now look like Figure 3.21.

Figure 3.21: Adding text of a different style

Notice that this text has a three-dimensional look to it. You want to keep the taper, but lose the 3-D. You can experiment with some of the different settings before turning the 3-D effect off.

SYLLABUS

Ref: AM6.3.2.2
Apply 3-D effects to a drawn object.

Make the **FM** text larger and, with it selected, try out the different options in the **3-D Style** menu on the **Drawing** toolbar (see Figure 3.22). When you've finished experimenting, select **No 3-D**.

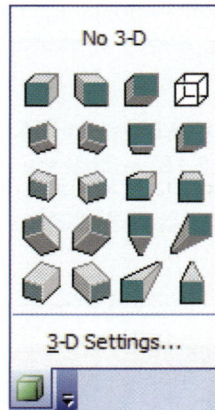

Figure 3.22: The 3-D options

Use the **Format Painter** to apply the text style from **BLAST** to **FM**.

Your finished logo should look something like Figure 3.23.

Figure 3.23: The completed logo

Now is a good time to save the logo.

➡ Save your file as **Blast FM Logo.ppt**.

You can also save slides as graphics, which can be useful if you want to put them on the Web or to edit them in a graphics application.

📘 SYLLABUS

Ref: AM6.2.2.1
Save a slide in gif, jpeg, bmp format to a location on a drive.

➡ From the menu, select **File**, **Save As**. The **Save As** dialogue box appears. Change the **Save as type** to **Device Independent Bitmap (*.bmp)** and press the **Save** button. The dialogue box shown in Figure 3.24 appears. Press **Current Slide Only**.

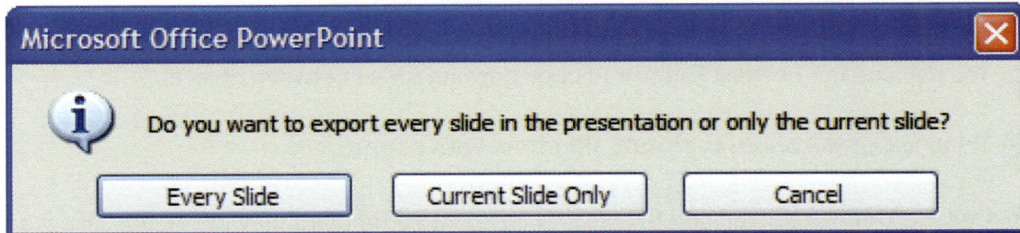

Figure 3.24: Choosing what to save

TIP

To save a slide in gif or jpeg format instead, simply choose a different **Save as type**.

📘 SYLLABUS

Ref: AM6.3.3.6
Convert an image into a file format such as: bmp, gif, jpeg format.

Note that the technique in the step above saves the whole slide. If you only want to save part of the slide, first make sure that the objects you want to save are grouped and then simply right-click the group and select **Save as Picture** from the menu that appears.

TIP

As well as being able to save drawing objects in image formats, you can convert between these formats. For example, you can insert a gif image into your slide, right-click it and save it as a jpeg.

TIP

PowerPoint is not really the best tool for converting high-quality images between different types. You might prefer to use an external piece of software to do this conversion. Some suitable tools are listed in the next chapter.

Conclusions

This exercise has demonstrated the following points.

- You can fill shapes with sophisticated fill designs – you are not limited to solid colours.

- You can use the **Format Painter** to copy drawing styles between objects.

- There is a useful option to **Rotate fill effect with shape**.

- Use the **Ungroup** command to convert clip art into a grouped drawing object. Use it again if you really wish to ungroup the object.

- You can use **Save As** to convert slides into graphics. When you save using one of the graphics formats, PowerPoint will ask whether you wish to save the current slide or the whole presentation.

- To save an individual drawing object as a graphic, right-click it and select **Save as Picture** from the menu that appears.

Test yourself

1. Create a new PowerPoint presentation. Search for **Earth** in the clip art – you should find the image shown on the left of Figure 3.25. Use this to create the earth grouping shown in the right of Figure 3.25. You will have to convert the clip art to a drawing object, break it apart, delete the bits you don't need and change the colouring (practise using the **Format Painter** for this).

Figure 3.25: Creating a globe from existing clip art

2. Add a 3-D effect to the land. Click the **3-D Style** button on the **Drawing** toolbar and then select **3-D Settings** from the menu that appears. This will display the **3-D Settings** toolbar. This toolbar will allow you to fine-tune the 3-D effect (for example, by reducing its depth, as shown in Figure 3.26). Use the **Lighting** control to set the lighting source to be coming from the top left for all the land (see Figure 3.27).

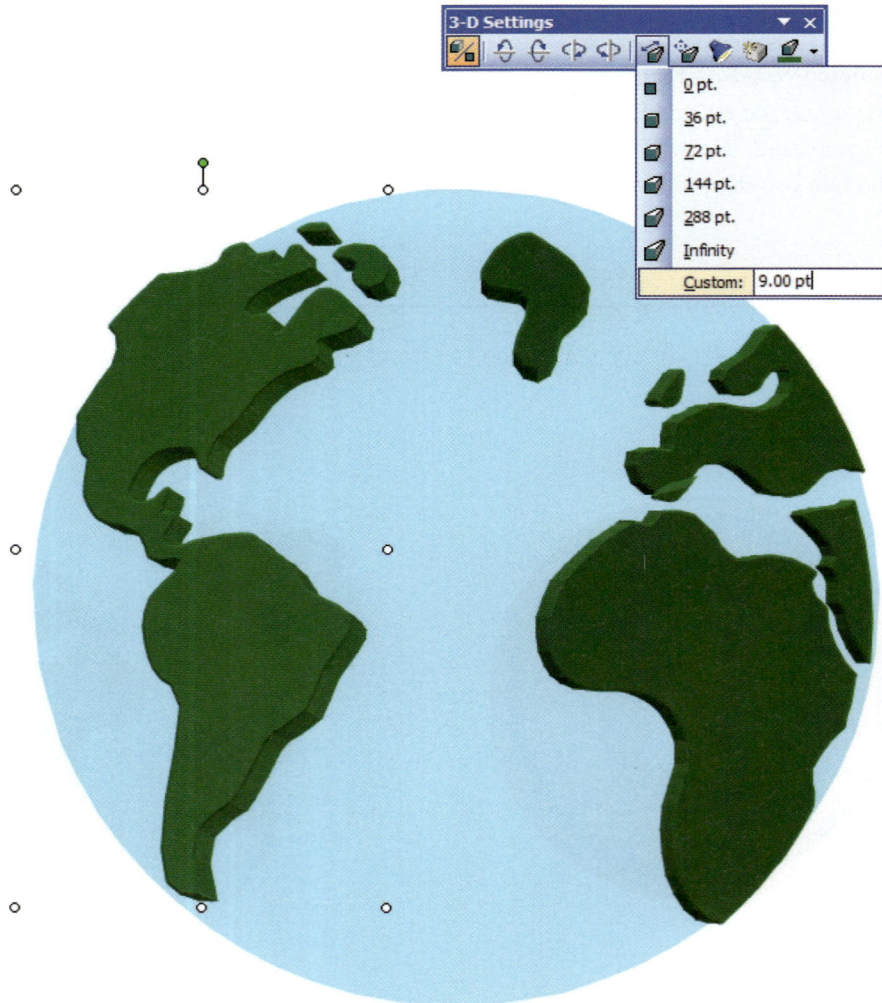

Figure 3.26: Adding a 3-D effect to the land

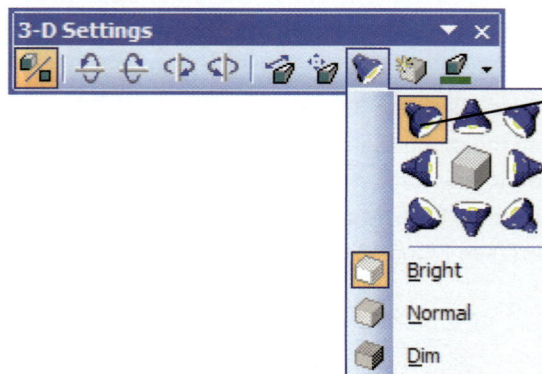

**Click here t
set the ligh
come from
top left**

Figure 3.27: Setting the lighting source

3. Delete the current water, which is composed of two shapes, and replace it with a single circle drawing object. Send this new circle behind the land objects (right-click it and select **Order**, **Send to Back**). Give it a graduated fill that changes from a light blue at the top left to a dark blue at the bottom right (to match the lighting source for the land – see Figure 3.28).

Figure 3.28: Adding a graduated fill effect to the water

4. Experiment with some other fill and shadow effects, as shown in Figure 3.29. Make sure you remember how to nudge the shadow.

Figure 3.29: Applying fill and shadow effects

5. Save your presentation as **Earth slide.ppt** and then save it again as **Earth slide.jpg**. Create a second slide in your presentation and set it to have a **Title and Content** layout. Set the title to **My Earth Slide** and insert your saved **Earth slide.jpg** picture, as shown in Figure 3.30. Edit the properties of the imported picture to give it a black outline.

Figure 3.30: Saving a slide as a graphic and inserting it into another slide

6. On your original slide, remove the shadow from the earth and then make sure that all its other components are grouped together. Save just this object as **Earth.gif**. Use this image to create a third slide with four copies of the earth at different angles, as shown in Figure 3.31.

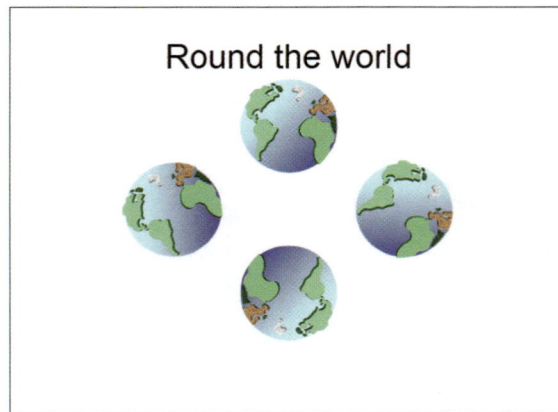

Figure 3.31: Rotating an image

TIP

You only need to insert the image onto the slide once. After that, you can select it and press **Ctrl + D** to duplicate it.

4 Editing images II

Introduction

In this chapter, you will discover how to edit bitmap images using PowerPoint and Photoshop Elements. You will make various modifications to the Blast FM logo image you saved at the end of the last chapter.

In this chapter, you will

- use Photoshop Elements to apply **effects** (negative, blurred, sharpened, stained glass and embossed) to the logo image

- use Photoshop Elements to change the **colour depth** (palette size) of the logo image

- set the **position of objects** accurately in PowerPoint

- **distribute objects** relative to each other or the slide

- set the **drawing order** for objects to control how they overlap one another

- apply total and partial **transparency** to images and drawing objects

- **crop** an image to remove an unwanted border

- learn how to **convert images to greyscale or black and white**.

Editing images outside PowerPoint

Versions of Microsoft Office prior to Office 2003 came bundled with an application called Microsoft Photo Editor. You could use this tool to edit bitmap images in various ways, including the use of special effects. For Office 2003, this tool has been replaced by Microsoft Office Picture Manager, which does not include some of these features. Therefore, to cover some of the items from the ECDL Advanced syllabus, you will have to choose another application to make these modifications to images outside PowerPoint.

The Web has a wealth of tools that you could use to edit images for your presentations. Here are some possibilities (prices are subject to variation):

- Irfan Skiljan's **Irfanview** (www.irfanview.com) [free for non-commercial use].

- The GIMP Team's **GIMP** (**GNU Image Manipulation Program**, www.gimp.org) [free].

- Cerious Software's **ThumbsPlus** (www.thumbsplus.com) [from US$49.95, trial version available].

- ULead's **PhotoImpact** (www.ulead.co.uk) [£29.99 (download)/£49.99 (CD), trial version available].

- Adobe's **Photoshop Elements** (http://www.adobe.co.uk/products/photoshopelwin/) [£49 + VAT (download)/£59 + VAT (CD), trial version available].

- Corel's **Paint Shop Pro** (www.corel.co.uk) [£77 + VAT (download)/£85 + VAT (CD), trial version available].

In this book, we will be using Photoshop Elements because it's often installed in schools and colleges, its filters are easy to apply and it comes with a stained glass filter built in (unlike, for example, Irfanview). However, the techniques covered are very similar in each of the other applications listed above.

- Load Photoshop Elements and open the file **Blast FM Logo.bmp**, which you saved in the previous chapter.

Special effects

SYLLABUS

Ref: AM6.3.3.4
Apply different available effects such as: negative effect, blurred, sharpened, stained glass, embossed etc. to an image.

From the menu, select **Filter**, **Adjustments**, **Inverse**. This reverses all the colours in the image, leading to the negative effect shown in Figure 4.1.

Figure 4.1: Negative effect

From the menu, select **File**, **Save As**. If you get a warning about the **Organizer** not being initiated, press **OK**. Save the file as a JPEG, specifically as **Blast FM Logo (inverted).jpg**. It will be fine for our purposes to set the **Quality** to **Low**, as shown in Figure 4.2.

From the menu, select **Edit**, **Undo Invert**. The logo changes back to orange.

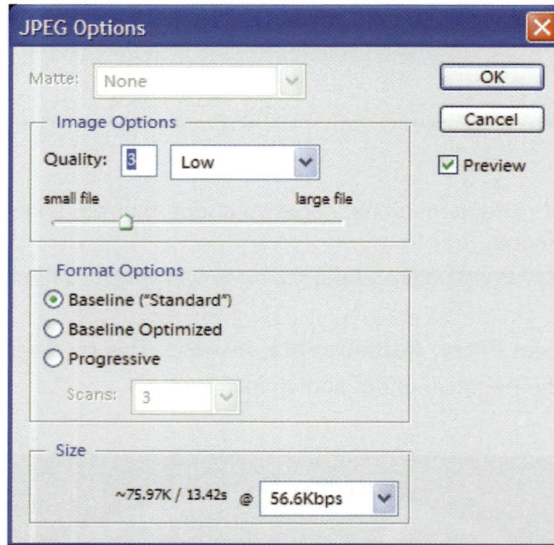

Figure 4.2: Saving the altered image as a JPEG

From the menu, select **Filter**, **Blur**, **Blur More**. Save the modified image as **Blast FM Logo (blurred).jpg** and then undo the filter.

From the menu, select **Filter**, **Sharpen**, **Sharpen More**. Save the modified image as **Blast FM Logo (sharpened).jpg** and then undo the filter.

From the menu, select **Filter**, **Texture**, **Stained Glass**. Set the **Cell Size** to **5**, the **Border Thickness** to **2** and the **Light Intensity** to **5**, as shown in Figure 4.3, then press **OK**. Save the modified image as **Blast FM Logo (stained glass).jpg** and then undo the filter.

Figure 4.3: Applying a stained glass filter

⊙ From the menu, select **Filter**, **Stylize**, **Emboss**. The **Emboss** dialogue box appears. Experiment with different settings until you find one you like, then save the modified image as **Blast FM Logo (embossed).jpg** and undo the filter.

Changing the colour depth

The colour depth of an image is the number of bits used to describe the colour of any pixel. Each additional bit increases the physical size of the file on disk, but doubles the number of available colours: a 4-bit image can have $2^4 = 16$ unique colours; a 24-bit image can have $2^{24} = 16,777,216$.

The logo you saved from PowerPoint is 24 bit at the moment (although it only uses a few thousand different colours). Observe how the quality degrades as you reduce the colour depth.

📘 SYLLABUS

Ref: AM6.3.3.1
Change colour depth of an image, such as: 4 bit, 8 bit, 24 bit.

⊙ From the menu, select **Image**, **Mode**, **Indexed Color**. The **Indexed Color** dialogue box appears (Figure 4.4).

⊙ Set the **Colors** to **256** (8 bit) and the **Dither** to **None**. If **Preview** is ticked you will be able to see the effect this has on your image. Other than some banding on the red bits of the **FM**, the quality is acceptable.

Figure 4.4: Reducing the image to an 8-bit (256) colour depth

Reduce the **Colors** down to **16** (4 bit). With **Dither** set to **None**, the effect is not acceptable – there aren't enough colours to go around, so the graduated fill becomes a series of stripes (see Figure 4.5(a)).

Change the **Dither** to **Pattern**. This improves things by stippling the colours so that they blend together better (see Figure 4.5(b)).

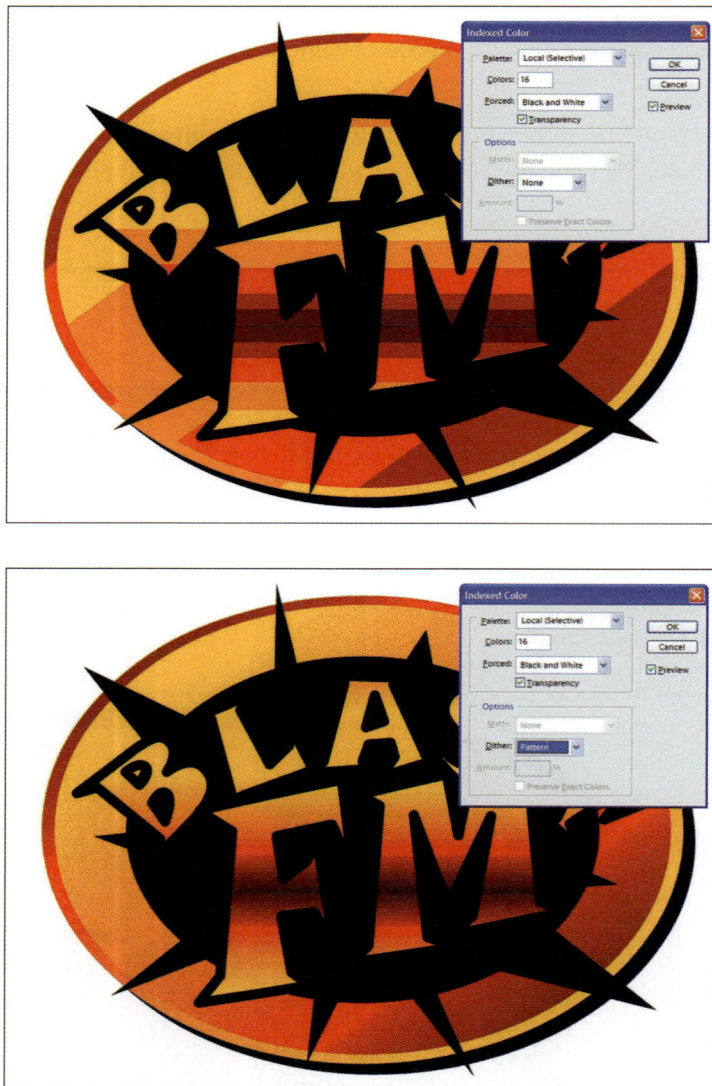

Figure 4.5: Reducing the image to a 4-bit (16) colour depth (a) without dither and (b) with pattern dither

Press **Cancel** on the **Indexed Color** dialogue box and exit Photoshop Elements without saving.

Designing a montage

You will now import these images back into PowerPoint and look at some of the ways you can manipulate them.

➡ Open your presentation **Blast FM Logo.ppt** if it isn't already open.

➡ Press **Ctrl + M** to create a new slide. Set its **Layout** to **Title Only** and set the title to **Special effects**.

➡ From the menu, select **Insert**, **Picture**, **From File**. Navigate to the folder in which you saved your graphics from Photoshop Elements. Select **Blast FM Logo (stained glass).jpg**, as shown in Figure 4.6, and press **Insert**.

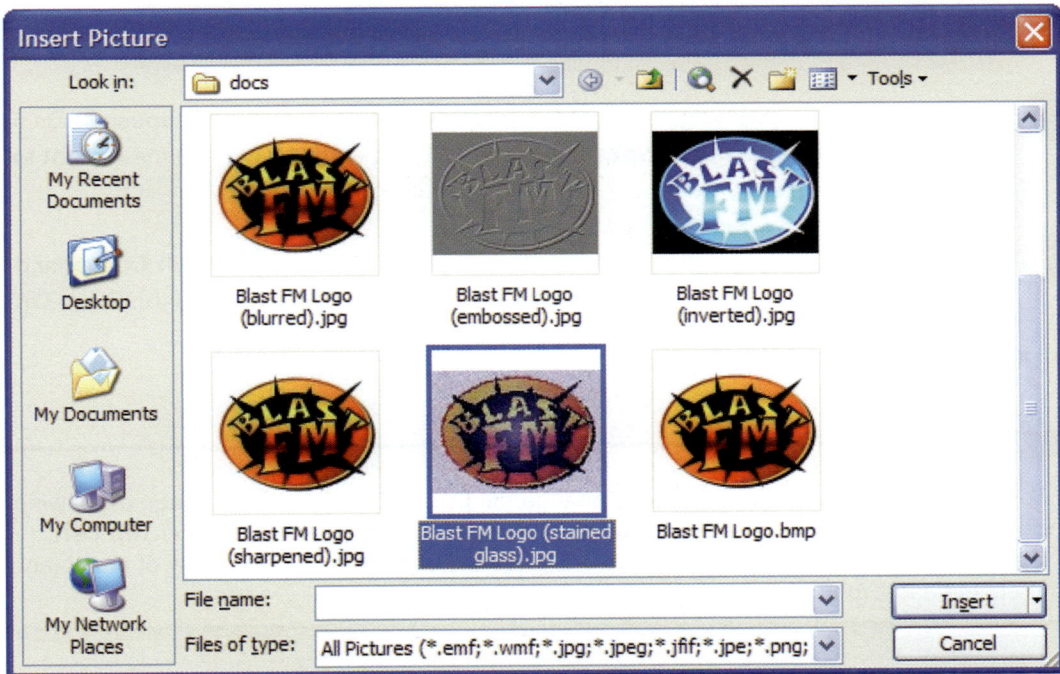

Figure 4.6: Inserting an image

The logo appears on the slide, filling it.

SYLLABUS

Ref: AM6.3.1.4
Position a picture, image, drawn object on a slide horizontally and/or vertically using specified co-ordinates.

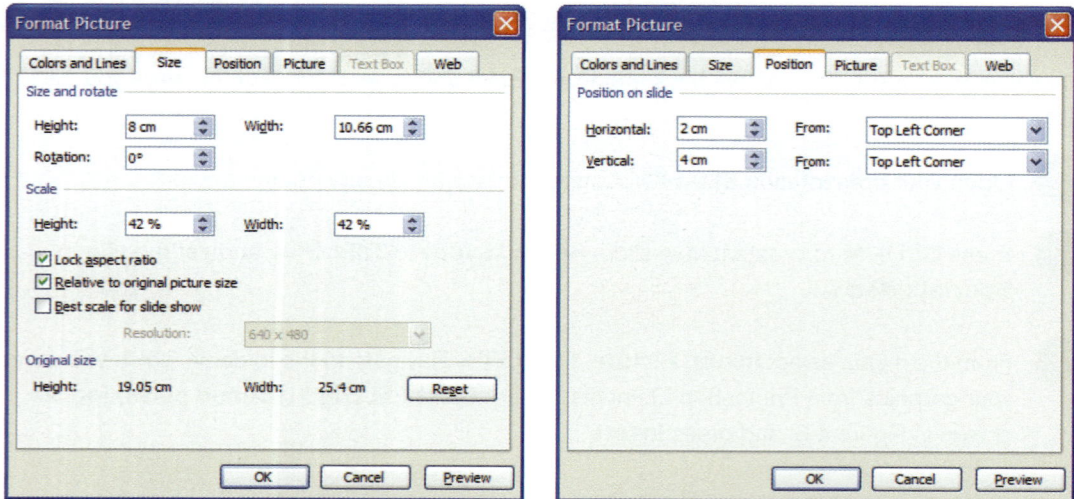

Figure 4.7: Manually setting the size and position of the picture

Double-click on the stained glass logo. The **Format Picture** dialogue box appears. On the **Size** tab, make sure the **Lock aspect ratio** box is ticked and then change the **Height** to **8 cm**, as shown in Figure 4.7(a).

On the **Position** tab, change the **Horizontal** setting to **2 cm** from **Top Left Corner** and the **Vertical** setting to **4 cm** from **Top Left Corner**, as shown in Figure 4.7(b). Press **OK**.

Your slide should now look like Figure 4.8.

TIP

You can use this technique to resize or change the position of any picture, image or drawing object in PowerPoint. You have the choice of whether to position relative to the **Top Left Corner** or the **Center** (although the co-ordinates will be for the top-left corner of the object in either case). You can supply negative values if necessary.

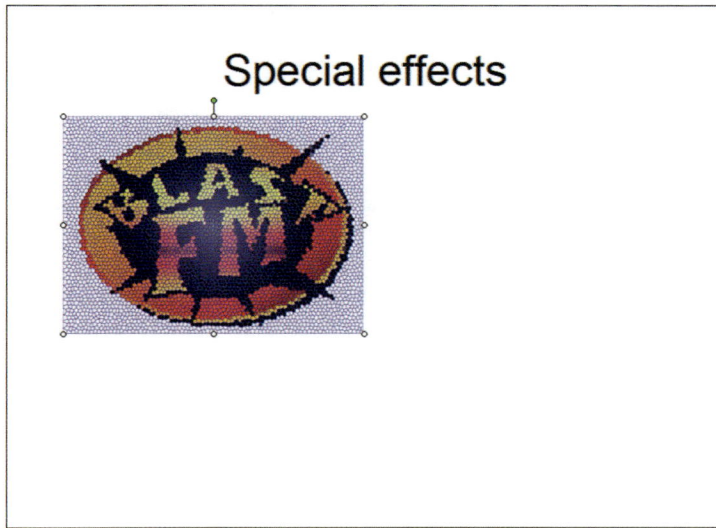

Figure 4.8: The resized, repositioned picture

Repeat this process for **Blast FM Logo (embossed).jpg**. Set the size the same as before, but position the new image **13 cm** across and **10 cm** down the page.

Do the same again for **Blast FM Logo (inverted).jpg**. Set the size the same as before, but position the new image **5 cm** across and **6 cm** down the page.

Your slide should now look like Figure 4.9.

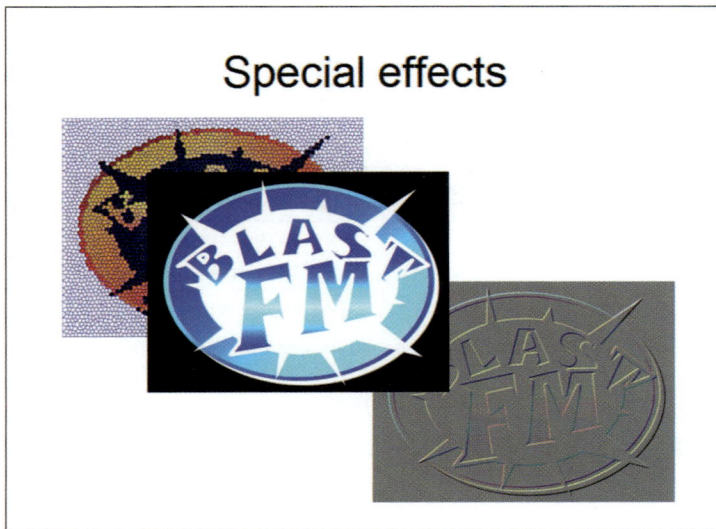

Figure 4.9: The three logo effects resized and positioned on the page

Distributing objects

Notice that the middle logo is off-centre. You can get PowerPoint to distribute the logos across the slide automatically.

SYLLABUS

Ref: AM6.3.1.5
Distribute selected pictures, images, drawn objects horizontally, vertically relative to a slide.

➡ Click in the grey border around the slide to clear the selection. Hold down the **Ctrl** key and click in each of the three logos in turn. All three of them should acquire selection handles.

➡ Click the **Draw** button on the **Drawing** toolbar and hover your mouse pointer over **Align or Distribute** to expand the menu. If **Relative to Slide** is not already ticked, then tick it now and expand the menu again. Select **Distribute Horizontally**, as shown in Figure 4.10.

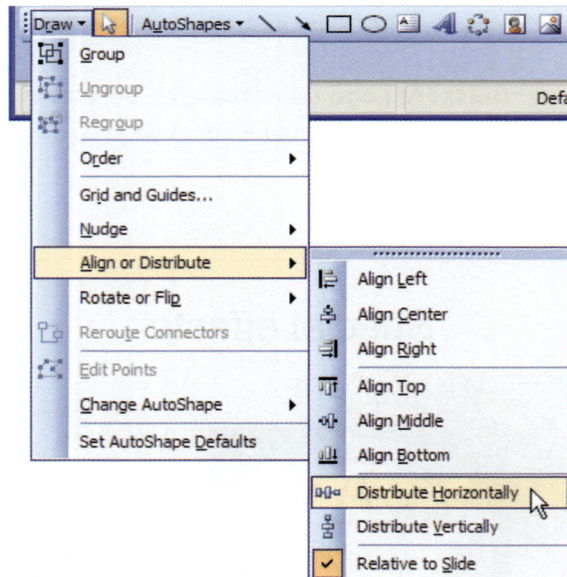

Figure 4.10: Distributing the images across the slide

➡ Select **Draw**, **Align or Distribute**, **Distribute Vertically**.

Your slide should now look like Figure 4.11. Because the **Relative to Slide** option was set, PowerPoint distributes the slides equally across the whole slide.

➡ Press **Ctrl + Z** twice to undo the vertical and horizontal distributions.

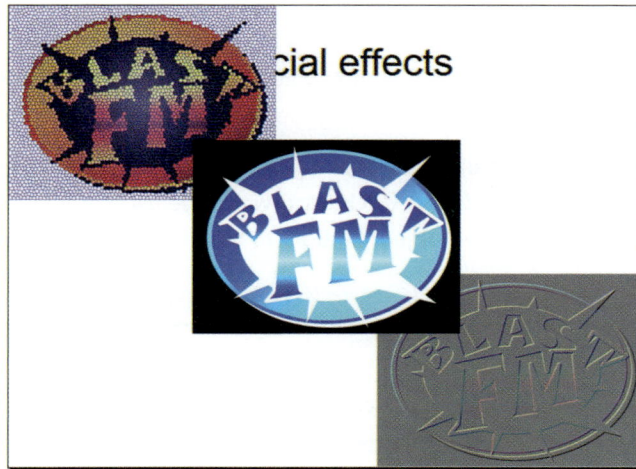

Figure 4.11: Distributing the logos across the whole slide

It would be better if you could rearrange the objects across only the area they already cover. This is what will happen if you distribute them with the **Relative to Slide** option turned off.

Select **Draw**, **Align or Distribute**, **Relative to Slide** to turn this option off.

Distribute the three logos horizontally and vertically again. Your slide should look like Figure 4.12.

Figure 4.12: Distributing relative to the bounding area already covered by the objects

TIP

You can use this same technique to distribute any floating objects in PowerPoint.

Object drawing order

By default, PowerPoint draws each new object you add to a slide on top of the existing objects. You can move any of the objects without affecting the drawing order.

You can use the **Order** menu to change the drawing order of any picture, image or drawn object in PowerPoint. **Bring Forward** and **Send Backward** work one layer at a time; **Bring to Front** and **Send to Back** move the selected object straight in front of or behind all the other objects.

> **SYLLABUS**
>
> **Ref: AM6.3.1.3**
> Bring a picture, image, drawn object, backward or forward within a grouped selection.

Right-click on the centre image and select **Order**, **Send Backward** from the menu that appears.

The image tucks in behind the embossed logo, but remains in front of the stained glass, as shown in Figure 4.13.

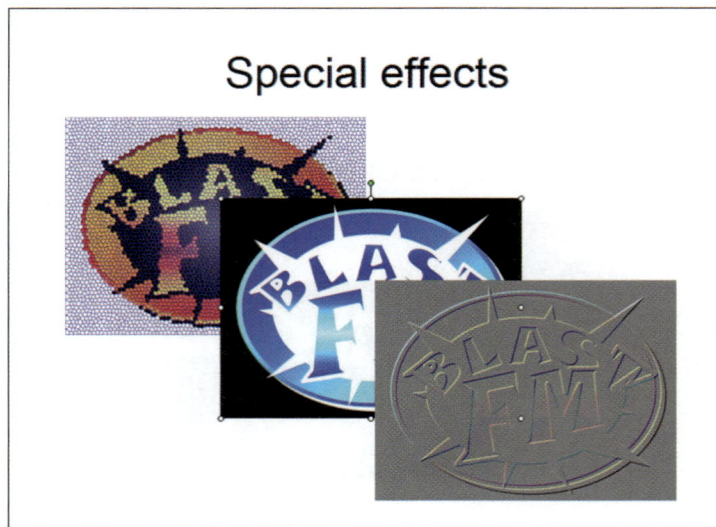

Figure 4.13: Changing the order of an object

Now change the embossed logo into a type of background.

Resize the embossed logo image so that it completely covers the slide.

Use **Order**, **Send to Back** to send the embossed logo behind everything else on the slide.

Figure 4.14: Sending an object to the back

Your slide should now look like Figure 4.14.

Transparency

Total transparency

For a picture, you can nominate one (and only one) of the colours to become transparent so that whatever is behind shows through. The black border of the inverted logo would be ideal for this treatment.

Select just the inverted (blue) logo. Select the **Set Transparent Color** tool from the **Picture** toolbar and then click anywhere on the black border of the inverted logo. The border disappears, giving the logo an oval edge.

Repeat this to set the transparent colour for the stained glass logo to white.

Copy the explosion drawing object from the main logo slide to the **Special effects** slide. Resize the new explosion shape (holding down **Shift** to keep it in proportion) so that it doesn't hide the logos.

Set Transparent
Color

Figure 4.15: After applying a transparent colour and copying a shape

Your slide should now look like Figure 4.15.

Semi-transparency

You can alter the transparency of a drawn shape's fill colour between totally opaque (as the explosion is now) and totally transparent (which can be useful for adding hyperlink hotspots to images – see page 157–158).

Double-click on the explosion shape. The **Format AutoShape** dialogue box appears. Set the **Fill Color** to **yellow** and set the **Transparency** to **90%**, as shown in Figure 4.16. Press **OK** to apply the change.

Figure 4.16: Setting semi-transparency for an AutoShape

Resize the explosion so that it sits on top of the explosion in the engraved background.

Move the explosion back in the drawing order so that it is just above the background.

Your slide should now look like Figure 4.17.

Figure 4.17: Transparent explosion added to the background

You can add a semi-transparent effect to pictures as well, but it will only affect their fill colours. You will only be able to see a picture's fill colour if it already has one of its colours set to transparent.

> **TIP**
>
> You can achieve semi-transparency for pictures by creating a rectangle and setting its fill to use a picture. The **Test yourself** section at the end of this chapter demonstrates this.

Remember that you have already set the white colour in the stained glass logo to be transparent, so you can add a fill colour to it now.

➡ Double-click on the stained glass logo. The **Format Picture** dialogue box appears.

➡ On the **Colors and Lines** tab, set the **Fill Color** to **Lime**. Press the **Preview** button to see what this look like (the glass colour used for the border becomes lime).

➡ Set the **Transparency** to **75%** and press **OK**.

You can now see the background through the green-tinted border. Because the background is dark, increasing the transparency has toned down the lime to a mid-shade green.

➡ Use **Draw**, **Align or Distribute** to distribute the two small logos horizontally relative to the slide and to align them to the middle relative to the slide.

Your slide should now look like Figure 4.18.

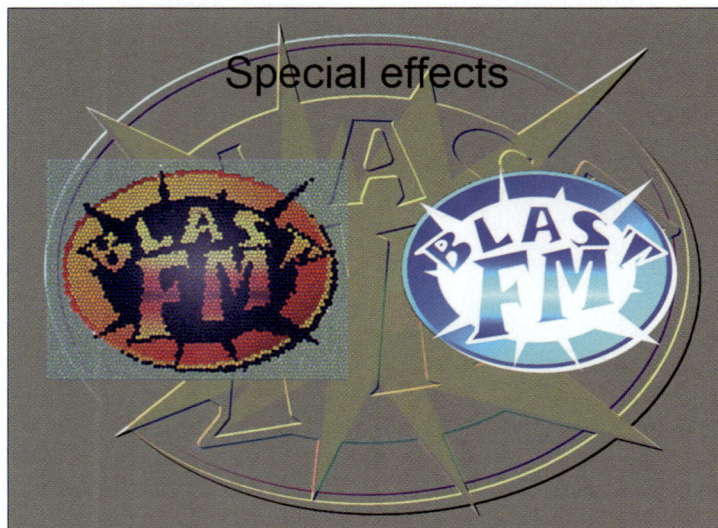

Figure 4.18: Tidied slide layout showing a semi-transparent picture

Cropping pictures

Because of the transparent border around the right-hand logo, the left-hand one looks slightly larger. Crop it to remove some of the border.

SYLLABUS

Ref: AM6.3.3.2
Crop and proportionately re-scale an image.

Select the stained glass logo. Click the **Crop** tool in the **Picture** toolbar. The selection handles around the picture change to thick black lines.

Crop

Click and drag the thick black handles to trim off any excess green border, as shown in Figure 4.19. Press the **Esc** key to apply the change.

Figure 4.19: Cropping the stained glass logo

TIP

To re-scale an image, simply drag any of its selection handles; If you drag a corner selection handle it will automatically be scaled proportionately; if you drag a top/bottom/side selection handle it will be scaled disproportionately. To scale an image disproportionately, use the **Size** tab of the **Format Picture** dialogue box and untick the **Lock aspect ratio** box (see page 74)

You can use the **Compress Pictures** button on the **Picture** toolbar to delete the cropped areas of your pictures from your presentation, which will reduce its size. By default, PowerPoint keeps the trimmed areas in case you later wish to restore them.

Compress
Pictures

Changing an image to black and white

The final item to cover is how to convert images into greyscale and black and white.

SYLLABUS

Ref: AM6.3.3.5
Convert an image into greyscale, black and white format.

Select both the small logos (click one, hold down **Ctrl** and then click the other).

Color

Click the **Color** icon on the **Picture** toolbar. Select **Black & White** from the menu that appears.

Figure 4.20 shows the effect, which is not very attractive. Every pixel in the two logos has been converted either to pure black or pure white, whichever it was closest to. Notice that the green transparent fill of the stained glass logo has not been affected by this change.

Figure 4.20: Converting to black and white – not very attractive

Use the **Color** menu again, but this time choose **Grayscale**.

The colours are now converted to an appropriate shade of grey so that the graduated colour fills of the original images appear much smoother than they did in black and white (Figure 4.21).

Use the **Color** menu again, and select **Automatic** to revert to full colour.

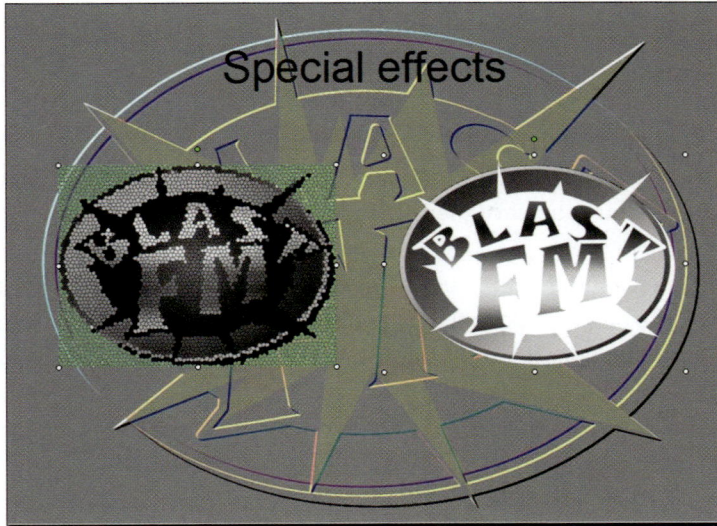
Figure 4.21: Converting to greyscale

There's one more option on the **Color** menu – **Washout** – which you can use to improve the background.

Select the background logo. Click **Color**, **Washout** from the **Picture** toolbar.

This automatically changes the brightness and contrast of the image to produce a washed-out effect (Figure 4.22).

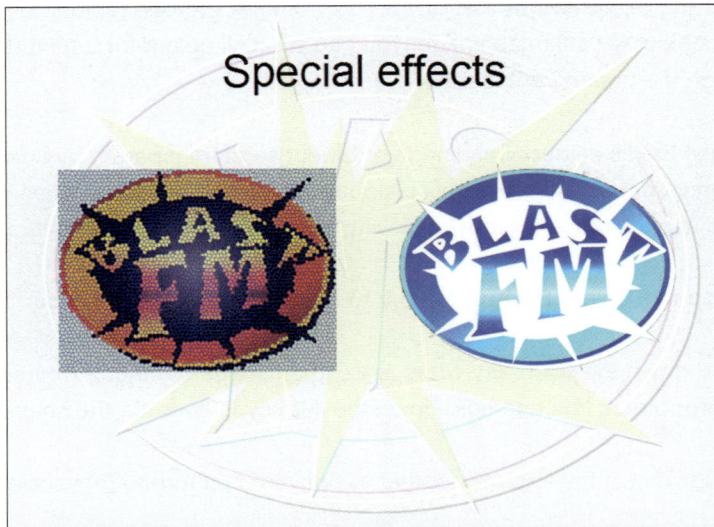
Figure 4.22: Using Washout to improve the background

Save your presentation again.

Conclusions

This exercise has demonstrated the following points.

PowerPoint no longer comes bundled with software for applying special effects to images or for changing their colour depth. Instead, you can use an external application, such as Photoshop Elements, to achieve these results.

Colour depth is measured in the number of bits used to store each pixel's colour. The number of colours can be calculated as two to the power of the colour depth. For example, an image with 4-bit colour depth can contain at most $2^4 = 16$ unique colours.

You can use a **dither** to reduce the bands of colours that can form when you reduce the colour depth of an image.

You can use the **Size** and **Position** tabs on the **Format** dialogue box to resize or reposition an image or drawing object accurately.

When distributing objects, set the **Relative to Slide** option to distribute them across the whole slide, and unset this option to redistribute them across only the area they already take up.

Right-click on an object and use the **Order** menu to control how it overlaps other objects.

You can use the **Set Transparent Color** tool from the **Picture** toolbar to nominate a transparent colour for a bitmap image. You can set a fill colour for a picture, but it will only show through the transparent areas.

You can make the fill colour of an image or object semi-transparent by adjusting the **Transparency** control in the **Format** dialogue box. This also works when you set the fill of an object to use a picture, thereby achieving semi-transparency for pictures.

Use the **Crop** tool on the **Picture** toolbar to remove an unwanted border from an image.

You can hold down the **Shift** key when resizing an image or object to force PowerPoint to resize it in proportion. You can hold down the **Alt** key to override the snap-to-grid setting.

Use the **Color** tool in the **Picture** toolbar to convert a picture to greyscale or black and white.

Test yourself

Preparation

To practise the techniques in this chapter, you need a picture with lots of colours in it. For this, we can 'borrow' the coloured hexagon from PowerPoint's **Colors** dialogue box.

→ Create a new blank PowerPoint presentation.

→ Set the **Slide Layout** to **Blank**.

→ From the menu, select **Format**, **Background**, then select **More Colors** from the drop-down list. Press **Alt + PrintScrn** to copy this dialogue box to the clipboard, then cancel both dialogue boxes.

→ Press **Ctrl + V** to paste the copied dialogue box into your empty slide. It should now look like Figure 4.23.

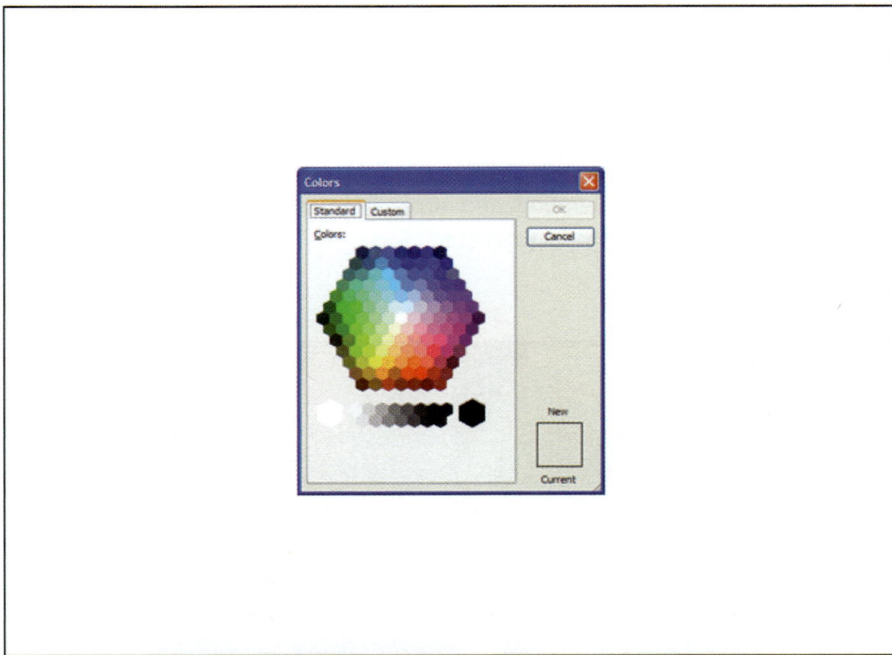

Figure 4.23: Pasting a copy of a dialogue box into a slide

Exercises

1. Crop this image so that only the hexagon and the white, grey and black areas beneath it remain. Resize the remaining image to make it half the width of the slide, keeping it in proportion. Repeat this for the **Custom** tab of the **Colors** dialogue box (this will contain a cross shape, but you can ignore this). Your slide should look like Figure 4.24.

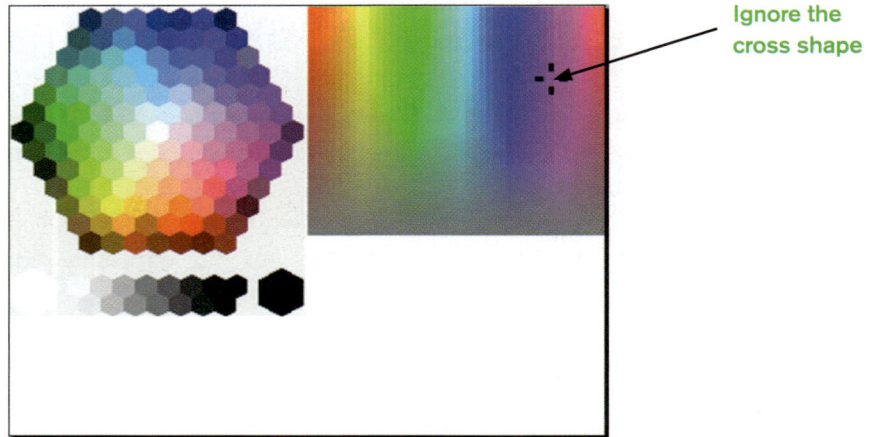

Ignore the cross shape

Figure 4.24: A slide full of colours

2. Save the slide as a presentation (**Colours.ppt**) and then again as an image (**Colours.jpg**). Load the image into Photoshop Elements and apply an **Invert** filter to it. The result should look like Figure 4.25. Save this as **Colours (inverted).jpg**.

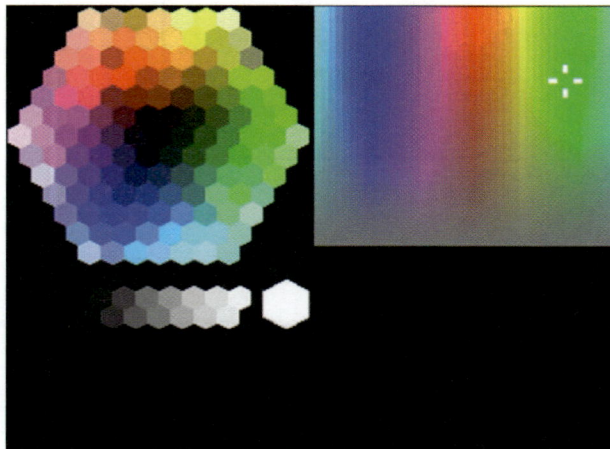

Figure 4.25: Colours inverted in Photoshop Elements

3. Change the colour depth to 8 bit (**256** colours) with a **75% Diffusion** dither. Save this as **Colours (inverted 8-bit).gif** (Figure 4.26).

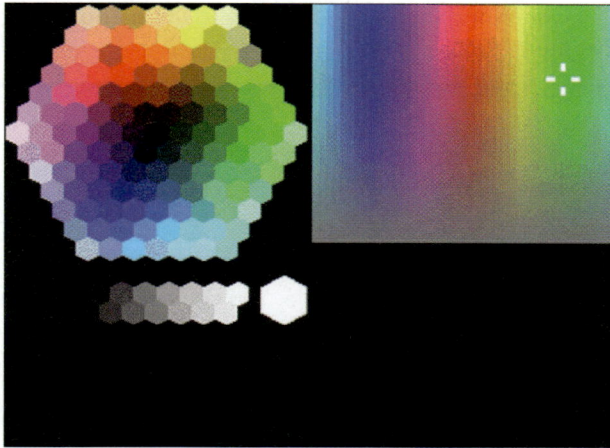

Figure 4.26: The same image with a lower colour depth (note the speckling)

4. Now try to get the original image and the inverted image to cancel one another out. Create a new slide with a blank layout in your PowerPoint presentation and draw a rectangle that fills the slide. Edit the rectangle's properties – change the **Fill** to use a **Picture Fill Effect** (add **Colours.jpg**) and set the **Transparency** to **33%**. Draw a second rectangle and fill it with **Colours (inverted).jpg** with **Transparency** set to **67%**. Your slide should look like Figure 4.27.

Figure 4.27: The two pictures average out to grey

> **Note!**
>
> You might think that the transparency of both images should have been set to 50% to achieve this effect. However, PowerPoint gives more emphasis to the part of the combined colour coming from the higher layer.

5. Swap the drawing order of the two images. Notice how they no longer balance each other out into grey. Swap them again and the image returns to grey.

6. Click on the second slide in the list on the left of the PowerPoint window – this selects the whole slide. Press **Ctrl + D** to duplicate the slide. You can now work on the third slide without losing the effect from the previous step. Resize both images proportionally to 30% of their size. Set the position of the normal image to **2 cm** across, **3 cm** down. Set the position of the inverted image to **8 cm** across, **4 cm** down. Set the **Transparency** back to **0%** for both images. Your slide should look like Figure 4.28.

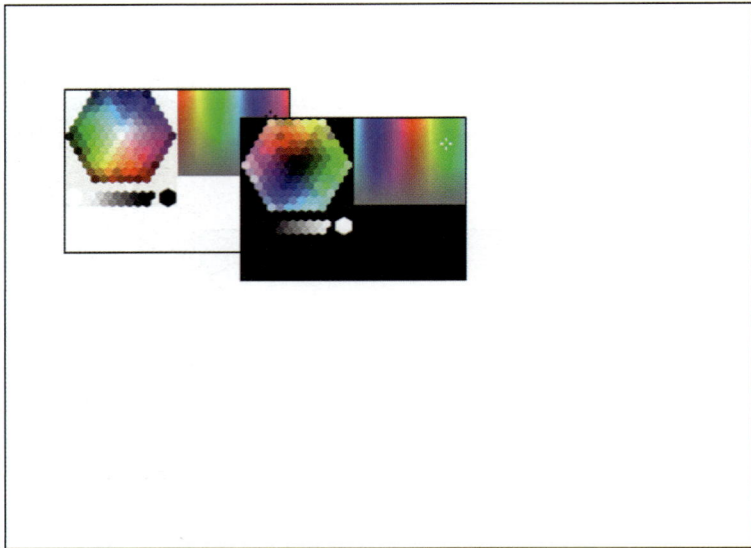

Figure 4.28: Resizing and positioning images accurately

7. Select the image with the white background and press **Ctrl + D** to duplicate it. Convert the duplicate into greyscale.

8. Draw another rectangle covering the whole screen. Set its background to the **Colours (inverted 8-bit).gif** file you saved earlier. Resize it to 30% and position the four images

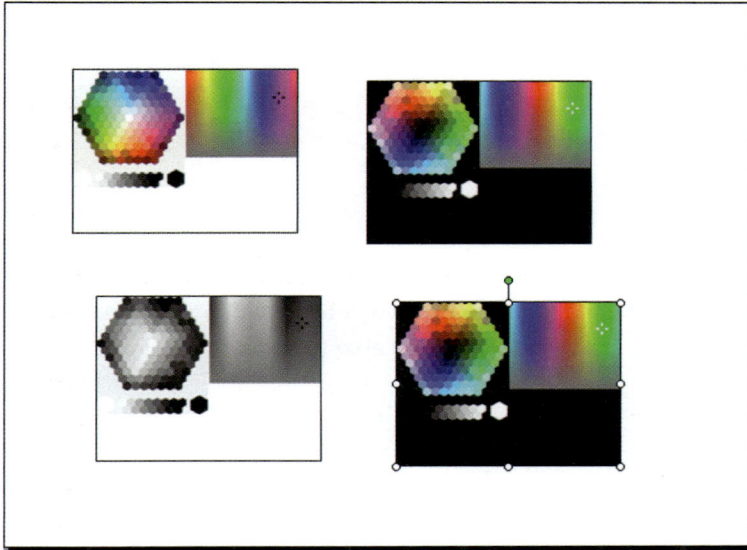

Figure 4.29: Four versions of the same image

roughly as shown in Figure 4.29. (The one you have just added is shown selected in the bottom right.)

9. Select the top two images and distribute them horizontally relative to the slide. Repeat this for the bottom two images. Select the left two images and distribute them vertically relative to the slide. Repeat this for the right two images. All four should now be spread out neatly, as shown in Figure 4.30.

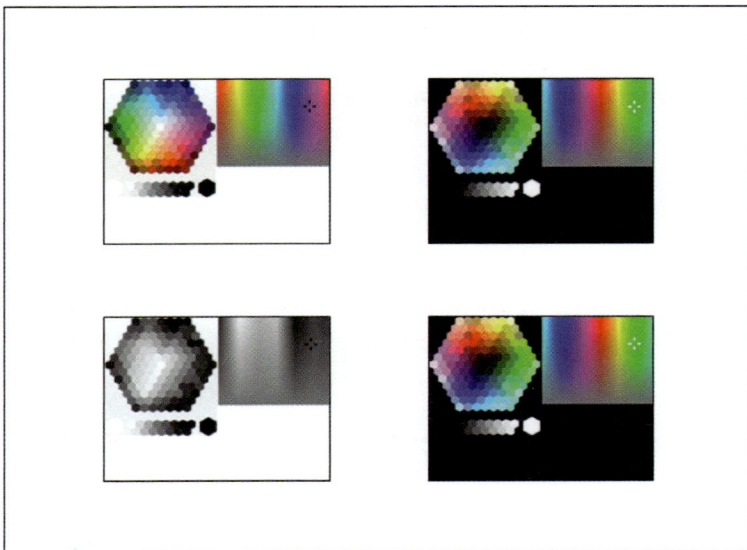

Figure 4.30: The four images after they have been distributed evenly

5 Charts and graphs

Introduction

In this chapter, you will create two types of chart in PowerPoint: a graph showing listener numbers and advertising income for Blast FM over a two-year period, and a flow chart showing how listeners to the Internet radio station will be able to upload their own music selections.

In this chapter, you will

insert a column chart into a slide

change the chart type to a mixed line/column chart using two axes

change the chart type of a data series

customise axes on your chart by setting their range and the frequency of their labels

apply the built-in feature to **display y-axis units in multiples**, such as thousands and millions

learn how to **draw a flow chart** using AutoShapes

discover how to **change or delete flow chart shapes**

learn how to **change connector shapes** in a flow chart.

PowerPoint graphs

➡ Create a new PowerPoint presentation based on **Blast FM.pot**.

➡ Change the slide layout to **Title and Content**. Click on the **Insert Chart** icon, as shown in Figure 5.1.

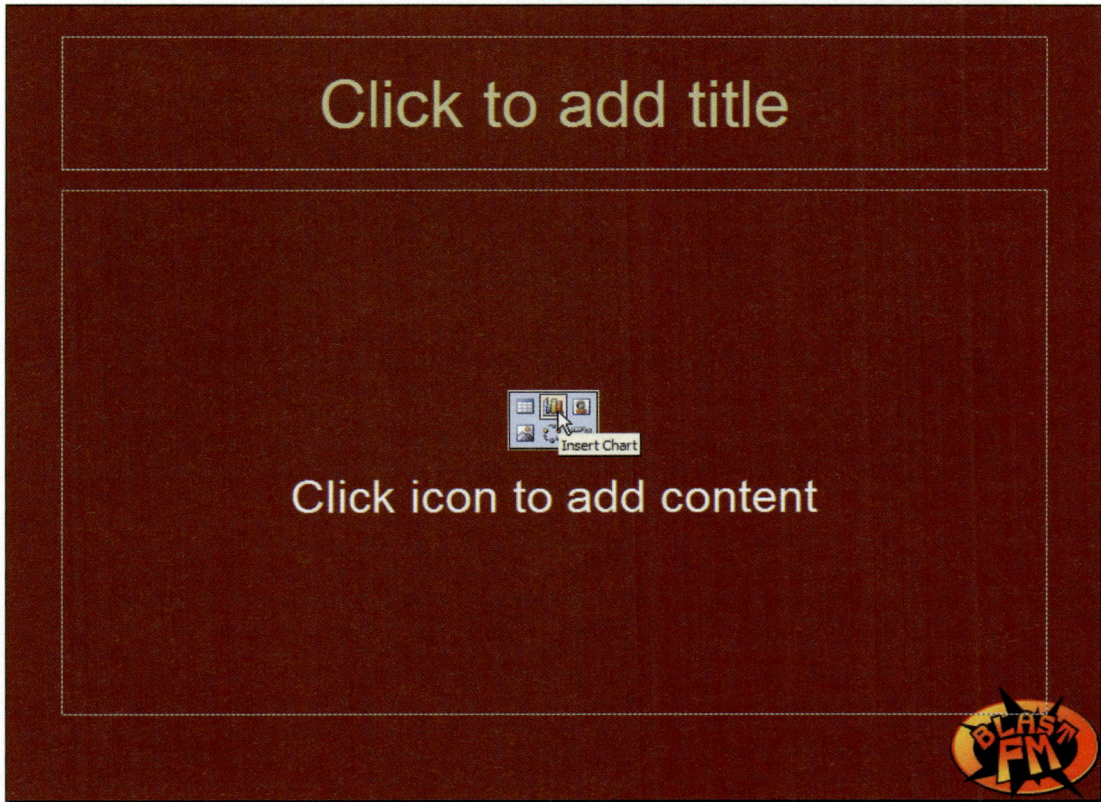

Figure 5.1: Inserting a chart

Note!

An alternative way of inserting a chart is to use **Insert**, **Chart** from the main menu.

A chart containing dummy data will be created, as shown in Figure 5.2.

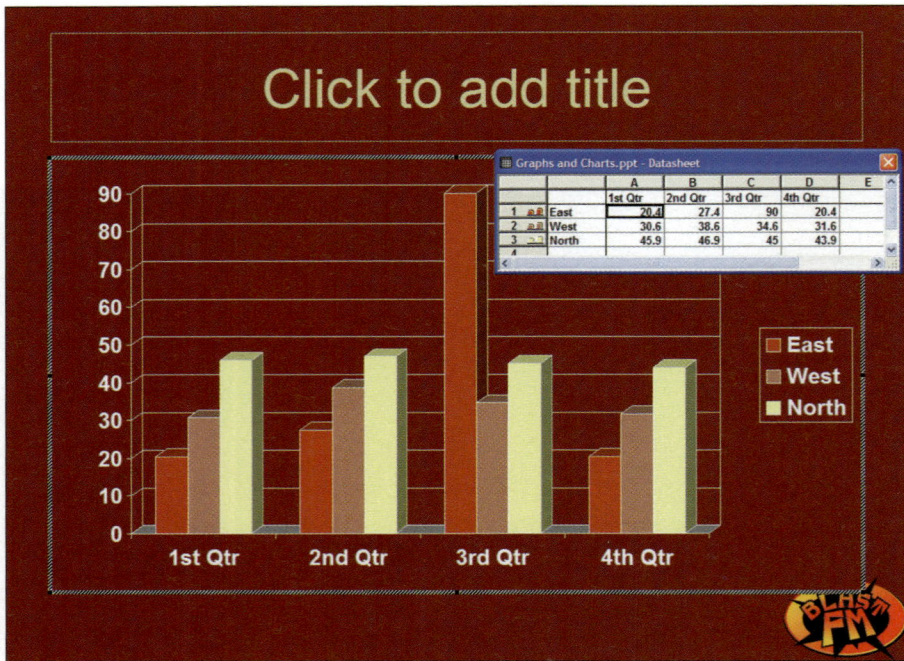

Figure 5.2: Initial chart with dummy data

Right-click in the row header numbered **3** and select **Delete** from the menu that appears. The chart updates to show only the remaining two dummy data series.

Edit the **Datasheet** to contain the numbers of listeners and the amount of advertising income for the last two years, as shown in Figure 5.3. You may need to resize some of the columns by dragging between them in the column header.

		A	B	C	D	E	F	G	H	I
		Q1 2005	Q2 2005	Q3 2005	Q4 2005	Q1 2006	Q2 2006	Q3 2006	Q4 2006	
1	Listeners	420,000	435,000	444,000	481,500	568,500	531,000	532,500	525,000	
2	Advertising income	£900,000	£909,000	£1,051,000	£1,065,000	£1,232,000	£1,179,000	£943,000	£915,000	
3										

Figure 5.3: Listener and advertising numbers

➤ Click in the grey area surrounding the slide to deselect the chart and thereby stop editing it.

➤ Change the title to **Listeners and advertising income**.

Your chart should now look like Figure 5.4.

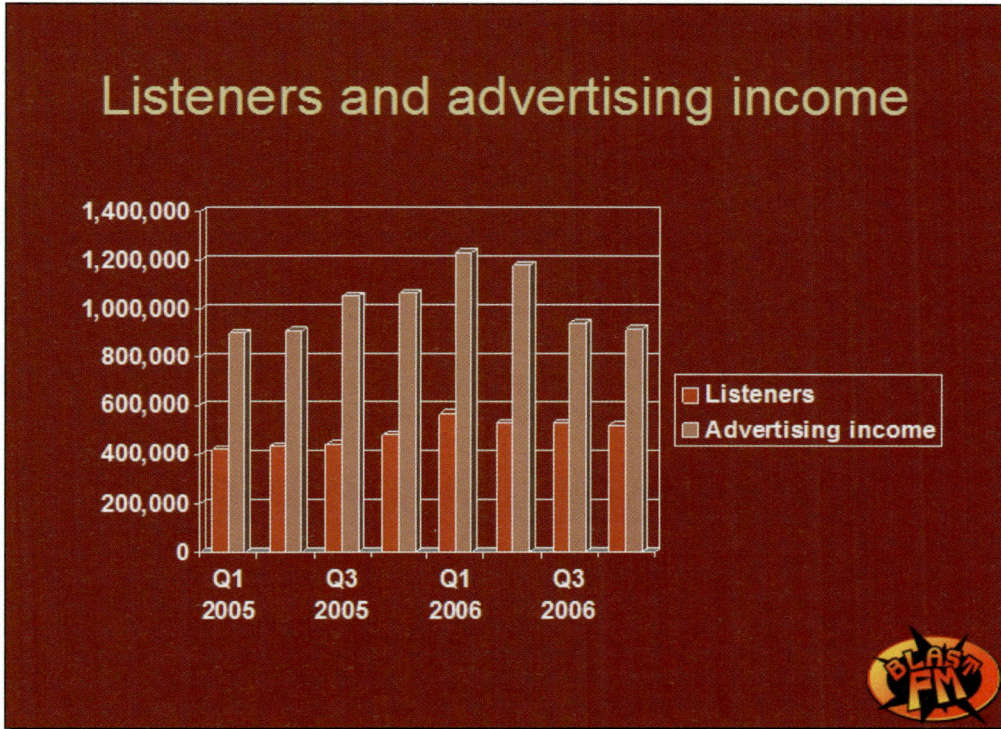

Figure 5.4: The initial chart

Independent axes and chart types for data series

The **Listeners** data series is difficult to read because the **Advertising income** figures are much larger, so they are dominating the y-axis. This chart can be improved by adding a second y-axis so that both the data series have their own y-axes.

SYLLABUS

Ref: AM6.4.1.1
Create a line – column on two axes/mixed chart/graph.

SYLLABUS

Ref: AM6.4.1.2
Change graph/chart type such as: a column chart/graph to a line – column on two axes/
mixed chart/graph.

Double-click on the chart to edit it.

TIP

If the **Datasheet** doesn't appear automatically (usually because you closed its window
before), then select **View**, **Datasheet** from the menu.

From the main menu, select **Chart**, **Chart Type**. The **Chart Type** dialogue box appears.

Change to the **Custom Types** tab and select **Line – Column on 2 Axes** from the **Chart
type** list, as shown in Figure 5.5. Press **OK**.

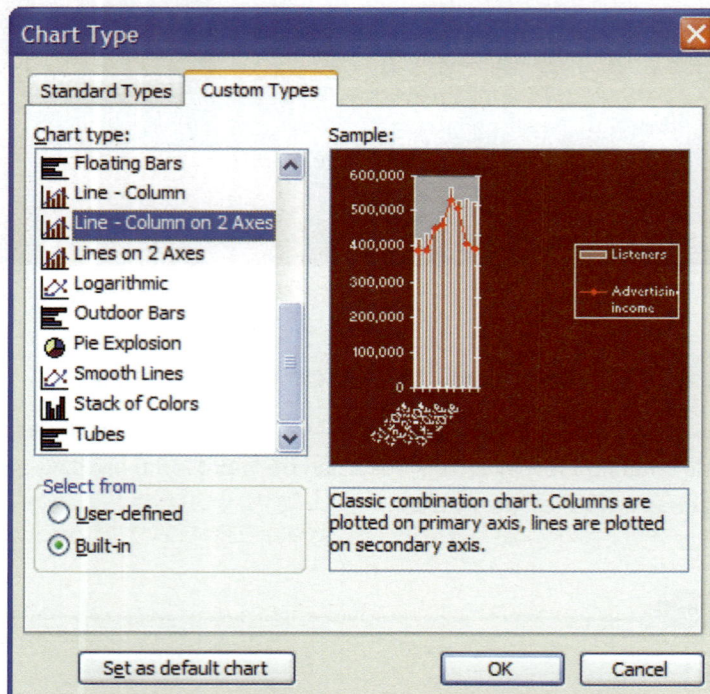

Figure 5.5: Changing the chart type

Even if you know from the outset that you want a particular type of chart, it is still easiest to create a default column chart (as you have done) and then to change its type later.

➡ Click in the grey area around the slide again.

Your chart should now look like Figure 5.6.

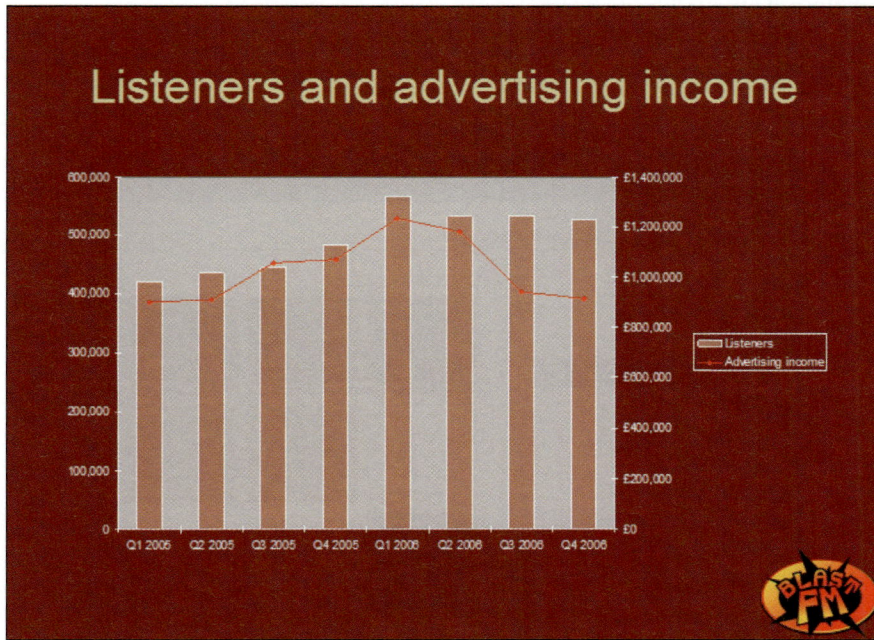

Figure 5.6: A mixed chart type

Notice that the listener numbers are plotted as columns against the left-hand y-axis and the advertising income is plotted as a line against the right-hand y-axis.

You may think that the chart type applies to the chart as a whole. However, each data series has a chart type associated with it – changing the chart type for the whole chart is simply a shortcut to setting the chart type for each data series in turn.

This can be demonstrated by changing the **Listeners** data series from columns to a line.

SYLLABUS

Ref: AM6.4.1.3
Change a chart type format to a named chart style, format. Change chart/graph type for a data series in a chart/graph.

Double-click on the chart to edit it.

Right-click on any of the columns and select **Chart Type** from the menu that appears. The **Chart Type** dialogue box appears.

In the **Standard Types** tab, select **Line** (as shown in Figure 5.7) and press **OK**.

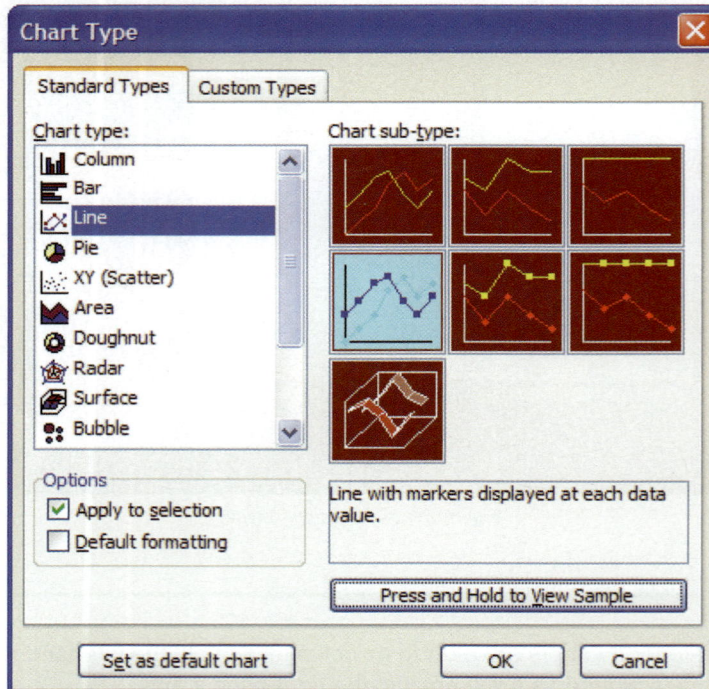

Figure 5.7: Changing the chart type for a single data series

Click in the grey area again. Your chart should look like Figure 5.8.

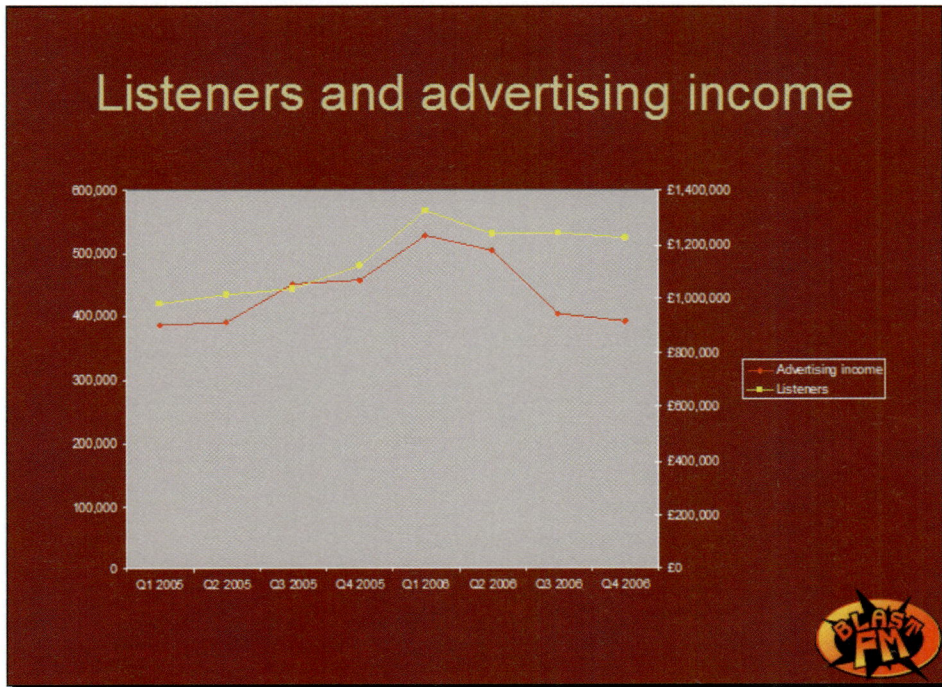

Figure 5.8: The result of changing the columns into a line

Customising axes

Because there is a lot of wasted space under the two lines, you can change the scale.

SYLLABUS

Ref: AM6.4.1.4
Change scale of value axis (y-axis), minimum, maximum number to display, major interval between plotted numbers in a chart/graph.

Double-click on the chart to edit it.

Double-click on the left-hand y-axis. The **Format Axis** dialogue box appears.

Click on the **Scale** tab. Change the **Minimum** to **420000** and the **Major unit** to **20000**, as shown in Figure 5.9. (The corresponding **Auto** checkboxes will automatically clear themselves.) Press **OK**.

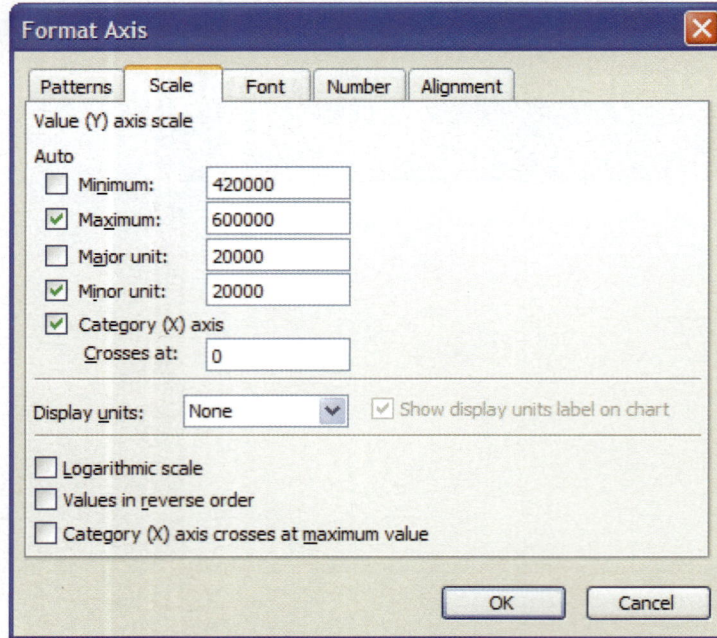

Figure 5.9: Customising the axis

Minimum is the lowest value to plot on the chart.

Maximum is the highest value to plot on the chart.

Major unit is the frequency with which to add numerical labels to the axis (in this case, they will increase in jumps of 20,000).

Minor unit is the frequency with which unnumbered tick marks should be added to the axis. We won't be using this feature.

Category (X) axis Crosses at is the y-axis value at which to draw the x-axis.

The values with their **Auto** checkboxes ticked will be automatically calculated by PowerPoint (their current values will be updated in the light of your changes).

Make a similar change to the right-hand y-axis, setting **Minimum** to **900000** and **Major unit** to **100000**.

Click in the grey border again. Your chart should now look like Figure 5.10.

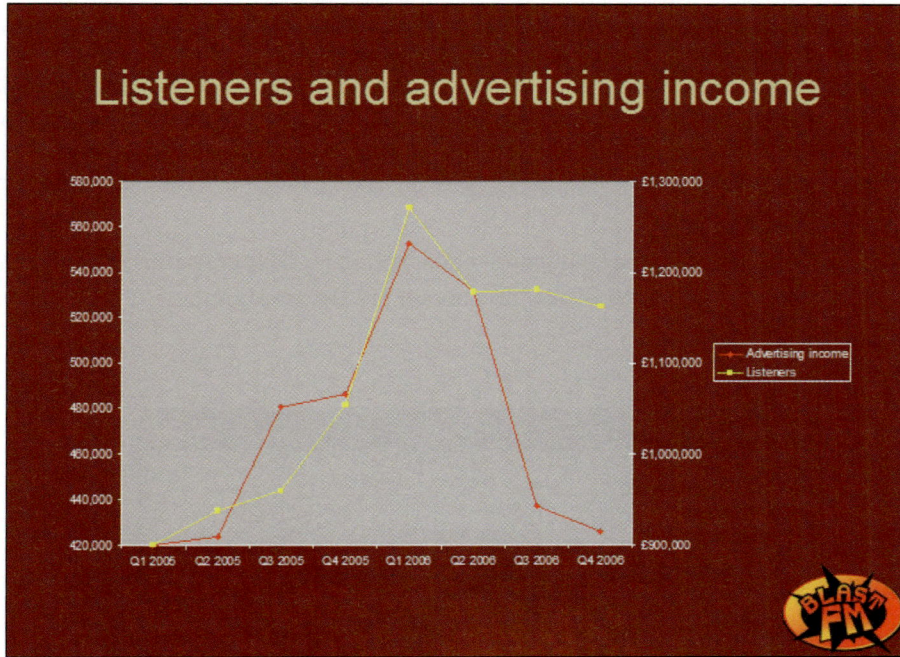

Figure 5.10: Customised range and major tick values for the axes

This has made it much clearer that listener numbers are stabilising after a period of good growth, and that advertising income has fallen sharply in the last two quarters of 2005.

Changing the display units

You can improve the axes still further by simplifying the numbers. There is a built-in feature to display the number of thousands, millions or other multiples.

SYLLABUS

Ref: AM6.4.1.5
Apply built-in feature to display y-axis units in a chart/graph in hundreds, thousands, millions on value axis, not changing numbers in data grid.

Double-click on the chart to edit it.

Double-click on the left-hand y-axis to edit it. The **Format Axis** dialogue box appears, with the **Scale** tab selected automatically (since this was the last one you used).

Change **Display units** to **Thousands** and untick the **Show display units label on chart** box. Press **OK**.

Note!

If the **Show display units label on chart** box were ticked, the word **Thousands** would appear just beneath the axis title. Instead, you will add your own axis title, specifying that the values are in thousands.

Make a similar change to the right-hand y-axis, changing **Display units** to **Millions**. This time, also change the **Number** tab and set the **Decimal places** to **1**, as shown in Figure 5.11. Press **OK**.

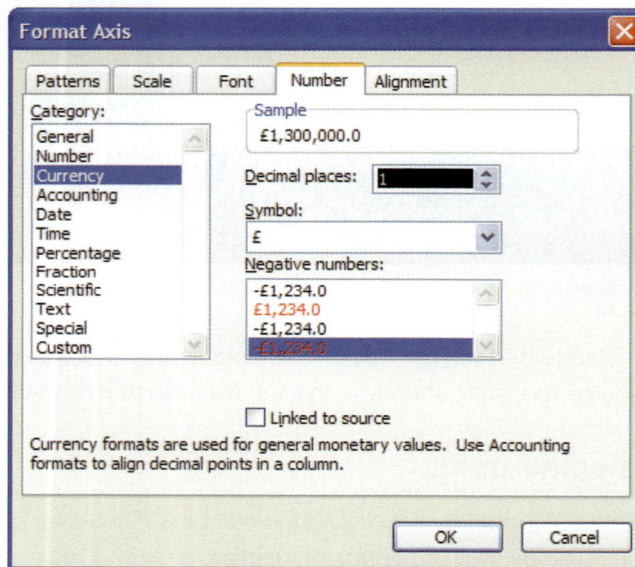

Figure 5.11: Increasing the number of decimal places

Note!

The values in the **Datasheet** haven't changed, just the way they are represented on the axes. You can use this technique to display values in hundred, thousands, millions, billions or trillions!

From the main menu, select **Chart**, **Chart Options**. The **Chart Options** dialogue box appears.

On the **Titles** tab, set the **Value (Y) axis** to **Listeners (thousands)** and the **Second value (Y) axis** to **Advertising income (£m)**, as shown in Figure 5.12. You can make better use of the space by moving the legend to the bottom: change to the **Legend** tab and select the option **Bottom**. Press **OK**.

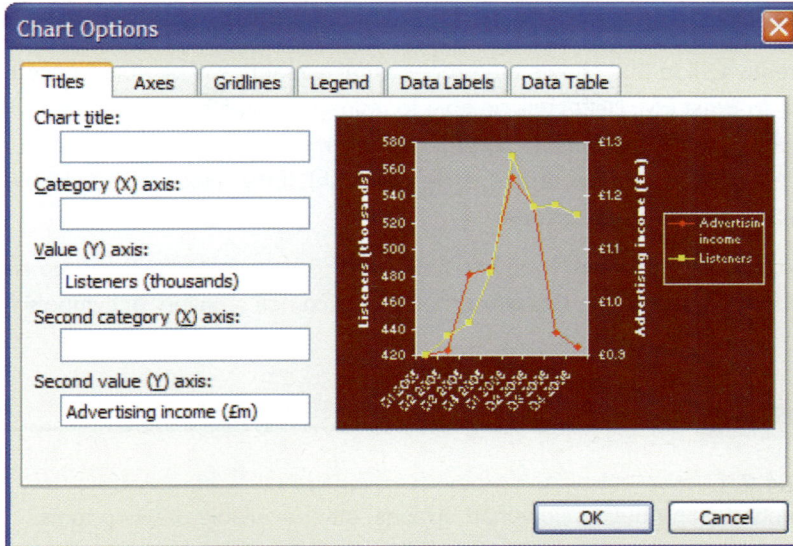

Figure 5.12: Adding y-axis titles

Your finished chart should look like Figure 5.13.

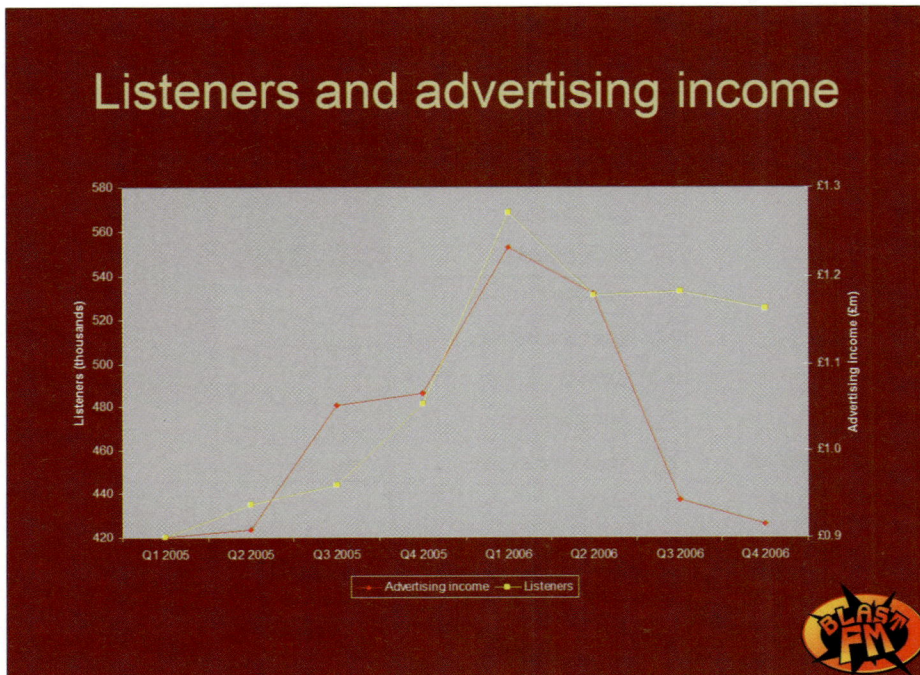

Figure 5.13: Completed chart

Flow charts

We will now create a slide that shows the process that listeners will be able to use to submit their own music to Blast FM. Users will be able to upload music files via Blast FM's website. The DJ will then check that the quality is acceptable (for example, that it is the sort of music Blast FM plays and that the quality of the recording is high enough). If the music is acceptable, it will be added to the play list and broadcast later.

We will capture this process in the form of a flow chart. The easiest way to create simple flow charts in PowerPoint is to use the **Drawing** toolbar, which has a gallery of symbols for flow charts.

SYLLABUS

Ref: AM6.4.2.1
Draw a flowchart using built-in flowchart options, other available drawing tools.

Create a new slide and set its layout to **Title Only**. Set the title to **User-submitted music.**

From the drawing toolbar, select **AutoShapes**, **Flowchart** and select the **Terminator** symbol, as shown in Figure 5.14.

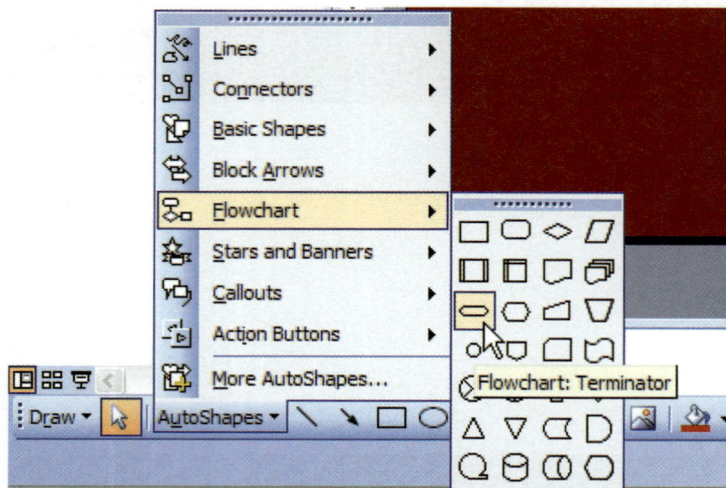

Figure 5.14: Starting to draw the flow chart

Click and drag on the slide to create a flow chart terminator shape, as shown in Figure 5.15.

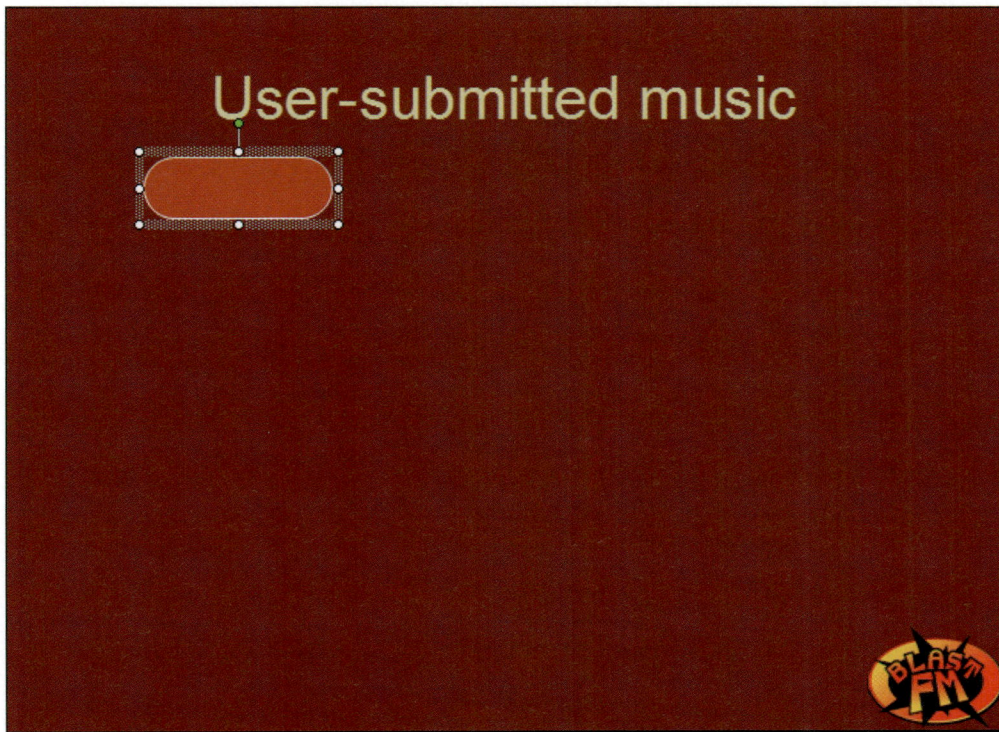

Figure 5.15: Adding the first shape to the flow chart

Right-click on the shape and select **Add Text** from the menu that appears. Type **Start** and then click anywhere outside the shape to clear the selection.

> **TIP**
>
> You can use **Add Text** to add a label to any AutoShape, not just flow chart elements.

This symbol represents the entry point into the flow chart. We need one more terminator at the exit point, so we can create this as a copy.

Click the **Start** symbol and then hold down the **Ctrl** key and drag the edge of the shape (not the handles) to start the copy. Your mouse pointer acquires a **+** sign to show that you are copying instead of moving, and a dotted outline shows where the copied shape will appear. Drop the symbol in the bottom right of your slide before releasing the **Ctrl** key. Change the new shape's text (just click in it) to **End** (Figure 5.16).

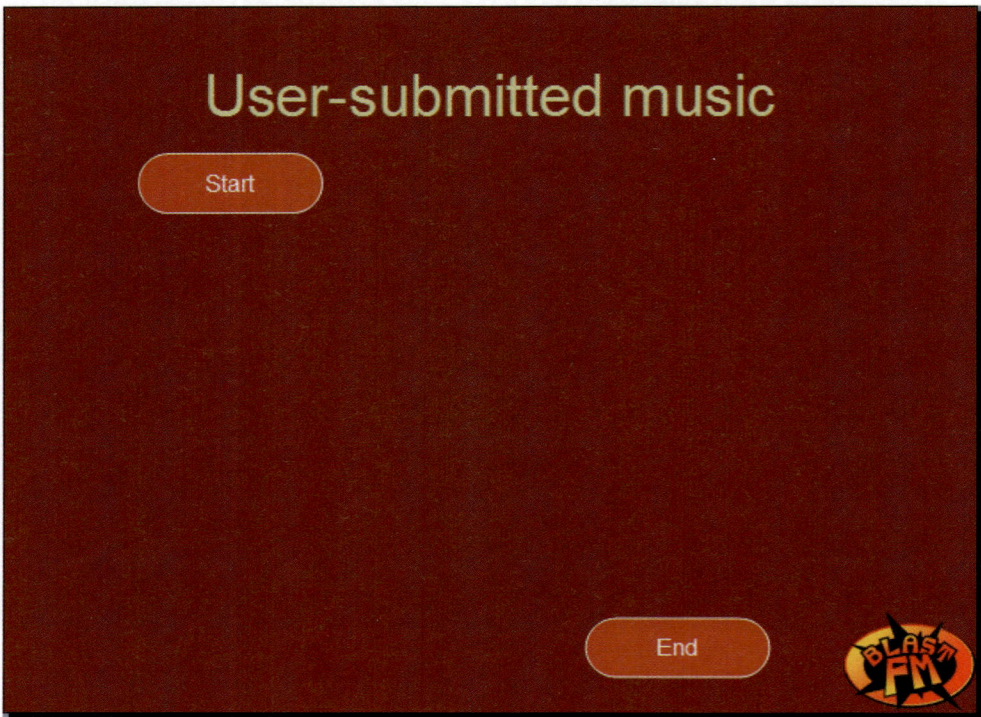

Figure 5.16: Adding text and copying shapes

Add a square (**Process**) flow chart AutoShape below the **Start** shape. Add the following text **Load and fill in [Enter] submission [Enter] Web page**, pressing the **Enter** key where indicated to break the lines.

Straight
Arrow
Connector

From the **Drawing** toolbar, select **AutoShapes**, **Connectors** and pick the **Straight Arrow Connector** (the middle one on the top row). Hover your mouse pointer over the **Start** shape and you will find that some blue connection points appear around it. Click on the bottom connection point and drag to the top connection point of the shape below it (as shown in Figure 5.17), then release your mouse. An arrow appears.

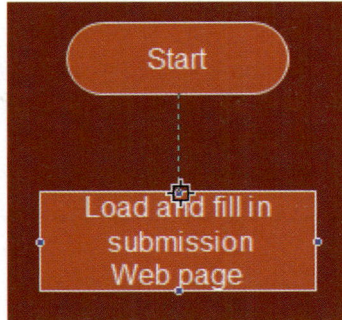

Figure 5.17: Drawing a connector between two drawing objects

A connector is different from a normal line or arrow because it is attached to the shapes you have drawn it between.

Move the bottom box slightly. You should find that the connector moves with it.

Add the other boxes and connectors shown in Figure 5.18. Two different types of connector are needed: a **Curved Arrow Connector** between **Upload music file** and **Quality OK**, and an **Elbow Arrow Connector** for the two **No** connectors. There are also some text boxes containing **Yes** and **No** for the two **Decision** boxes.

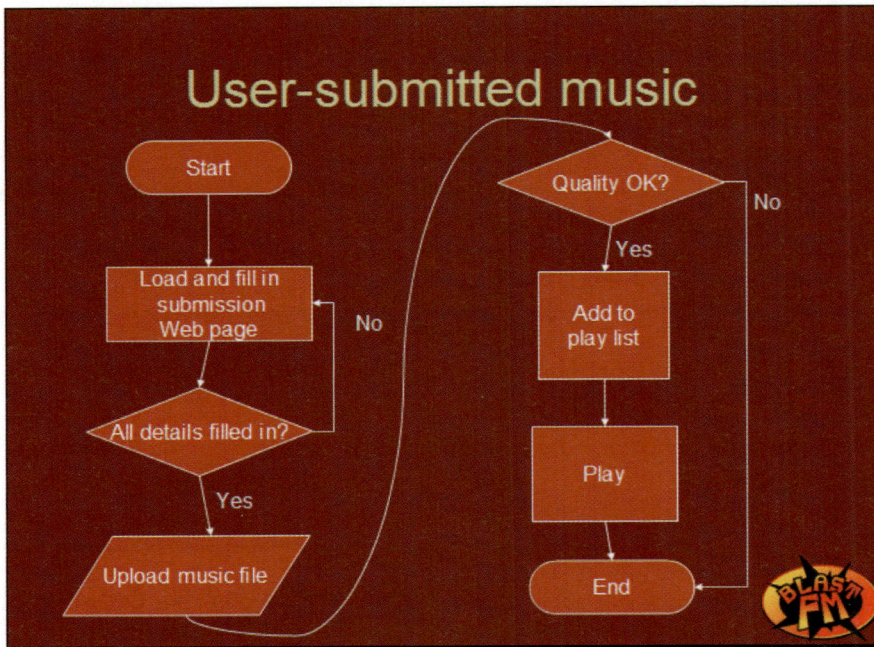

Figure 5.18: The flow chart before tidying

Use the **Align or Distribute** commands to tidy up the flow chart.

Modifying shapes

It's straightforward to change an AutoShape from one type to another without losing its formatting.

SYLLABUS

Ref: AM6.4.2.2
Change, delete flowchart shapes in a flowchart.

Click the **Add to play list** shape to select it.

D

Delay

From the **Drawing** toolbar, select **Draw**, **Change AutoShape**, **Flowchart**, **Delay**. The shape changes to a D-shaped box.

TIP

To delete a shape from a flow chart, simply select it (click on the shape's border so you are not editing its text) and press the **Delete** key.

Changing connector types

SYLLABUS

Ref: AM6.4.2.3
Change connector types between flowchart shapes.

Select the curved connector, right click it and select **Elbow** from the menu that appears.

TIP

To change the arrow heads, you could use the **Arrow Style** tool on the **Drawing** toolbar.

Your final flow chart should look like Figure 5.19.

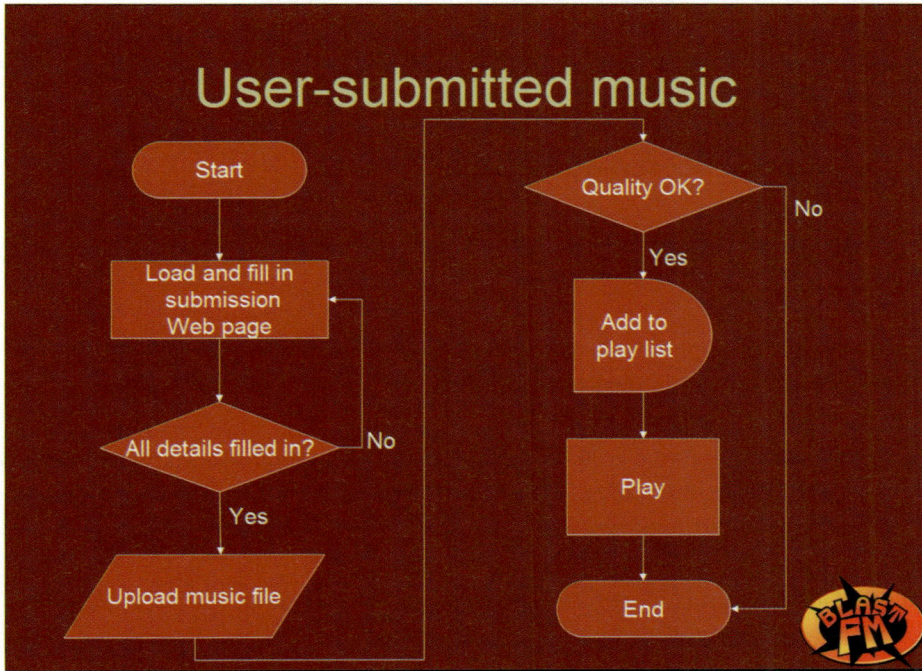

Figure 5.19: The tidied flow chart

Save your presentation as **Charts.ppt**.

Conclusions

This exercise has demonstrated the following points.

- You can use **Chart**, **Chart Type** to change the type of chart. You can set the chart type for each data series individually to create mixed-type charts.

- The quickest way to edit a chart is to double-click on it.

- Click outside a chart (for example, in the grey area around the edge of the slide) to finish editing it.

- You can double-click on an axis to customise it. You can change the **Minimum** and **Maximum** values, and the **Major unit**, which controls the frequency of the text labels.

- The easiest way to create a flow chart is to draw it using the AutoShapes on the **Drawing** toolbar. The menu **AutoShapes**, **Flowchart** contains the main symbols, which you can join together with arrowed **connectors**.

- You can add a text label to an AutoShape by right-clicking on it and selecting **Add Text** from the menu that appears.

- To change the type of an AutoShape (such as a box on a flow chart), select it and choose **Draw**, **Change AutoShape** from the **Drawing** toolbar. To delete an AutoShape, select it (by clicking on its border) and press the **Delete** key.

- You cannot change a connector shape in this way. Instead, you have to right-click it and select a new type – Straight Connector, Elbow Connector or Curved Connector – from the menu that appears.

Test yourself

Internet radio trial data usage

Blast FM kept records about the amount of data they transmitted at different times of day during their Internet radio trial. They offered 50 high-bit-rate data streams and 50 low-bit-rate data streams for people to listen to. Figure 5.20 shows the amount of data they transmitted in megabytes, on average, across different times of day. They can use this information to work out what their bandwidth bills are likely to be if they decide to go ahead with the Internet radio station.

1. Add a new slide to **Charts.ppt** containing a chart set up with the data shown in Figure 5.20.

		A	B	C	D	E	F	G	H	I	J	K	L	M
		M'night	2	4	6	8	10 Noon	2	4	6	8	10	
1	High bit rate	406	383	148	231	299	567	659	523	599	717	682	595	
2	Low bit rate	102	91	36	51	85	136	183	152	140	193	173	159	
3														

Figure 5.20: Data about the Internet radio trial

2. Give the chart a title and set the legend to display at the top of the chart. Add titles for both axes. Make sure that the horizontal axis shows all the values (on its **Scale** tab, change **Number of categories between tick mark labels** to **1**). Set the vertical axis to extend to **1000** megabytes (approximately 1 gigabyte) and to display its results in **Thousands**. Your chart should now look like Figure 5.21.

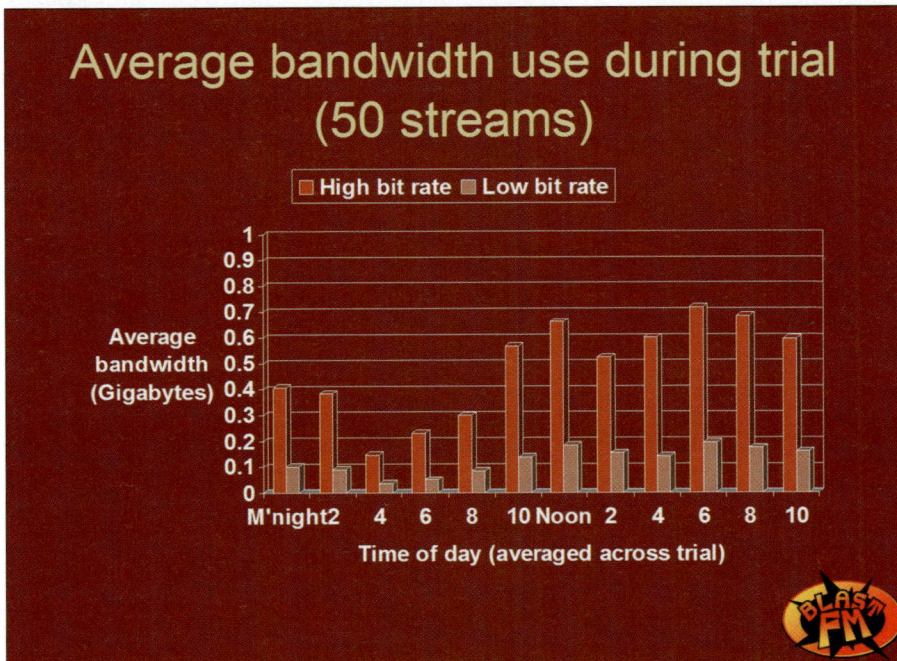

Figure 5.21: Initial bandwidth chart

3. Change the chart type for the whole chart to any of the two-axis chart types, and then change the two data series one at a time to have the **Area** chart type. Move the legend back to the top (if it has moved) and type in the axis titles shown in Figure 5.22.

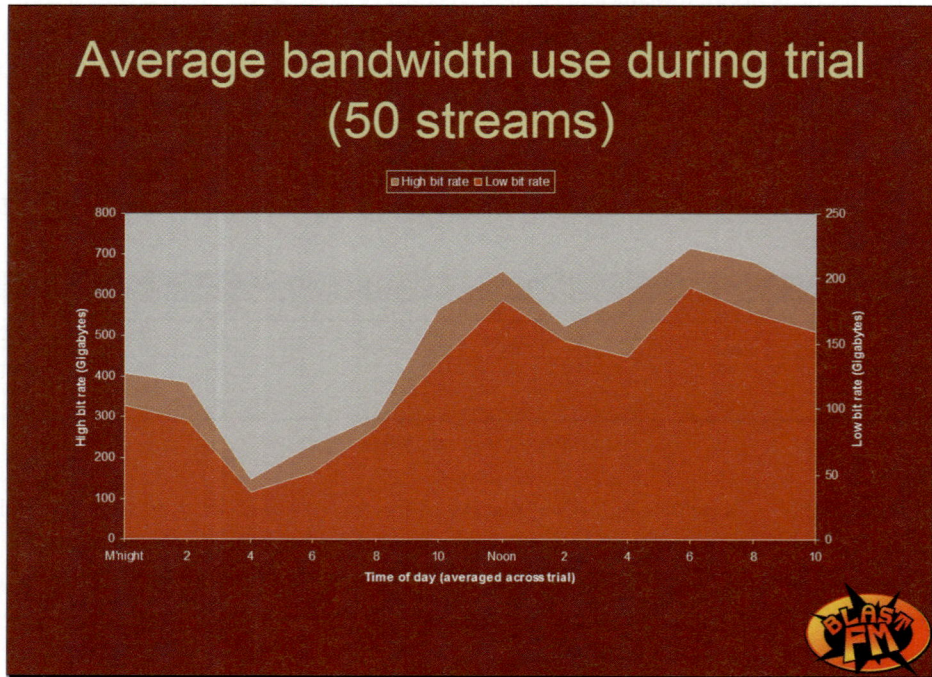

Figure 5.22: The same chart represented as two areas

4. Practise drawing a flow chart for an everyday activity, such as making a cup of tea. Make sure you are confident adding and deleting the flow chart shapes and their connectors, and that you remember how to change the type of a flow chart shape or connector without having to delete it.

6 Animation and multimedia

Introduction

In this chapter, we will use PowerPoint's animation capabilities to add entrance and exit effects to slide components such as bullets, drawing objects and charts. Then we will see how to add multimedia components – sound files and movie clips – to presentations, and how to control them. (You might like to check that you have some headphones attached to your PC if you are learning with other people.)

In this chapter, you will

add entrance animation to objects, triggered either by a mouse click or a time delay

learn how to make objects **dim** after they appear

change the order of animations in a slide using the **Re-Order** buttons

create a simple column chart and use it to learn how to **animate chart elements** by series, by category, by elements in a series or by elements in a category

insert sounds to represent the types of music that are liked and loathed by Blast FM, and learn how to control their **animation style** and **timing**

insert a movie showing an explosion, as a more interesting start to the slide show, and add animation effects to make it fade out while the Blast FM logo fades in.

Animation

Animation on click

SYLLABUS

Ref: AM6.5.2.1 (Part 1 of 2)
Introduce animated objects by mouse click, automatically after a specified time.

Open the **Investment.ppt** presentation you created in Chapter 2.

Change to the **History** slide.

We will make these bullets appear one by one in response to key presses.

First, the easy way.

Click anywhere in the list of bullets and then select **Slide Show**, **Animation Schemes** from the menu. The **Slide Design** task pane appears, containing a list of animation styles.

Select **Appear**, as shown in Figure 6.1.

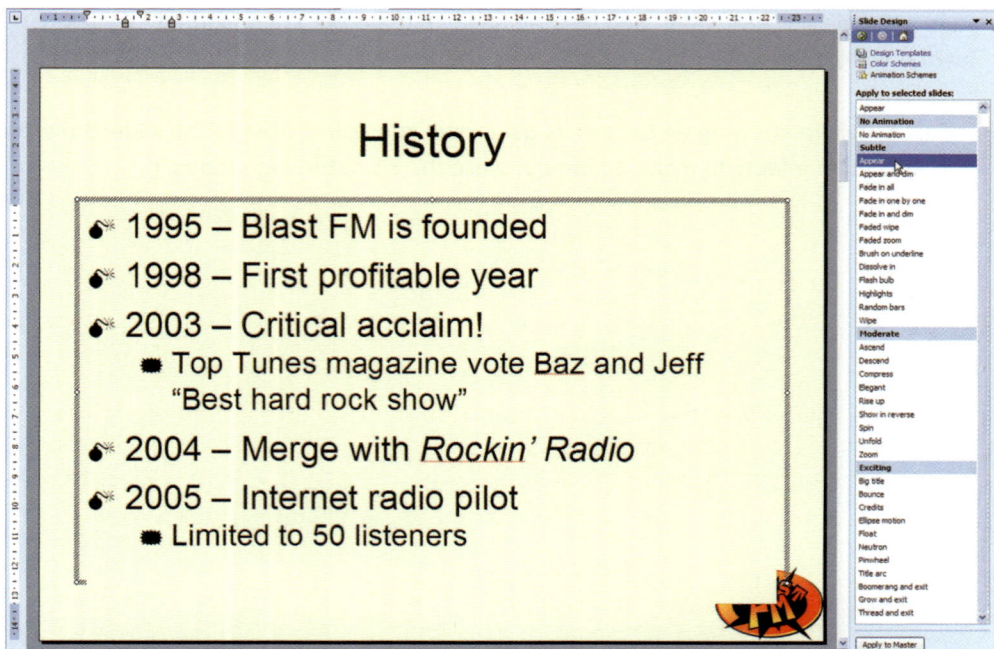

Figure 6.1: Setting a simple animation style for a slide

Press the **Slide Show** button at the bottom of the task pane to test the slide.

Slide Show

TIP

Shift + F5 is the shortcut key for starting the presentation from the current slide.

First you should get a slide containing only the **History** title and the Blast FM logo.

Press **Space**. The first bullet point appears. Repeat this four times for the other bullets.

TIP

If you prefer, you could **click the mouse** or use the **down arrow** key instead of **Space**.

Press **Space** again. The slide show progresses to the next slide.

Press **Esc** to quit the slide show, and then change back to the **History** slide.

That was the easy way!

TIP

You can use the **Play** button at the bottom of the task pane to get a quick preview of the effect without having to press any more keys. Try it!

Play

Dimming after animation

SYLLABUS

Ref: AM6.5.2.3
Apply automatic settings so that bulleted points, drawn objects in a presentation will dim to a specified colour after animation.

It's just as easy to get the earlier bullets to dim each time a new one appears.

➜ Click in the bulleted list again and this time choose **Appear and dim** as the animation style.

➜ Test the slide show again to check the effect. Each new bullet should cause the previous one to dim, as shown in Figure 6.2.

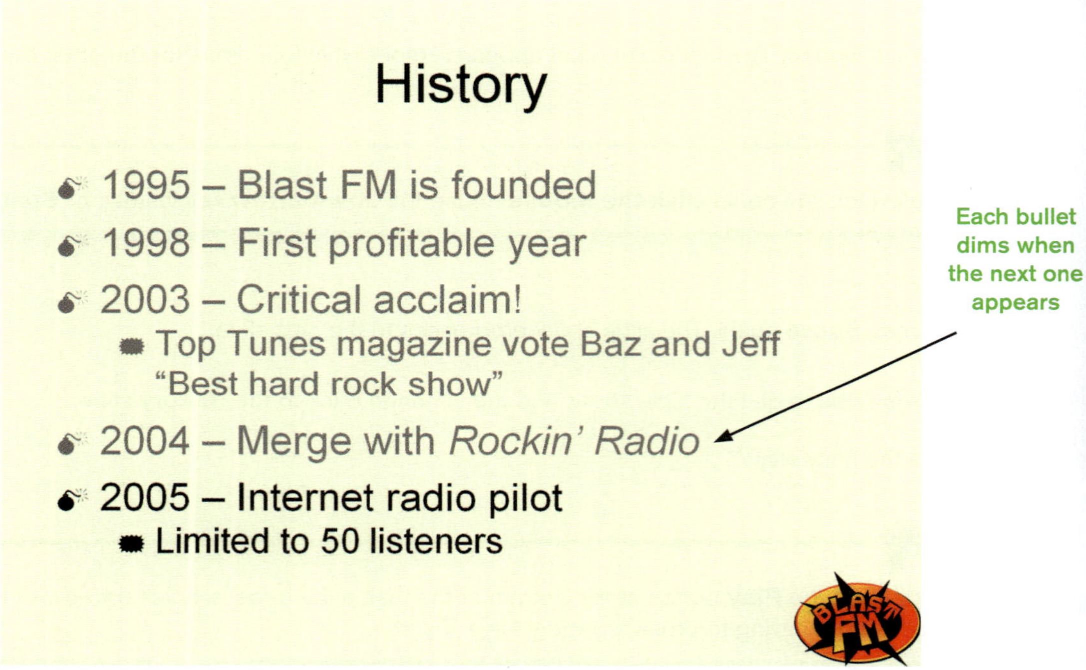

History

- 1995 – Blast FM is founded
- 1998 – First profitable year
- 2003 – Critical acclaim!
    - Top Tunes magazine vote Baz and Jeff "Best hard rock show"
- 2004 – Merge with *Rockin' Radio*
- 2005 – Internet radio pilot
    - Limited to 50 listeners

Each bullet dims when the next one appears

Figure 6.2: Dimming 'stale' bullets

You can see from the list in the task pane that there are lots of different styles to experiment with. You can also choose different styles for individual bullets, as you'll now see.

By default, the bullet points change to the colour scheme's **Shadows** colour when they dim. To change the colour, you can either edit the colour scheme (see Chapter 2) or edit the effect options (see Figure 6.3) – you will have plenty of practice in editing the effect options in the rest of this chapter.

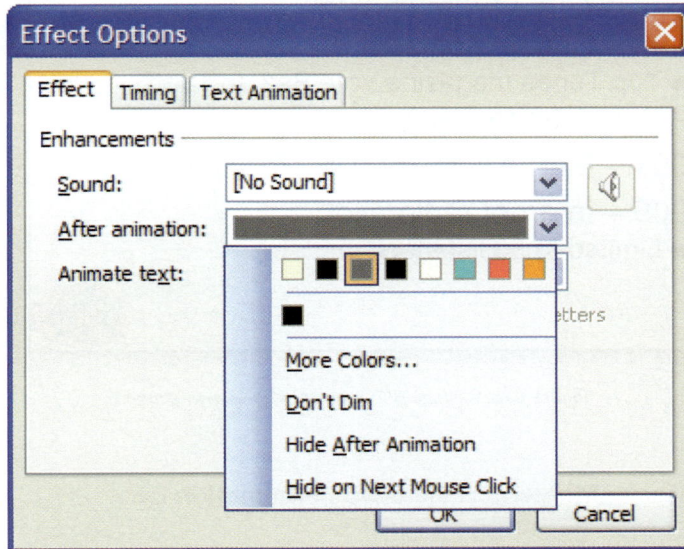

Figure 6.3: Changing the dim colour

You can use the same techniques to cause drawing objects to dim after they appear.

Custom animation

From the menu, select **Slide Show**, **Custom Animation**. The **Custom Animation** task pane appears, together with numbers beside the bullet points, as shown in Figure 6.4.

Animation numbers beside the bullets

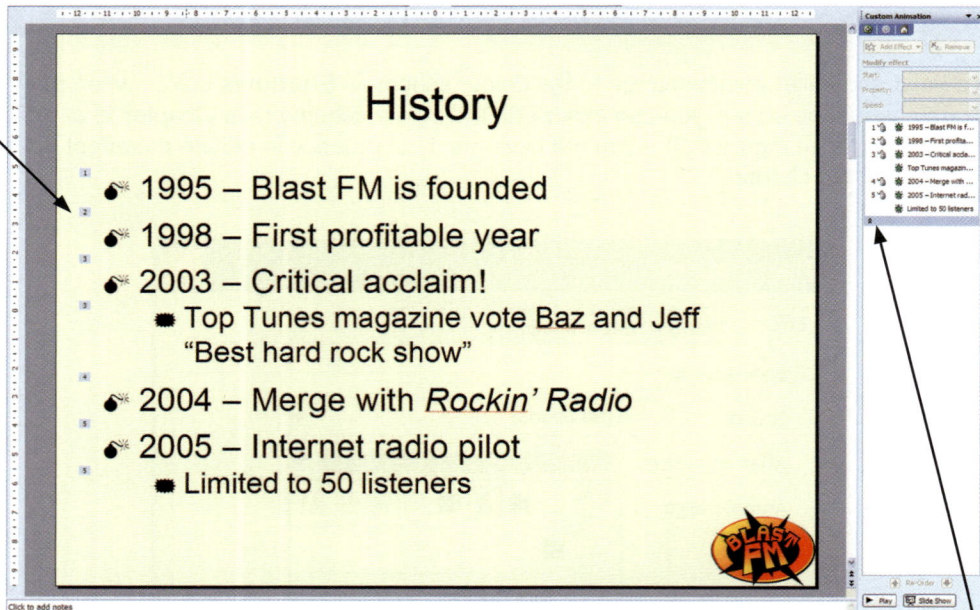

Figure 6.4: Switching to a custom animation scheme

You may need to click here to expand the list

Select animation 4 (**Merge...**) in the **Custom Animation** list.

Press the **Change** button at the top of the task pane and select **Entrance**, **Checkerboard** from the menu that appears.

Press **Shift + F5** to test the slide again. This time, when you get to the **Merge with Rockin' Radio** bullet, it should fade in with a checkerboard pattern, as shown in Figure 6.5.

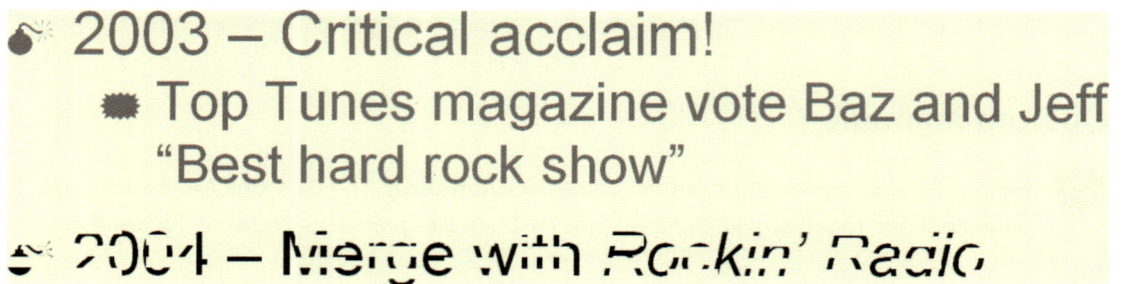

2003 – Critical acclaim!
● Top Tunes magazine vote Baz and Jeff "Best hard rock show"
2004 – Merge with *Rockin' Radio*

Figure 6.5: Checkerboard effect

You can use this custom animation to trigger animation at specific times instead of in response to keypresses, as you'll see in the following section.

Save **Investment.ppt** and close it.

Time-delayed animation

SYLLABUS

Ref: AM6.5.2.1 (Part 2 of 2)
Introduce animated objects by mouse click, automatically after a specified time.

Open **Charts.ppt**, which you created in Chapter 5.

Change to the flow chart slide (**User-submitted music**).

We're going to animate this so that each new box appears at ten-second intervals, which will allow the person giving the presentation to talk without having to keep pressing buttons to introduce the new boxes.

From the menu, select **Slide Show**, **Custom Animation**.

Select the **Load and fill in submission Web page** box.

Click the **Add Effect** button at the top of the task bar and select **Entrance**, **More Effects** from the menu. The **Add Entrance Effect** dialogue box appears.

Make sure that the **Preview Effect** checkbox at the bottom of the dialogue box is ticked and then try out some of the different effects by clicking on their names. When you've finished experimenting, select **Faded Zoom** from the **Subtle** section and press **OK** (Figure 6.6).

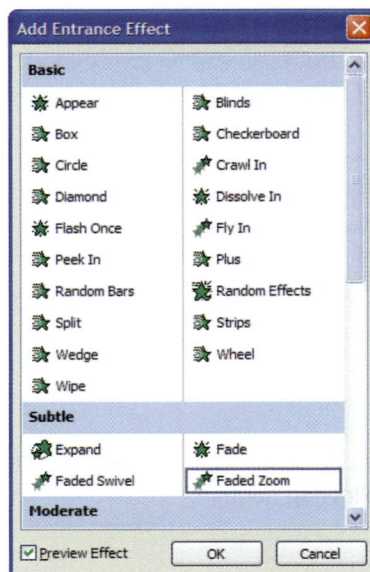

Figure 6.6: Adding an entrance effect from the list

➡ Change **Start** to **After Previous**.

This tells PowerPoint to wait until the previous animation has finished before starting this one. You can go one step further and specify the delay.

➡ Click the arrow to the right of the new effect (**0**) in the task pane and select **Timing** from the menu that appears, as shown in Figure 6.7.

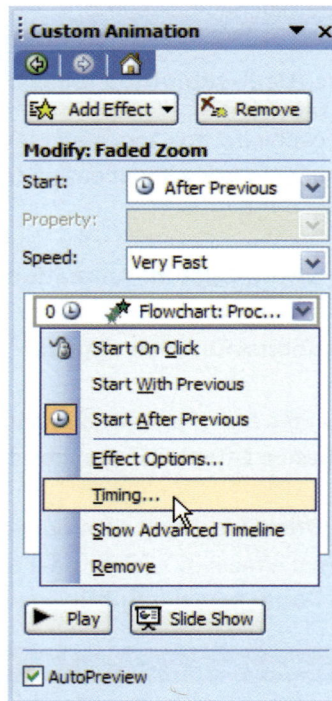

Figure 6.7: Setting custom timing for an animation effect

A dialogue box named after the effect (**Faded Zoom**) appears. There are three tabs, but the **Timing** tab is automatically selected.

➡ Change the **Delay** to **5** seconds, as shown in Figure 6.8, and then press **OK**.

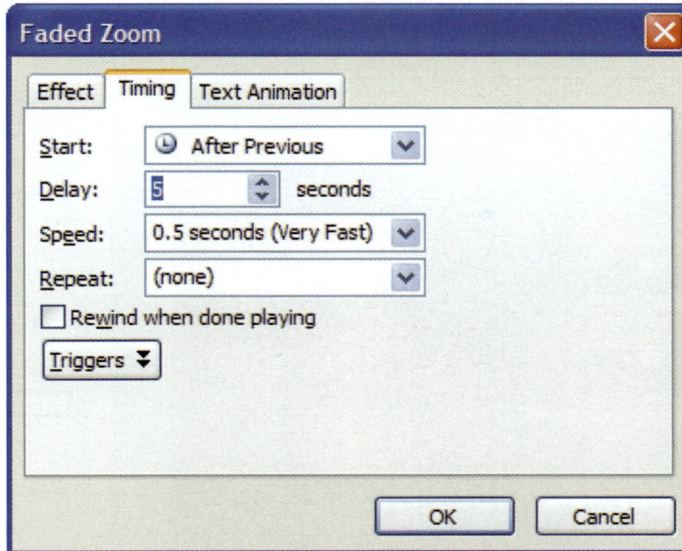

Figure 6.8: Adding a five-second delay

> **Note!**
>
> If you add a **Delay** to an animation effect and the effect that follows is set to start **With Previous**, then it will start at the beginning of the delay period, not at the end. Therefore, if you have two or more effects that you wish to start simultaneously after a delay, you will need to add the same **Delay** setting to all of them.

Press the **Play** button to preview the animation. There is a five-second delay and then the box fades and zooms in.

 Play

We also want the arrow out of the **Start** box to appear.

Select the arrow that comes out of the **Start** box. Add an **Entrance** effect of type **Descend** to it. Change its **Start** setting to **With Previous**.

Preview the animation. If the arrow floats over the top of the **Start** box, right-click the border of the **Start** box and select **Order**, **Bring to Front** from the menu that appears. If you now preview the animation again, the arrow will appear to grow from one box to the other.

Repeat this process for the next box (**All details filled in?**). Give it a **Faded Zoom** entrance animation that occurs five seconds after the previous animation, and make the arrow from the previous box **Descend** at the same time.

Your slide should now look like Figure 6.9.

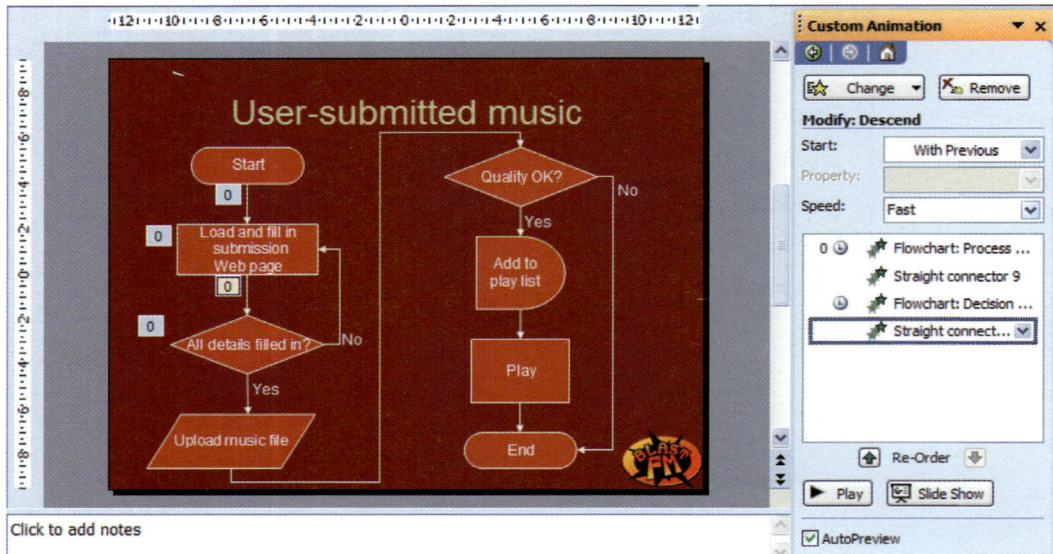

Figure 6.9: After animating two boxes and two lines

This is the first box with two lines coming out of it. We'll animate the **No** branch separately, and then the **Yes** branch with the **Upload music file box**.

Select both the **Yes** label and the **No** label (click one, hold down **Ctrl** and then click the other). Give them an **Appear** animation effect to take place **After Previous**.

This will make the labels appear at the correct time, without any fancy effect. The next step is to make the arrowed connector for the **No** branch appear to grow upwards.

Select the arrowed connector that represents the **No** branch. Give it a **Stretch** effect, occurring **After Previous** (don't worry that this doesn't look right yet).

Click the arrow to the right of the effect you have just added and select **Effect Options** from the menu. The **Stretch** dialogue box appears.

Change **Direction** to **From Bottom**, as shown in Figure 6.10(a). This will cause the arrow to grow upwards. Switch to the **Timing** tab and set the **Delay** to **5** seconds (Figure 6.10(b)). Press **OK** to confirm the new settings.

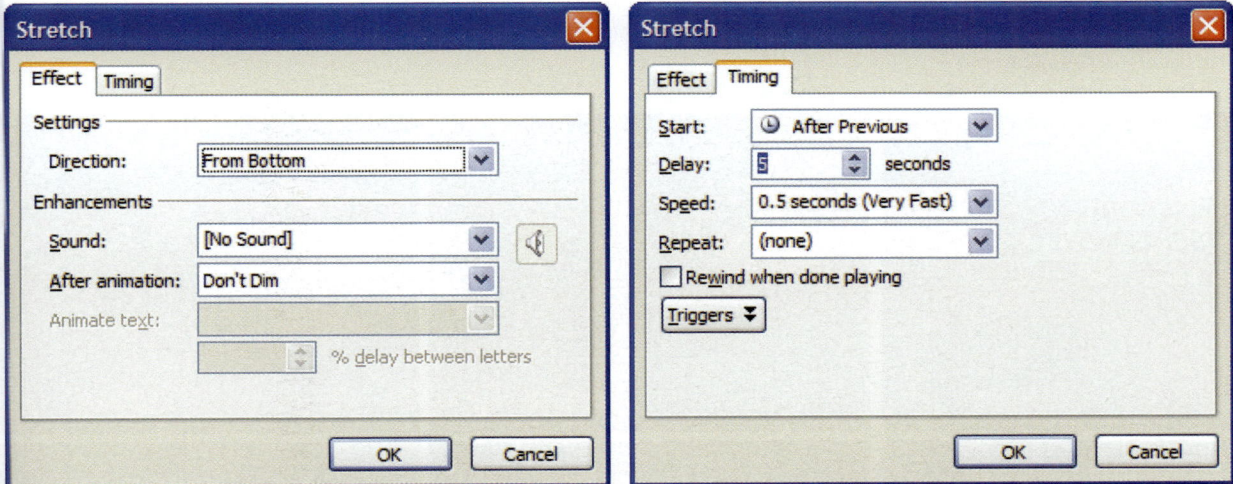

Figure 6.10: Changing the stretch options (a) the Effect tab and (b) the Timing tab

Use the **Play** button to test the slide's animation again.

Add a **Faded Zoom** effect to the **Upload music file** box and a **Descend** effect to the **Yes** branch arrow, using the same settings as before.

We're about half way there!

Add a **Faded Zoom** effect to the **Quality OK?** box, with a five-second delay.

Select the big connector linking the two columns. Give it a **Strips** effect. Edit the **Effect Options** and set its **Direction** to **Right Up**. Make sure it is set to start **With Previous**.

Make the **Yes** and **No** labels appear **After Previous**.

Make the **No** branch arrow **Stretch** downwards after a five-second delay (as you did for the other **No** branch, but this time stretching **From Top**).

The **Add to play list** box can appear like the others: animate it with a **Faded Zoom** delayed by five seconds, and slide its arrow in from the top.

Repeat this for the **Play** box and the arrow going into it.

Animate the final arrow using a **Descend** with a two-second delay.

Test your slide. You should find that it is animated, as shown in the storyboard in Figure 6.11.

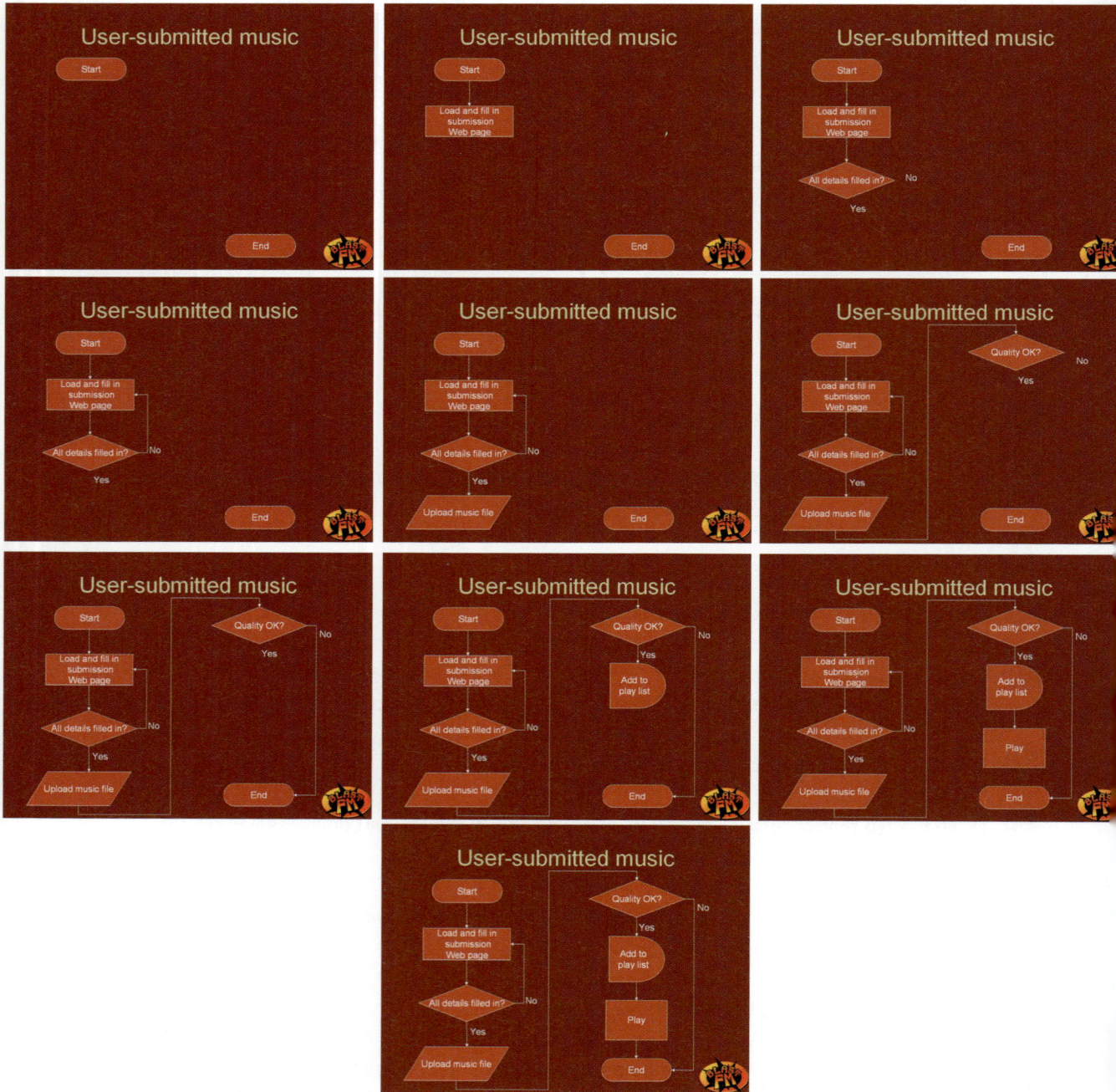

Figure 6.11: Storyboard showing the progress of the animation

This is a suitable point to save your work, if you haven't already done so.

Changing the sequence of animations

Let's modify the slide so that the **End** box appears only when it is needed: just as the **No** branch is being drawn from the **Quality OK?** box.

SYLLABUS

Ref: AM6.5.2.2
Change sequence of animations in a slide.

Add a **Faded Zoom** effect to the **End** box and set its **Start** to **With Previous**.

Preview the animation. It's not right – the **No** branch appears pointing into space and the **End** box appears only at the end of the presentation. We need to change the order.

Click on the right-hand **No** arrow and notice which of the effects becomes selected in the task pane (it will start with **Elbow**). We want to move the last effect up until it is just below the one you have just selected.

Click the **End** box and use the **Re-Order** buttons at the bottom of the task pane to move the animation until it is just below the one for the **No** arrow.

⬆ Re-Order ⬇

TIP

You can keep clicking between the two objects in your slide, but be careful to move only the **End** box's action.

Test your animation. The **End** box should be invisible and should reappear at exactly the same time as the **No** branch that ultimately connects to it.

Save the file again.

Note!

Instead of using the **Re-Order** buttons, you could drag and drop the animation effects in the list. A black horizontal line will appear to show where the dragged animation effect will end up. However, if you use this method then you are more likely to slip; if you don't notice and undo in time you could break your carefully crafted sequence of animations.

Animating charts

The best type of chart to use for demonstrating animation is a column or bar chart because other chart types do not support all the possible styles of animation. We'll create a new dummy chart to try out the options. The **Test yourself** section at the end of this chapter includes exercises about applying animated options to the Blast FM charts.

> ### SYLLABUS
>
> **Ref: AM6.5.2.4**
> Animate chart elements by series, by category, by elements in series.

Open your file **Charts.ppt**.

Press **Ctrl + M** to create a new blank slide.

Change the new slide's layout to **Title and Content** and give it a title of **Testing chart animation**.

Click on the **Insert Chart** icon to create a simple column chart. We'll just use the dummy data that is automatically added, so click away from the chart to stop editing it.

The chart should look like Figure 6.12 (the columns have been numbered because this will be useful in the discussion that follows).

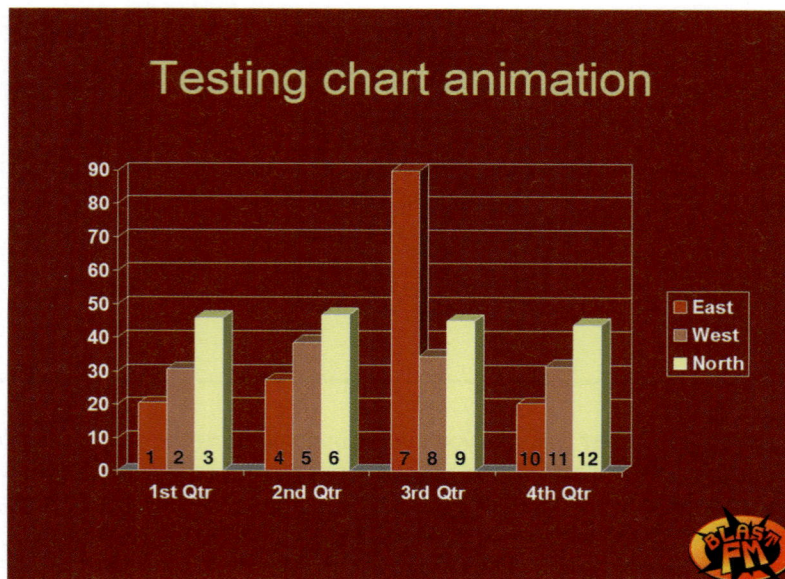

Figure 6.12: A default column chart to practise on

Right-click in the chart and choose **Custom Animation** from the menu that appears. The **Custom Animation** task pane is displayed.

Click the **Add Effect** button and then select **Entrance**, **Appear**.

Press **Shift + F5** to preview the animation. At first, only the slide's title and the Blast FM logo are displayed. After you press **Space** once, the whole chart appears. Pressing **Space** again advances to the next slide (in this case, the end of the presentation).

This is nothing new. However, there are some extra options that are specific to charts.

Click on the arrow to the right of your animation effect and select **Effect Options** from the menu. A dialogue box titled **Appear** is displayed. This is the same box we have already seen (for example in Figure 6.10), but with an extra **Chart Animation** tab.

Switch to the **Chart Animation** tab. The default option is **As one object** – we've just seen the effect of this setting. Change this to **By series**, as shown in Figure 6.13, and then press **OK**.

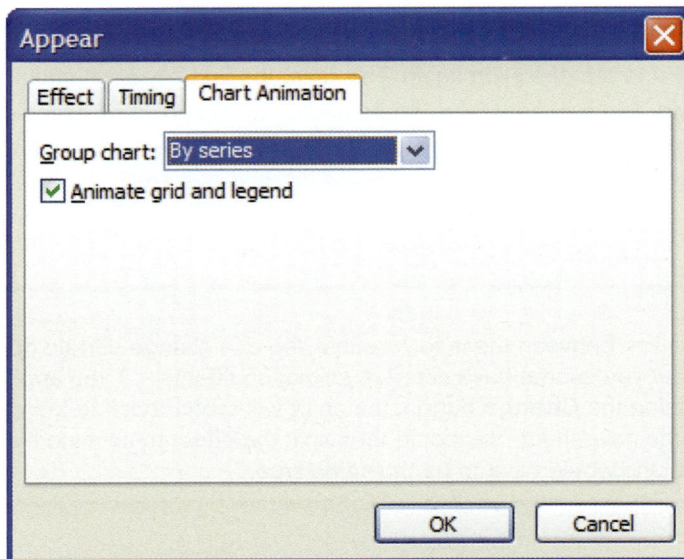

Figure 6.13: Animating a chart by series

Notice that there are now four separate animation effects, as shown in Figure 6.14 (you may have to click on the double-arrow to expand the list). The first effect makes the grid and legend invisible at first, and is there because we left the **Animate grid and legend** checkbox ticked (see Figure 6.13). After this, there is a separate animation effect for each of the three series (**East**, **West** and **North**).

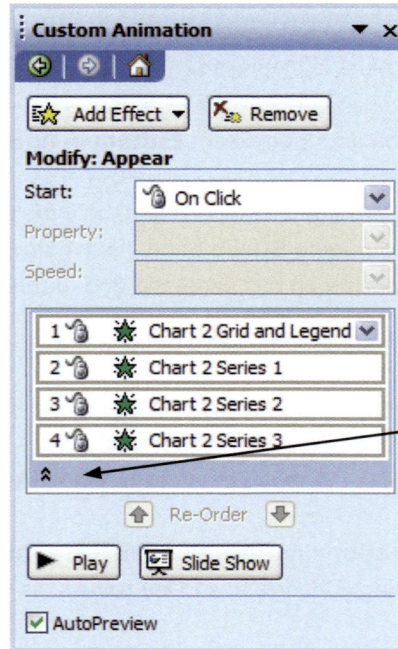

Figure 6.14: Each series has its own animation effect

Use **Shift + F5** to test the slide again. This time, the first keypress should activate the grid and the legend. The next keypress should display all the columns associated with the **East** region (numbers **1**, **4**, **7** and **10** in Figure 6.12). The next two keypresses should display the columns for **West** (**2**, **5**, **8** and **11**) and **North** (**3**, **6**, **9** and **12**).

> **Note!**
>
> There is an implicit link between these four series. You can change certain options (for example, timing) but you cannot have different animation effects – if you apply a new animation effect using the **Change** button, the chart will switch back to being animated **As one object** with the new effect. You could then split the effect to animate by series again, but each of the animations would have to be the same type.

Use the menu on any of the animations in the list to change the **Group chart** option to **By category**. This time, try unticking the **Animate grid and legend** checkbox.

Test the slide again. This time, PowerPoint reveals the columns quarter by quarter (as numbered in Figure 6.12, you get **1**, **2**, **3** then **4**, **5**, **6** then **7**, **8**, **9** then **10**, **11**, **12**).

Now try changing the **Group chart** option to **By element in series**. This time the columns appear in the following order, with a keypress between each: **1**, **4**, **7**, **10**, **2**, **5**, **8**, **11**, **3**, **6**, **9**, **12**.

Finally, try the **By element in category** option. This time the order is **1**, **2**, **3**, **4**, **5**, **6**, **7**, **8**, **9**, **10**, **11**, **12**.

You don't need this chart any more, so select **Edit**, **Delete Slide** from the main menu.

Multimedia

Inserting sounds

Open your presentation **Investment.ppt**, if it isn't already open.

Change to the **Our kind of music** slide.

You're going to insert a ten-second sound clip for each of the six different types of music. You can download the files **easy_listening.mp3**, **hard_rock.mp3**, **country.mp3**, **drum_and_bass.mp3**, **pop.mp3** and **hip_hop.mp3** from the ECDL section of the publisher's website (http://www.payne-gallway.co.uk/ecdl) if you haven't already done so. You will also need the file **explosion.mpg** for the **Inserting movies** section.

> **Note!**
>
> When you insert a WAV-format sound file into a presentation, it can either be embedded in the presentation itself or inserted as a link. In general, small files are embedded and large files are linked – this behaviour is controlled by an option on **Tools**, **Options**, **General**. Other sound formats, such as MP3, may only be inserted as links.

> **SYLLABUS**
>
> **Ref: AM6.5.1.1**
> Insert sounds with entry animation style, timing for automatically playing.

From the main menu, select **Insert**, **Movies and Sounds**, **Sound from File**. The **Insert Sound** dialogue box appears.

Navigate to the file **easy_listening.mp3** and double-click it. A speaker icon appears in the slide and the dialogue box shown in Figure 6.15 appears. Press the **Automatically** button. An entry for **easy_listening.mp3** appears in the **Custom Animation** task pane.

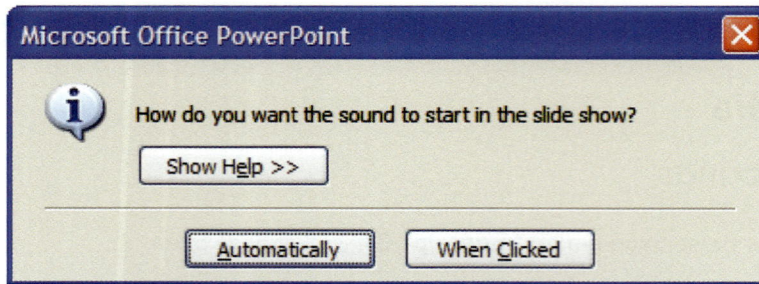

Figure 6.15: How will the new sound be triggered?

TIP

The **Automatically** option makes PowerPoint play the sound without user interaction. The **When Clicked** option does nothing until the person running the presentation clicks the speaker symbol, and then plays the sound.

We'll replace the explosion-style bullets with the speaker icons.

Bullets

Click anywhere in the **Easy listening** line and then press the **Bullets** button in the **Formatting** toolbar to remove the bullet. Click and drag the speaker icon next to the **Easy listening** bullet point. This will help you to keep track of the different sounds.

Delete the other bullets in the same way. Your slide should now look like Figure 6.16.

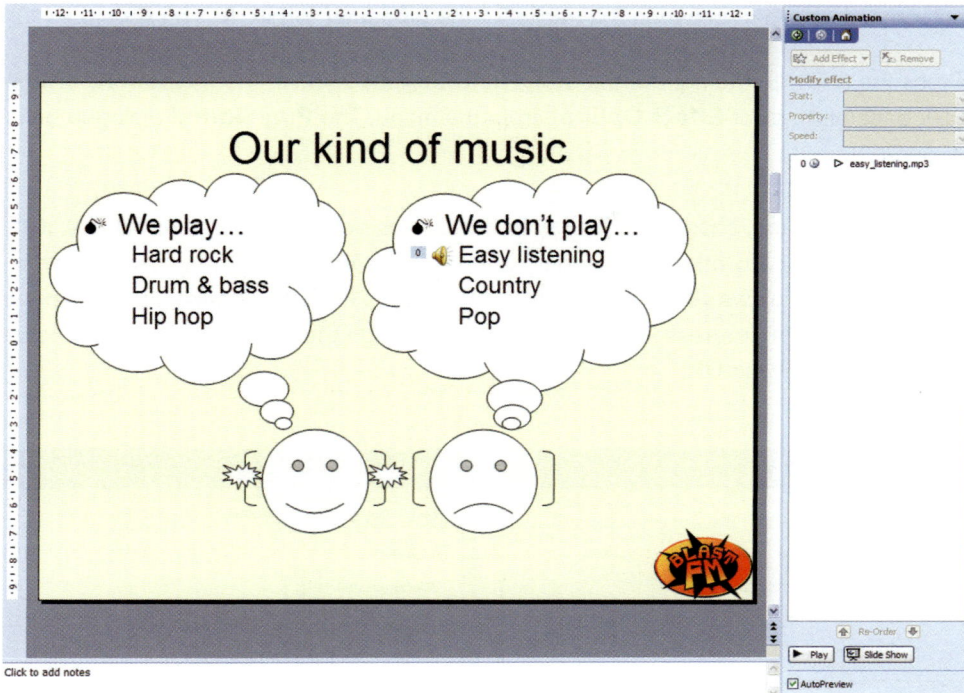

Figure 6.16: The slide after adding the first sound

TIP

If you are learning with other people, it may be a good idea to plug some headphones into your computer at this point!

Use the **Play** button to listen to the sound.

▶ Play

Add the sound **hard_rock.mp3** and move its speaker icon next to the **Hard rock** line.

Play the animation again. The hard rock should play immediately after the easy listening.

Add the other four sounds in the order **country.mp3**, **drum_and_bass.mp3**, **pop.mp3** and **hip_hop.mp3**, moving their speaker icons as appropriate.

The idea is that the presenter will say **We don't play** and then the music will start automatically; when it finishes, the presenter will say **But we do play** and there will be another burst of music. This will happen for each of the pairs of music styles.

Play the animation.

There isn't enough of a gap between the tracks for the presenter to talk, so you should add this in.

- Press the arrow to the right of the **easy_listening.mp3** line in the **Custom Animation** task pane and select **Effect Options** from the menu. The **Play Sound** dialogue box appears.

- On the **Timing** tab, change the **Delay** to **3** seconds, as shown in Figure 6.17(a), just as you would for any other animated component. The **Sound Settings** tab, shown in Figure 6.17(b), allows you to change the volume or to hide the speaker icon when the presentation is in progress – you don't need to change these, but it's useful to know that they are there. Press **OK**.

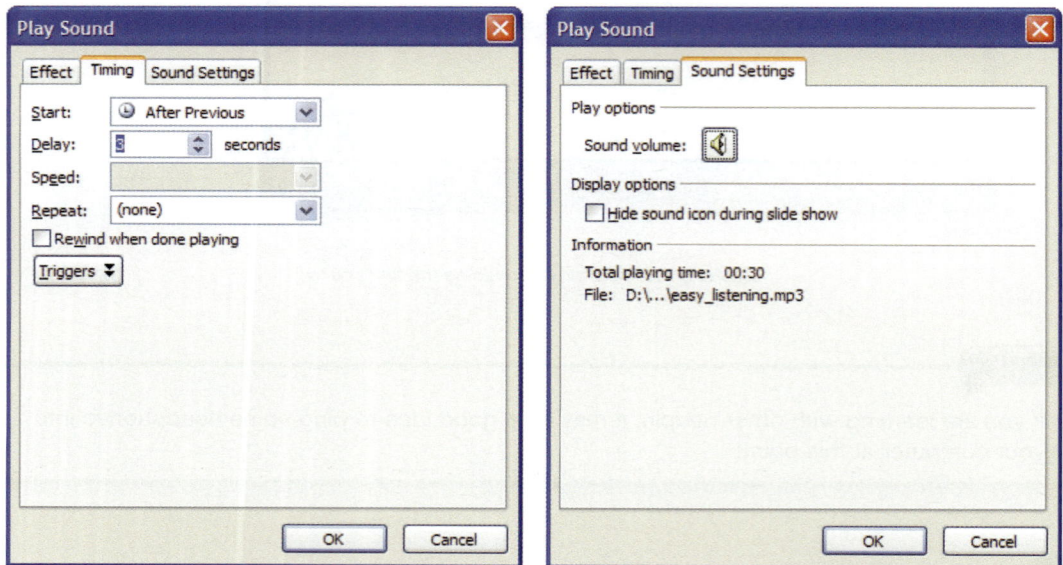

Figure 6.17: The Play Sound dialogue box (a) Timing and (b) Sound Settings tabs

- Press the **Play** button again to check that there is a three-second delay. You can press **Stop** once you have confirmed this.

- Add a **Delay** of **2** seconds to each of the other five sounds. Don't forget to test that this has worked.

The speaker icons are just pictures, so you can animate their appearance and disappearance.

- Select the speaker icon for **Easy listening**. In the **Custom Animation** task pane, select **Add Effect**, **Entrance**, **Faded Zoom**. Use the **Re-Order** buttons to move this effect up to just beneath the **easy_listening.mp3** play effect. Change its **Start** to **With Previous**.

Your task pane should now look like Figure 6.18.

Figure 6.18: Adding an entrance effect for the sound icon

Test your slide. After the initial delay, the easy listening music should start to play and the corresponding icon should disappear and then fade in again.

TIP

To hide the icon until it fades in, you could have added a **Disappear** effect to it and moved this to be the first effect in the sequence.

Add **Faded Zoom** effects to the other five buttons, so that they fade in at the appropriate times. Test your changes.

Note!

You may have noticed that the **Add Effect** menu for sounds includes an extra **Sound Actions** submenu, as shown in Figure 6.19. You can use this to pause or stop the playback of a particular sound, but only if it happens to be playing at the time (that is, this won't prevent delayed sounds from playing eventually).

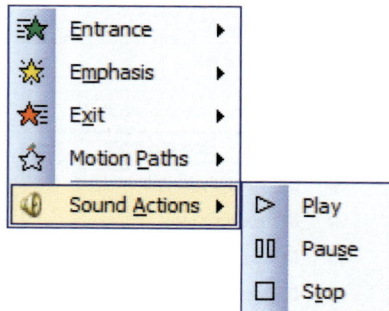

Figure 6.19: Controlling sound playback

Save your presentation and keep it open.

Inserting movies

Moving footage can be inserted in much the same way as sounds. We'll insert a video file of an explosion to make the first slide more interesting.

SYLLABUS

Ref: AM6.5.1.2
Insert movies with entry animation style, timing for automatically playing.

Change to the first slide in **Investment.ppt** – the one with the big Blast FM logo.

Make sure that the file **explosion.mpg** is in the same folder as **Investment.ppt**. This video file will not be embedded in the presentation (it will only be linked), so having both files in the same directory will make it easier to move the presentation between computers.

From PowerPoint's main menu, select **Insert**, **Movies and Sounds**, **Movie from File**. The **Insert Movie** dialogue box appears.

Navigate to **explosion.mpg** and double-click it. A dialogue box appears to ask whether you wish to start the movie automatically or when it is clicked. Choose **When Clicked** so that the person giving the presentation can start the effect when everyone is ready.

Your slide should now look like Figure 6.20.

Figure 6.20: Adding a movie to a slide

Press **Shift + F5** to run the presentation. Move your mouse and click on the movie to start it. Click on it again to pause it. Click on it a third time to resume. Press **Esc** to stop the presentation.

Note!

If you click without moving your mouse, you will just jump to the next slide. If you move your mouse first, the mouse pointer appears and PowerPoint knows you're clicking on the movie.

We'll modify the movie so that it starts when we press **Space** or click the mouse, even without waggling it about.

➡ Press the arrow to the right of the **explosion.mpg** effect and select **Timing** from the menu. The **Pause Movie** dialogue box appears.

➡ Expand the **Triggers** options if necessary (see Figure 6.21), and change them from **Start effect on click of explosion.mpg** to **Animate as part of click sequence**. Press **OK**.

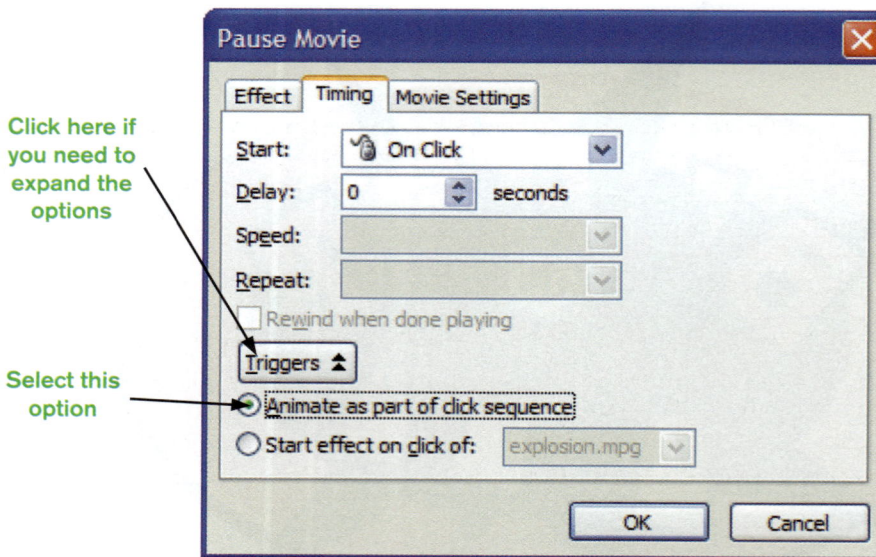

Click here if you need to expand the options

Select this option

Figure 6.21: Changing the movie to animate on any click

TIP

If, instead, you wanted the movie to play automatically after a delay, you could change the **Timing** options shown in Figure 6.21 in exactly the same way you have already done for sounds (changing **Start** to **With Previous** or **After Previous**, as appropriate).

We'll also expand the movie and make it fade in.

- Resize the movie so that it fills the whole slide. (You will have to drag the side handles as well as the corner handles; this will skew it slightly, but that doesn't matter.)

- With the movie still selected, press **Add Effect** on the **Custom Animation** task pane and select **Entrance**, **Fade** (look for **Fade** in **More Effects** if it isn't under the **Entrance** menu).

- Move the **Fade** effect to the top using the **Re-Order** buttons.

- Change the **Pause** effect to a **Play** effect using **Add Effects**, **Movie Actions**, **Play**. Set its **Start** to **After Previous**.

- Add an **Exit** animation effect of **Faded Zoom** to the movie. Set its **Start** to **After Previous**.

Note!

You have to add a style of exit animation that causes the movie to disappear from the slide, otherwise it will stay on top of the logo regardless of what is displaying on top in **Design** view.

- Use **Shift + F5** to play the animation again.

For one last effect, we'll remove the logo from the background and replace it with an animated logo that appears out of the exploding movie.

- With the first slide displayed, select **Format**, **Background** from the main menu. The **Background** dialogue box appears.

- Set the **Background fill** to **black**, as shown in Figure 6.22, and then press **Apply** (not **Apply to All** – you only want to change the background of this one slide).

137

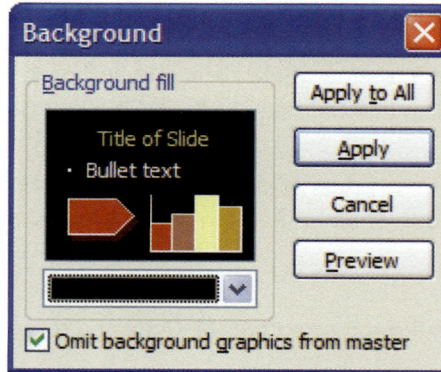

Figure 6.22: Removing the logo from the slide background

From the main menu, select **Insert**, **Picture**, **From File**. Navigate to **logo.tif** and double-click it to insert it into the slide.

Resize the logo to fill the slide (it doesn't matter if it isn't quite to scale).

Add an **Entrance Effect** of **Faded Zoom** to the logo and set it to occur **With Previous**.

Your task pane should now look like Figure 6.23.

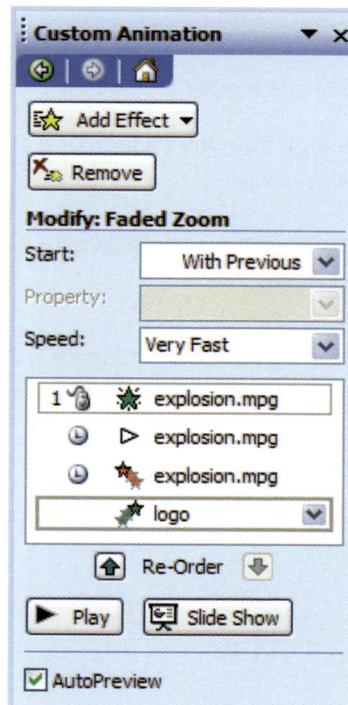

Figure 6.23: The Custom Animation task pane showing the movie and logo effects

Test the slide show. After you press **Space**, the video should fade in and then start to play automatically. As soon as it stops, it should fade and shrink and be replaced by a growing and darkening Blast FM logo. Pressing **Space** again should progress to the next slide.

That's it! Save your presentation.

Conclusions

This exercise has demonstrated the following points.

You can either click the left mouse button or press the **Space** key to move to the next animation effect on the current slide or to the next slide if there are no more animation effects.

Press the **Esc** key to exit a running presentation.

Press **F5** to start the presentation from the beginning, or **Shift + F5** to start it from the current slide.

You can control how an animated object dims by changing settings in its **Effect Options** dialogue box (see Figure 6.3).

Use the **Re-Order** buttons at the bottom of the **Custom Animation** task pane to change the sequence of animations in a slide.

To animate the elements of a chart, first add an animation effect to the chart as a whole and then use the animation's **Effect Options** dialogue box to change the **Group chart** setting.

Use the **Insert**, **Movies and Sounds** menu to add sounds or movie clips from files. PowerPoint will ask you whether you want them to play **Automatically** or **When Clicked**.

For sounds, you can animate the speaker icon (for example, making it fly in from off the slide). Alternatively, you can hide it completely.

Test yourself

1. Create a new blank slide in your **Charts.ppt** presentation and use PowerPoint's drawing tools to create a simple traffic light shape, as shown in Figure 6.24(a). Create three coloured circles and place them over the black ones, as shown in Figure 6.24(b). Add **Custom Animation** effects to show the order of traffic lights in the UK: red, red and amber, green, amber, red. Each transition should occur when you click the mouse, and all the affected lights should fade in and out together.

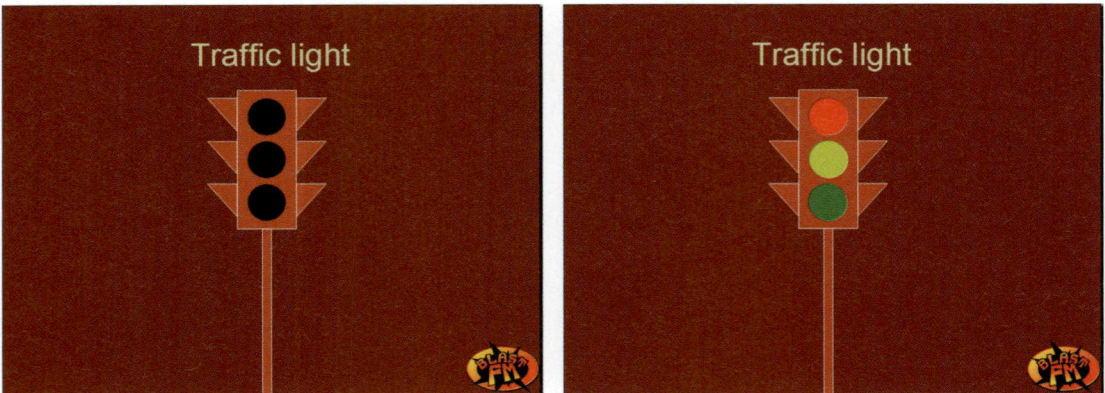

Figure 6.24: Drawing of a traffic light

> **TIP**
>
> The coloured lights look better if you use the **Drawing** toolbar to add **Shadow Style 18** to them. The transitions appear smoother if the fading-out lights are set to **Fast** and the fading-in lights are set to **Very Fast**.

2. Modify the slide you created in Exercise 1 so that the transitions after the first one happen automatically instead of when you press the mouse button or keyboard. Set the delays to **16** seconds of **red**, **2** seconds of **red and amber**, **12** seconds of **green** and **4** seconds of **amber**. (This is more difficult than it seems – if you can get this working, then you will definitely have mastered delayed animation effects!)

> **TIP**
>
> You may find it useful to add some text to the shapes to get some more meaningful labels, as shown in Figure 6.25(a). You can set the font to be small and the same colour as the background, so it doesn't actually show up on the slide itself. If you choose **Show Advanced Timeline** from one of the animation effects menus, then you will get the view shown in Figure 6.25(b), which can be useful for sorting out the dependencies.

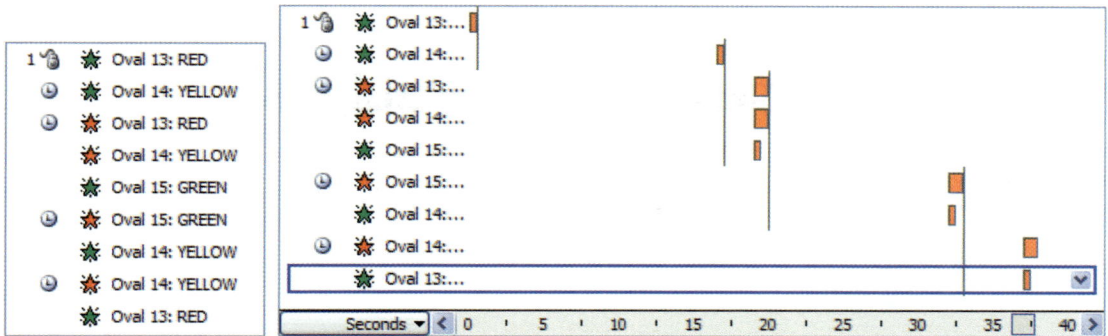

Figure 6.25: Two views of the Custom Animation task pane

3. Change the **Listener Demographics** slide in **Investment.ppt** to animate the bullets so that they **Appear** one by one. Make sure that all the animation effects, even for sub-bullets, are in response to mouse clicks (see Figure 6.26(a)). Set the main bullets to dim to **green** and the sub-bullets to dim to **light blue**, and try out the option to **Animate text By letter** (see Figure 6.26(b)). Figure 6.27 shows what your slide should look like part-way through animating the bottom line.

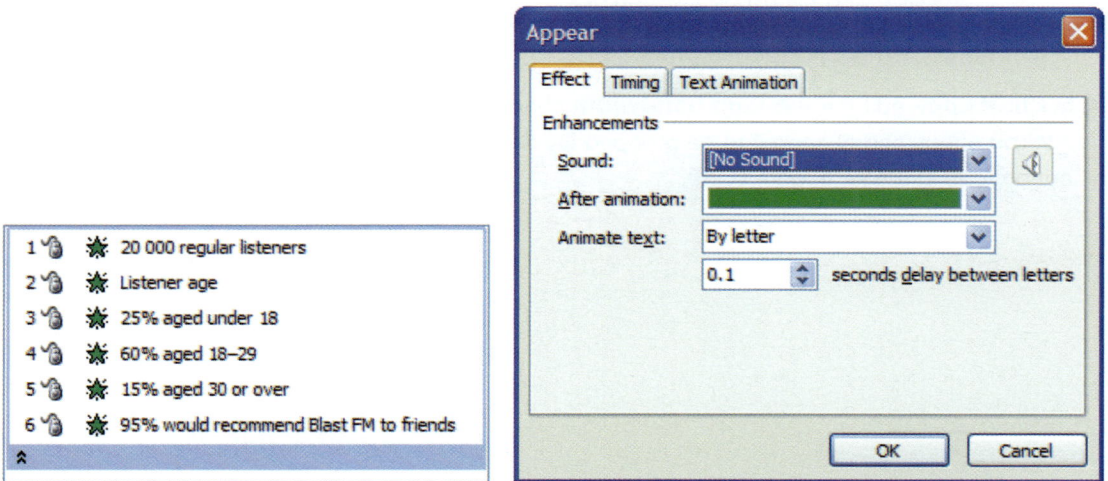

Figure 6.26: Changing the bullet animation effects

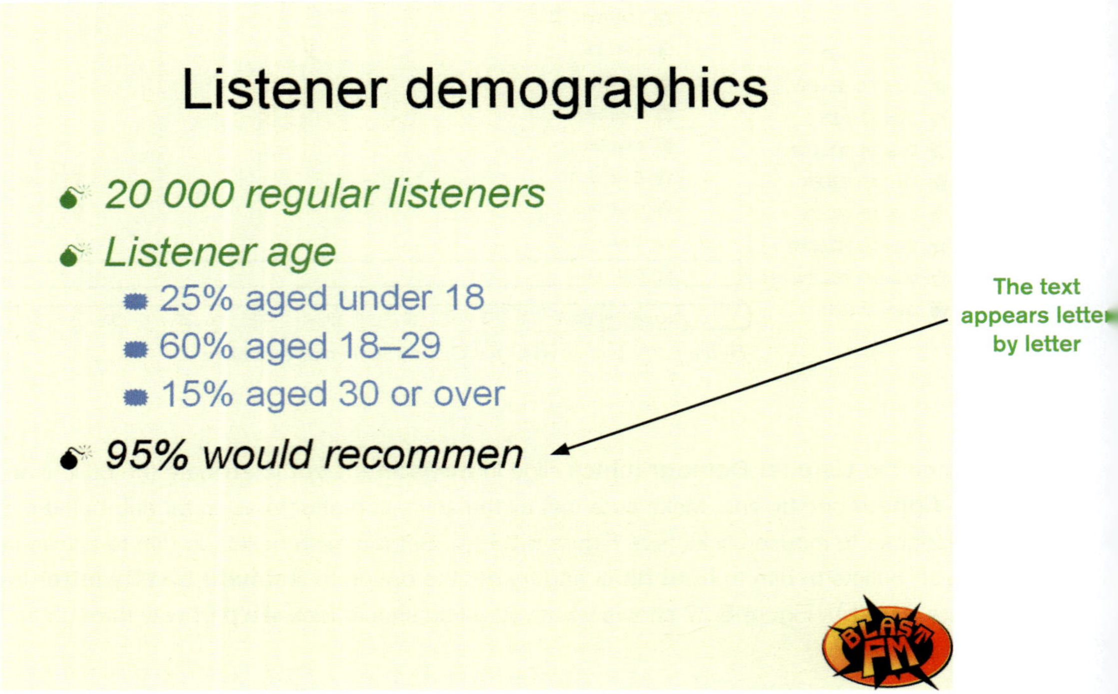

Figure 6.27: The Listener demographics slide part-way through animating the last line

4. In **Charts.ppt**, edit the **Average bandwidth** chart you created in Chapter 5, Exercise 3. Add a **Wipe** effect, and change it to be grouped **By Series** so that the areas wipe up from the bottom one at a time (Figure 6.28).

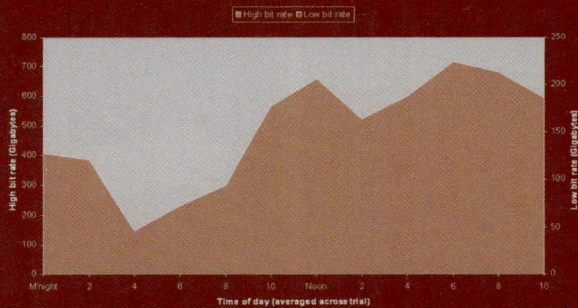

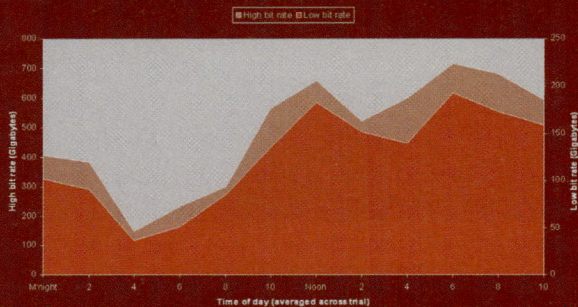

Figure 6.28: The three stages of the animation of the area chart

5. Create a slide with a chart. Keep the dummy data and change the chart into a 3-D pie chart using **Chart**, **Chart Type**. Add an **Entrance** animation effect of **Fade** and then change it to group by **Category** with **Animate group and legend** turned off. Check that the animation progresses as shown in Figure 6.29 with a click required between each animation.

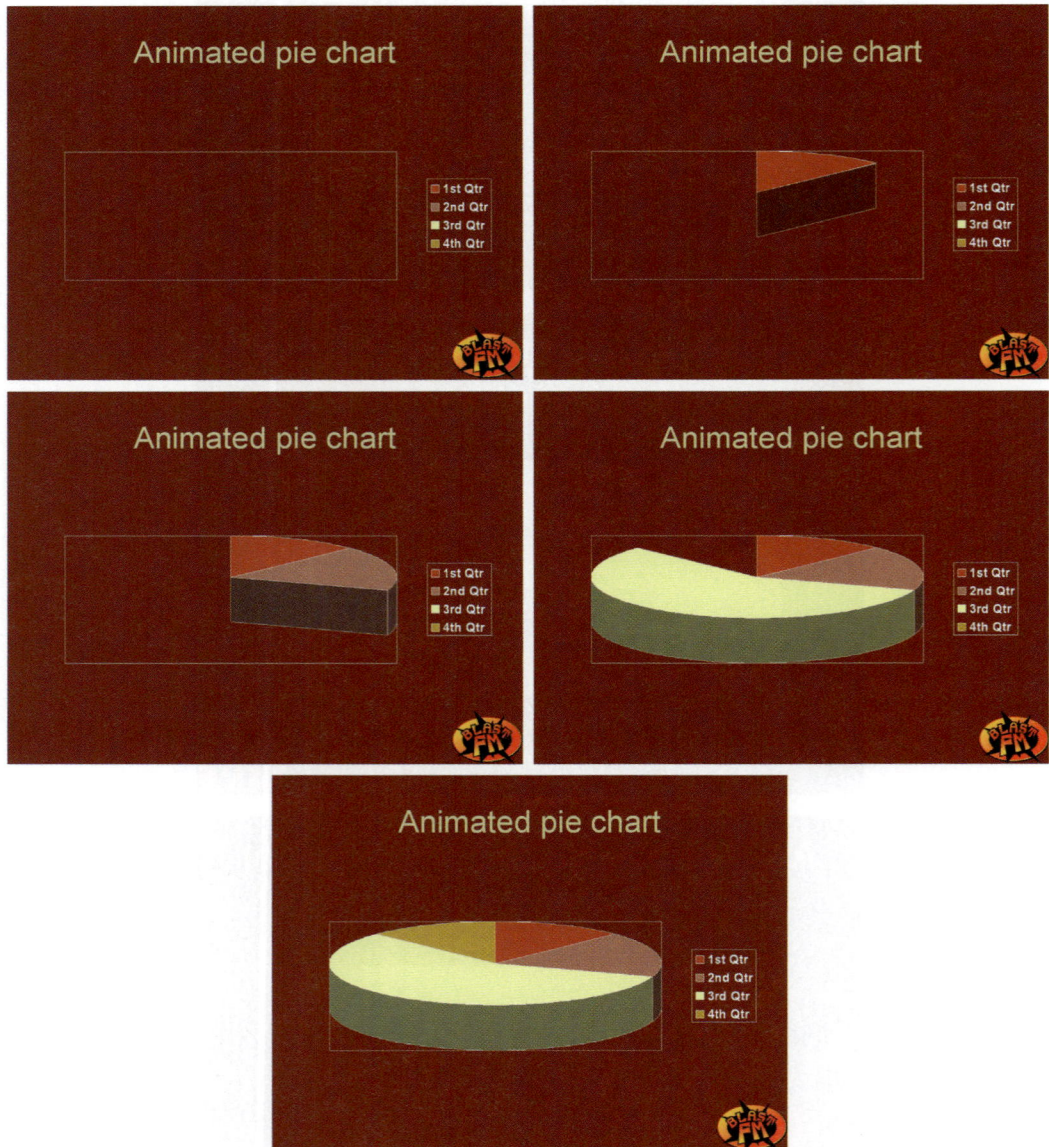

Figure 6.29: Five steps in the animation of the 3-D pie chart

6. Create a short presentation about one of your hobbies or interests. Search the Web for a few suitable sounds and movie clips, and add them to your presentation. Use a selection of different styles for the entrance and exit effects of the sounds and movies, and make some respond to mouse click, whereas others start playing automatically after a suitable delay. Make sure you practise changing the order of the animations by dragging them or using the **Re-Order** buttons.

> **TIP**
>
> A good place to look for sounds is **The Freesound Project**: http://freesound.iua.upf.edu. Good places to look for video clips are **Google Video**: http://video.google.com and **Moving Image Archive**: http://www.archive.org/details/movies.
>
> Alternatively, you can use your favourite search engine and include suitable file extensions in your search criteria, such as **wav**, **mid** and **mp3** for sounds, and **mpg**, **mpeg** and **wmv** for videos (make sure you turn on the search engine's **safe search** before searching for videos).

7 Presenting a slide show

Introduction

This chapter is about two extremes of user interaction with presentations: interactive components that users can click to control a presentation that they are viewing on their own computer or at a kiosk, and automation of presentations so that they can run without any user interaction at all.

First, we will add navigation buttons to the **Investment.ppt** presentation. Then we will see how to modify it so that it can play in a continuous loop in the Blast FM reception area. In the course of this, we will cover customised slide shows and macros.

In this chapter, you will

- learn how to use the **playback control** options, and how to turn their display on and off

- add **interactive buttons** to the presentation to move to specific slides, files or web pages

- create and use **customised slide shows** containing a subset of slides from the main presentation

- learn how to add automatic **timed transitions** between slides, how to remove them permanently and how to switch them on and off without losing the settings

- set the slide show to **loop continuously** until someone stops it

- record a pair of **macros** to switch between manual and automatic playback of the presentation, learning how to run them and how to add them to a custom toolbar.

Slide show control

Built-in controls

Load **Investment.ppt** and change to the last slide (**Website stats**).

Before going any further, we need to check some settings. Otherwise, you may get different effects from those described in this exercise.

From the main menu, select **Tools**, **Options**. Change to the **View** tab and make sure that all the **Slide show** options are ticked, as shown in Figure 7.1. Press **OK**.

Check that these are all ticked

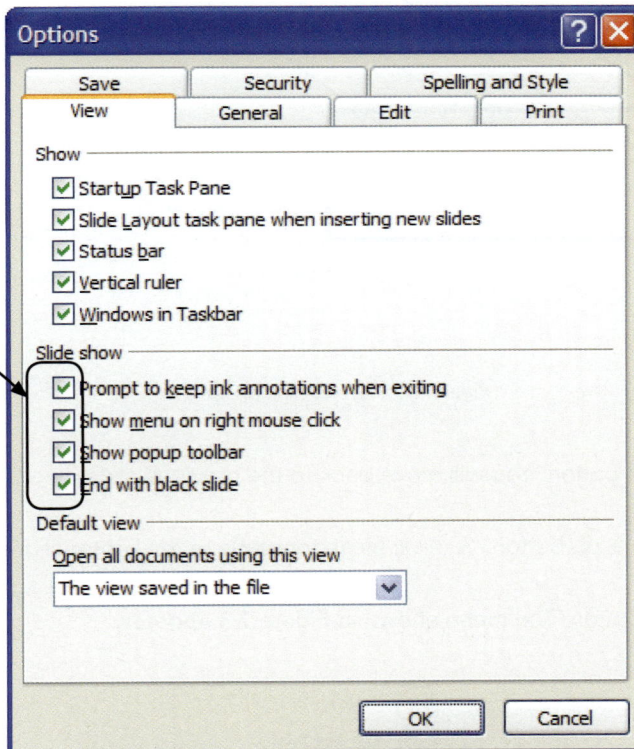

Figure 7.1: Checking the options for slide show behaviour

Press **Shift + F5** to view the slide. Move your mouse; the icons shown in Figure 7.2 should appear in the bottom left of the screen.

TIP

You won't get this unless **Show popup toolbar** is ticked in the **View** tab of the **Options** dialogue box, as shown in Figure 7.1.

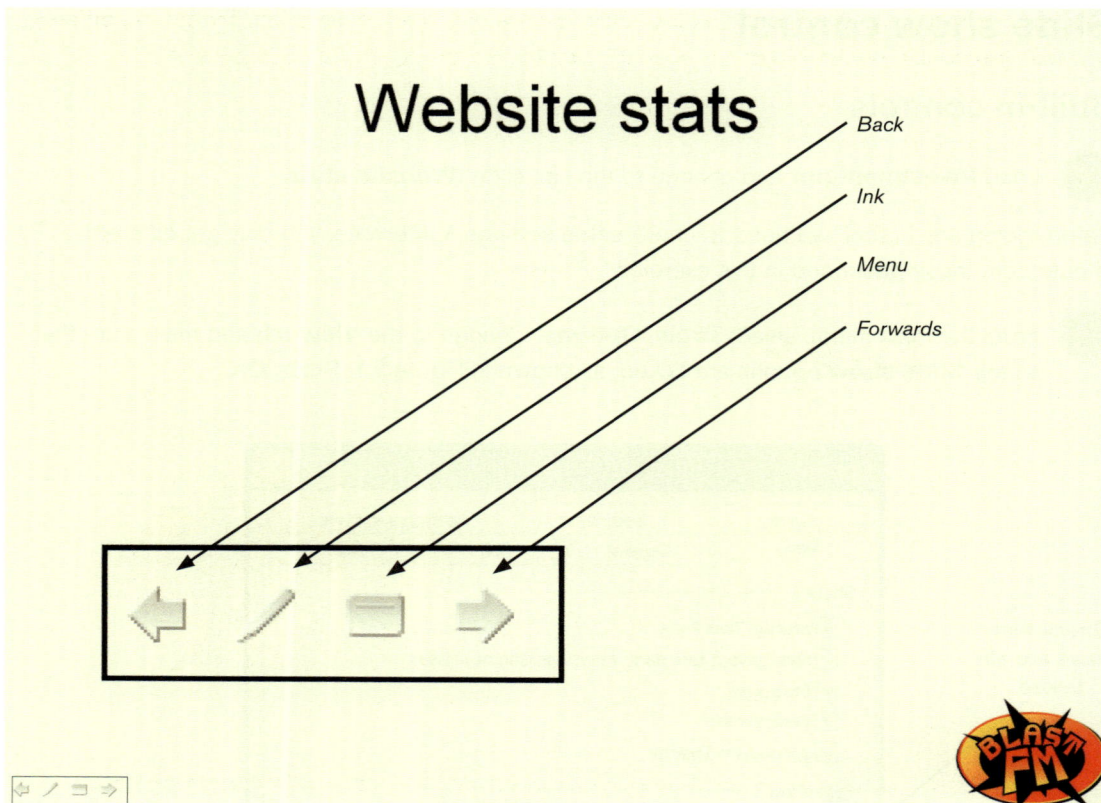

Figure 7.2: Playback control options

Press the **Back** button. You will move back to the previous slide.

Press the **Forwards** button. You will move forwards to the lighter slide.

Press the **Ink** button. The menu shown in Figure 7.3 appears.

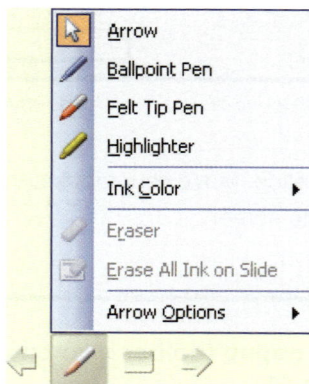

Figure 7.3: The Ink menu

You can use this menu to annotate slides while you are giving a presentation. Try out the different options. You should be able to come up with something more artistic than Figure 7.4.

Figure 7.4: Adding ink annotations to a slide

Now click on the **Menu** icon. Figure 7.5 shows the options available from this menu.

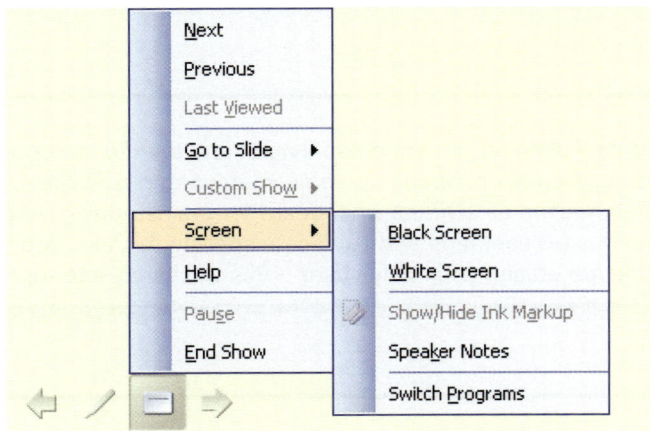

Figure 7.5: The menu, showing the Screen options

Try selecting **Screen**, **Black Screen** from this menu. Choose **Screen**, **Unblack Screen** to show the slide again.

Note!

Screen, **Show/Hide Ink Markup** applies only to markup that is already part of the presentation, not to the drawings you have just done. You cannot hide the drawings you have just done, but you can erase part or all of them using the **Erase** and **Erase All Ink on Slide** options on the **Ink** menu (see Figure 7.3).

Select **End Show** from this menu (as an alternative to pressing the **Esc** key). The dialogue box shown in Figure 7.6 appears. Select **Discard** to wipe the slide clean.

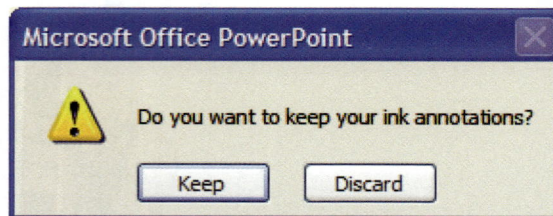

Figure 7.6: Warning that you have scribbled on your presentation

TIP

You won't get this unless **Prompt to keep ink annotations when exiting** is ticked in the **View** tab of the **Options** dialogue box, as shown in Figure 7.1. If this option is not selected, all annotations will be automatically discarded when you exit the presentation.

TIP

The ability to annotate a slide as you are presenting it, and then to incorporate those annotations into the presentation, opens up some interesting possibilities. For example, you could use a presentation as a virtual whiteboard for brainstorming. Alternatively, if you are doing a test run of a presentation and you find a spelling mistake, you can circle it so it stands out when you are editing your slides later – this will hardly interrupt your flow.

TIP

You can use the **Menu** icon to launch a custom show from the main presentation. How to create these customised slide shows is covered later in this chapter (see page 160).

If you use the **Help** option from this menu, you'll get the useful dialogue box shown in Figure 7.7.

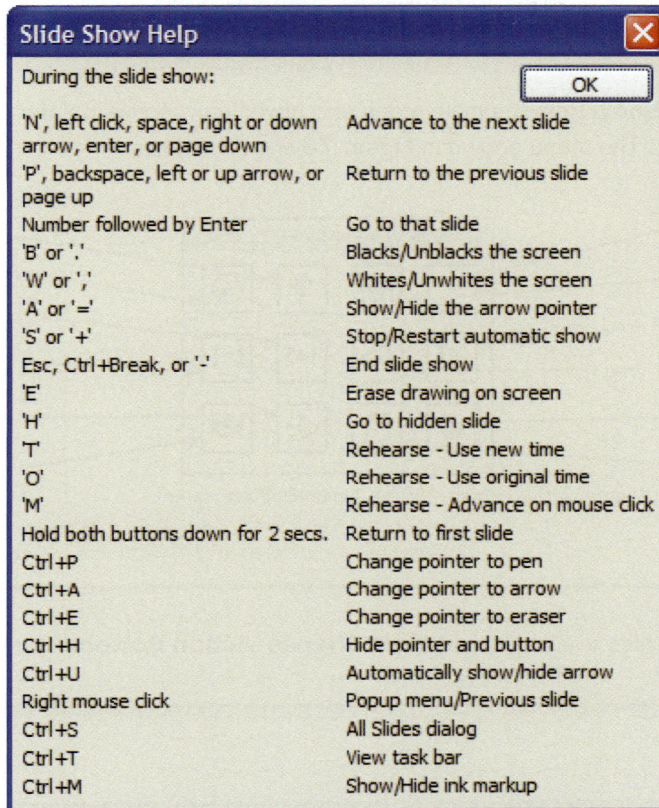

Slide Show Help	
During the slide show:	OK
'N', left click, space, right or down arrow, enter, or page down	Advance to the next slide
'P', backspace, left or up arrow, or page up	Return to the previous slide
Number followed by Enter	Go to that slide
'B' or '.'	Blacks/Unblacks the screen
'W' or ','	Whites/Unwhites the screen
'A' or '='	Show/Hide the arrow pointer
'S' or '+'	Stop/Restart automatic show
Esc, Ctrl+Break, or '-'	End slide show
'E'	Erase drawing on screen
'H'	Go to hidden slide
'T'	Rehearse - Use new time
'O'	Rehearse - Use original time
'M'	Rehearse - Advance on mouse click
Hold both buttons down for 2 secs.	Return to first slide
Ctrl+P	Change pointer to pen
Ctrl+A	Change pointer to arrow
Ctrl+E	Change pointer to eraser
Ctrl+H	Hide pointer and button
Ctrl+U	Automatically show/hide arrow
Right mouse click	Popup menu/Previous slide
Ctrl+S	All Slides dialog
Ctrl+T	View task bar
Ctrl+M	Show/Hide ink markup

Figure 7.7: PowerPoint's help about shortcut keys you can use when running a presentation

Adding interactive controls

Although these **Back** and **Forwards** icons are useful, you sometimes need more control. For example, you may want to be able to press a button to take you to a specific slide, or back to the beginning of the presentation, or to a slide in a different presentation entirely. It's easy to set up buttons to do any of these things, and more.

SYLLABUS

Ref: AM6.6.1.1 (Part 1 of 2)
Set up interaction on slide content to navigate to a slide, slides, presentation, file, URL.

Add some navigation buttons to each slide in the presentation by editing the **Slide Master**.

From the main menu, select **View**, **Master**, **Slide Master**. The presentation changes to show the **Slide Master**.

Select **Slide Show** from the main menu and hover your mouse pointer over the **Action Buttons** entry. The menu shown in Figure 7.8 should appear.

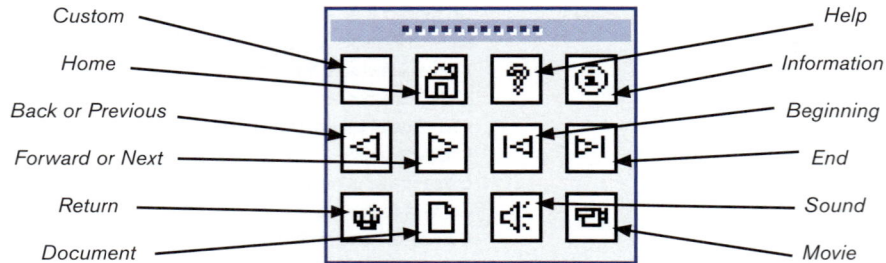

Custom	Help
Home	Information
Back or Previous	Beginning
Forward or Next	End
Return	Sound
Document	Movie

Figure 7.8: The Action Buttons menu

Note

These buttons are also available under **AutoShapes**, **Action Buttons** on the **Drawing** toolbar.

TIP

You can drag the dotted line at the top of the **Action Buttons** menu to make it float as a freestanding palette. This is useful if you need to add lots of action buttons.

Click on the icon for **Beginning** and then click anywhere on the slide. A button object appears on the slide and the **Action Settings** dialogue box is displayed, as shown in Figure 7.9. The default action for this button type is **Hyperlink to First Slide**: that's exactly what you want, so press **OK**.

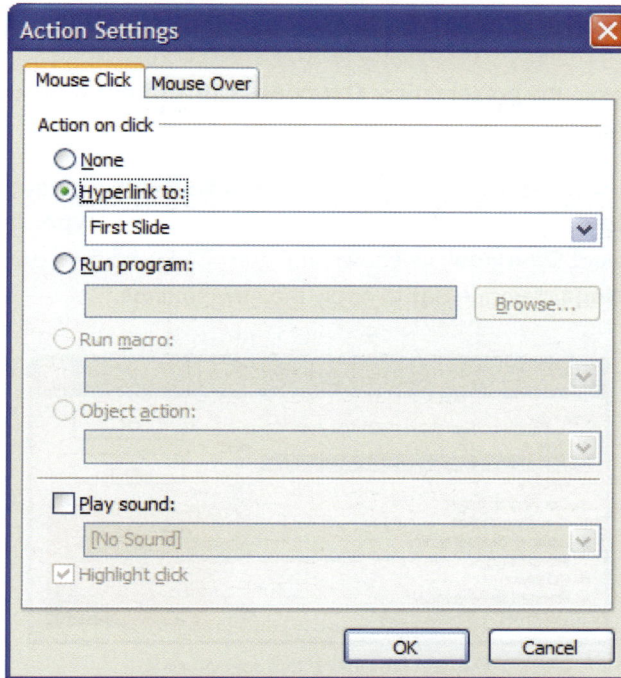

Figure 7.9: Default Action Settings for the Beginning button

Drag the button into the bottom left of the slide, which should then look like Figure 7.10.

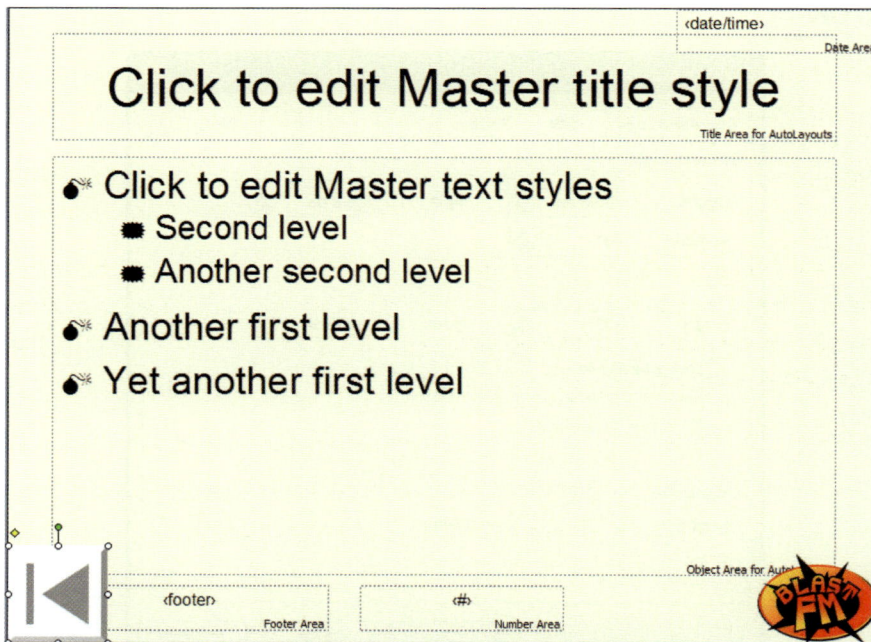

Figure 7.10: Slide with a single action button

Add a **Back or Previous** button next to this, accepting its default settings.

There are three sections in the presentation: **Overview**, **Current position** and **Planned development**. We'll add easy links to the beginning of each of these.

This time, add a **Custom** button. When the **Action Settings** dialogue box appears, select the **Hyperlink to** option and select **Slide...** from the list. The **Hyperlink to Slide** dialogue box appears. Select **Overview**, as shown in Figure 7.11, and then press **OK**. Press **OK** in the **Action Settings** dialogue box to apply the new settings.

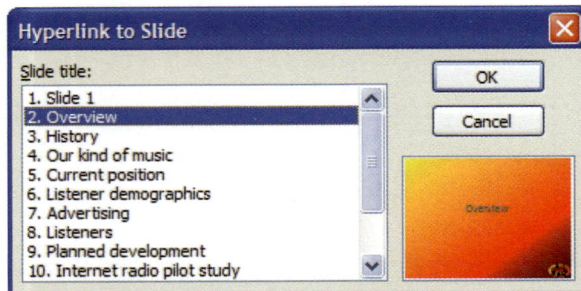

Figure 7.11: Linking to a specific slide

Now lay out the section buttons, one on top of the other.

Double-click on the new button to display the **Format AutoShape** dialogue box. Change to the **Size** tab and set the **Height** to **33%** and the **Width** to **200%**, as shown in Figure 7.12. Press **OK**.

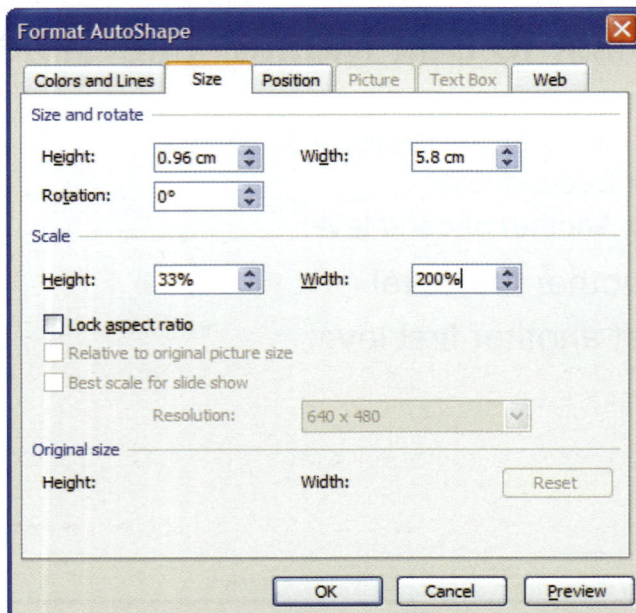

Figure 7.12: Resizing the button so it is twice as wide and a third as tall

Right-click the new button and select **Add Text** from the menu that appears. Type **Overview** and then click away to stop editing the text. Position the new button as shown in Figure 7.13. Use the **Overview** button's yellow selection handle to increase its bevel to match the other buttons.

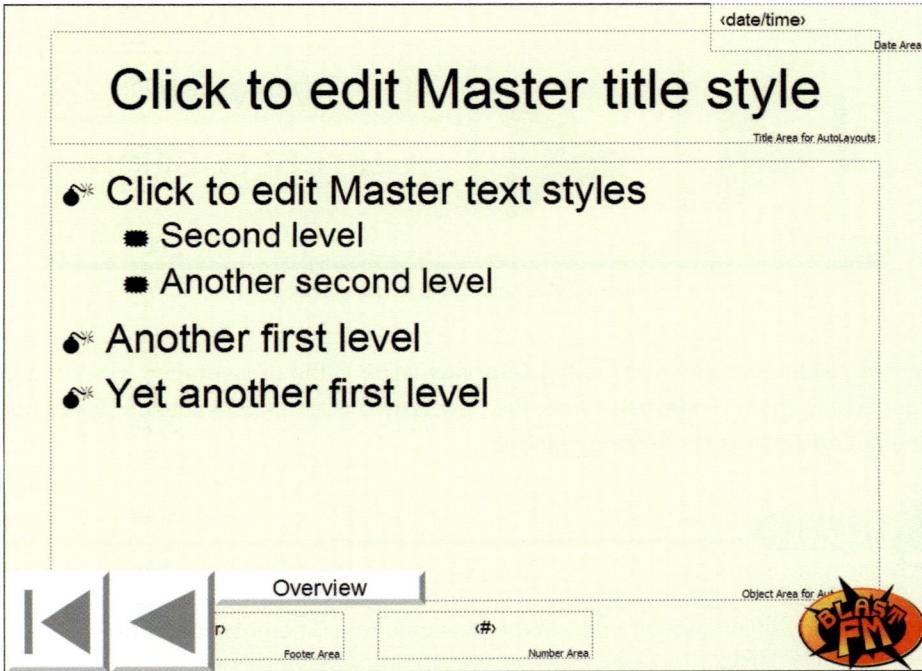

‹date/time›

Date Area

Click to edit Master title style

Title Area for AutoLayouts

- 🔨 **Click to edit Master text styles**
  - ✹ Second level
  - ✹ Another second level
- 🔨 Another first level
- 🔨 Yet another first level

Overview

Object Area for Au

BLAST FM

Footer Area

(#)

Number Area

Figure 7.13: Positioning the custom button

TIP

With **Overview** selected, hold down the **Ctrl** key and use the **arrow** keys to position it accurately to the pixel. You could use **View**, **Zoom** to get a clearer view.

Select the **Overview** button and then use **Format**, **Font** to set the text colour to grey (to match the images on the other buttons). This will be less distracting than the black text to people watching the presentation.

We want two more buttons under **Overview**. The easiest thing to do is to copy and then modify it.

Select the **Overview** button, if it isn't already selected (click on its border to make sure you have the button selected instead of editing its text).

155

Press **Ctrl + C** to copy the button and then press **Ctrl + V** twice to paste two new copies. Set the text of the two copies to **Current position** and **Planned development**, and arrange them as shown in Figure 7.14. (You will probably find that **Planned development** is too wide for the button, so select the text and reduce the font size slightly using **Format**, **Font**.)

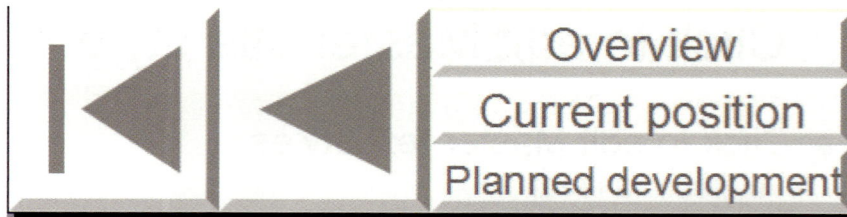

Figure 7.14: Arranging the section buttons

At the moment, all three buttons link to the **Overview** slide in the presentation, since the bottom two are identical to the top one, apart from the new text. This gives us a chance to see how to change the action settings for existing objects.

SYLLABUS

Ref: AM6.6.1.2
Change property of interaction on a slide to navigate to a different slide, slides, presentation, file, URL.

Right-click on the **Current position** button's border (not the text) and select **Action Settings** from the menu that appears. The **Action Settings** dialogue box is displayed. It works exactly as it does when adding a new action button.

Note!

The **Action Settings** dialogue box should show an existing hyperlink to the **Overview** slide. If **None** is selected instead, you have probably right-clicked on the text inside the button instead of on the button object itself. Close the dialogue box and right-click on the button's border.

Select **Slide...** from the drop-down list and choose the **Current position** slide instead. Press **OK** in both dialogue boxes.

Do the same thing to link the **Planned development** button to the **Planned development** slide.

Other interaction link types

These action buttons are not limited to linking to single slides in the current presentation. They can link to separate presentations, or load files or web pages.

Add an **Action Button** of type **Info** to your slide. Change the **Hyperlink to** option to **Other PowerPoint Presentation** and navigate to your **About Blast FM.ppt** file. Choose any slide you wish in the next dialogue box and then **OK** all the changes.

You can add action settings to any AutoShape; it doesn't have to be an **Action Button**.

Draw an oval over the top of the Blast FM logo in the bottom right of the slide.

Right-click in the oval and select **Action Settings**, just as you have been doing for the buttons. Set the **Hyperlink to** option to **URL**. The **Hyperlink To URL** dialogue box appears. Fill in a web address, as shown in Figure 7.15 (there isn't a real Blast FM website, so choose any real web address). Press **OK** in both dialogue boxes.

Figure 7.15: Linking to a web page

Double-click in the oval to display its **Format AutoShape** dialogue box. Change to the **Colors and Lines** tab and change the **Fill Color** to **No Fill** and the **Line Color** to **No Line**, as shown in Figure 7.16. Press **OK**.

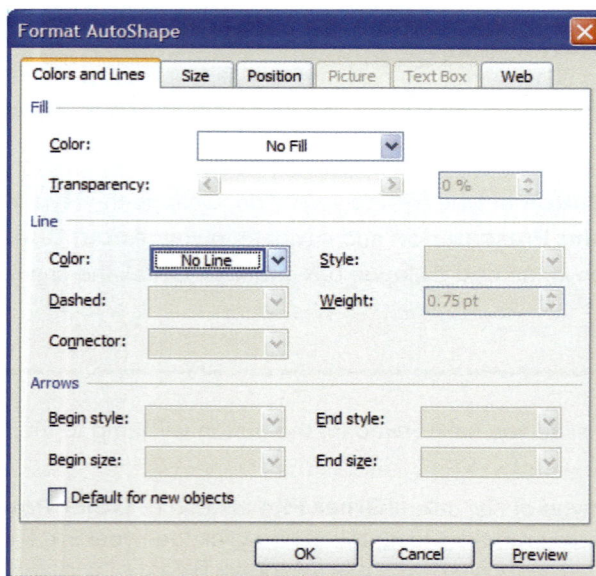

Figure 7.16: Making the oval into an invisible hotspot

Add one more **Action Button** to the right of your group, to advance the presentation one slide.

Your buttons won't work if a text area overlaps them (even if they are at the top of the drawing order). Select the **Object Area for AutoLayouts** and move it up so that it doesn't overlap your buttons. Your **Slide Master** should now look like Figure 7.17.

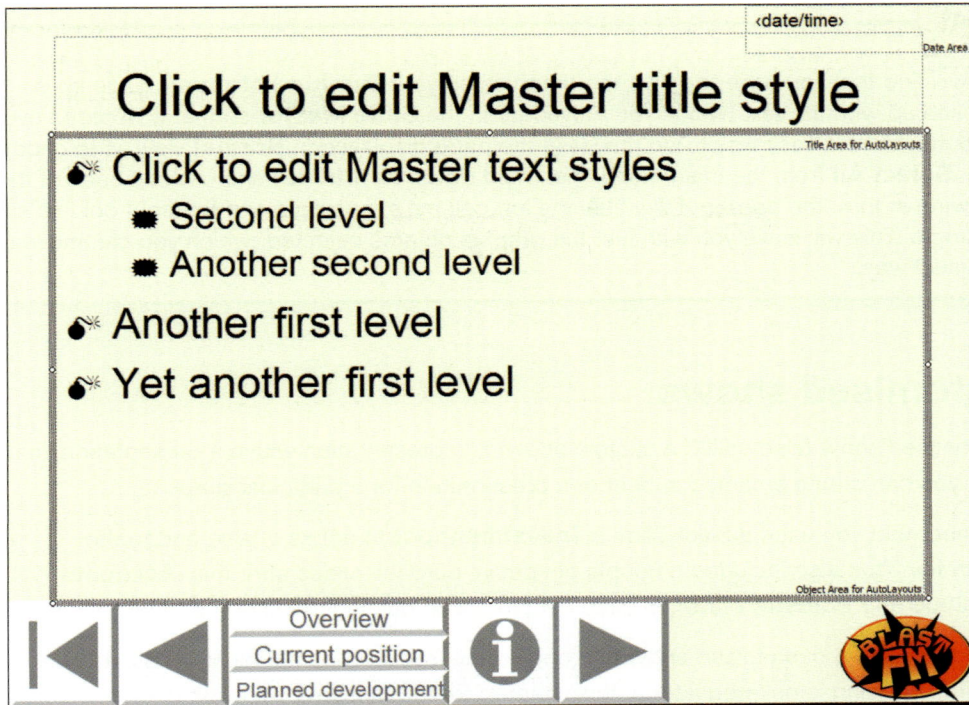

Figure 7.17: The completed set of navigation buttons

Note!

You can also link to a specific sequence of slides by creating a **customised slide show** and selecting **Custom Show** in the **Hyperlink to** list on the **Action Settings** dialogue box.

From the main menu, select **View**, **Normal** to stop viewing the **Slide Master**.

Run your presentation and test all the buttons, including the hyperlink over the Blast FM logo. Remember that one of the slides has sound effects, so you should probably plug in headphones or mute your PC's speaker if you are learning with other people.

TIP

You can use the left and right arrow keys to move between slides. The easiest way to advance past the title screens (which don't have the new navigation buttons) is simply to click on the slide.

Note!

You will find that you have to move the graphics on your **Our kind of music** page up so that they line up with the text (which you moved up in the **Slide Master** so that it wouldn't overlap the buttons). The easy way to do this, with the page displayed in **Normal** view, is to choose **Edit**, **Select All** from the main menu, then hold down the **Ctrl** key and click on each of the following in turn: the border of the title, the left column's rectangle and the right column's rectangle. This will leave you with just the graphic objects selected, which you can move up in the usual way.

Customised shows

A customised show (also called a custom show) is a presentation within a presentation. In other words, you can create a named subset of a presentation for a particular purpose.

Remember that you used a black slide in **Investment.ppt** to act as a false end to the presentation. You also included a couple of special-purpose slides after this (**Accounts 2005–2006** and **Website stats**), in case people asked questions about those specific points.

We'll now create a customised show that could be left to loop continuously in Blast FM's reception. Looping is covered later in this chapter; for the moment, we'll just decide which slides to show.

SYLLABUS

Ref: AM6.6.2.1
Create a customised slide show.

From the main menu, select **Slide Show**, **Custom Shows**. The **Custom Shows** dialogue box appears.

Press the **New** button. The **Define Custom Show** dialogue box appears.

Set the **Slide show name** to **Blast FM Reception**.

Click on the first slide in the **Slides in presentation** list and then press the **Add >>** button. The slide name is copied across to the **Slides in custom show** list.

Repeat this for each of the slides down to **Funding requirements**, as shown in Figure 7.18, and then press **OK**.

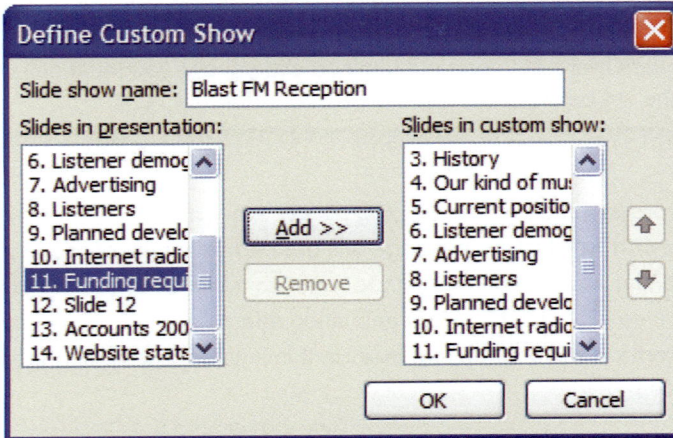

Figure 7.18: Selecting the slides for the customised show

The new customised show appears in the **Custom Shows** dialogue box, as shown in Figure 7.19.

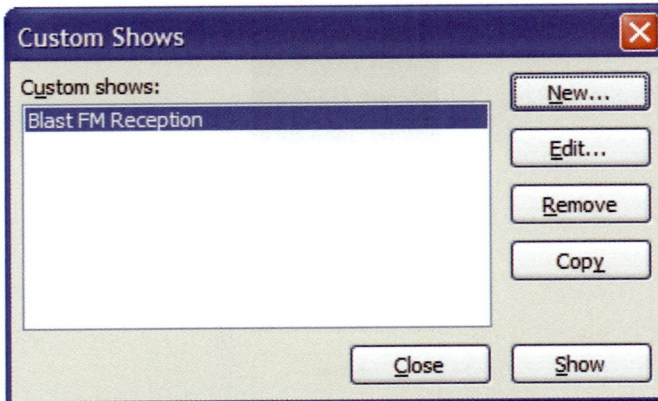

Figure 7.19: The new customised show

SYLLABUS

Ref: AM6.6.2.3
Run a customised slide show.

Press the **Show** button to run the customised show. Keep pressing **Space** to skip quickly through the presentation. You should find that the last slide shown is **Funding requirements**.

Note!

For presentations with more than one customised slide show, you must select the one you want to run from the list before pressing the **Show** button.

Remember that this presentation will be looping all day every day in Blast FM's reception. The sound effects on the **Our kind of music** page will get on the nerves of the reception staff in no time at all! You could just set the presentation to run with no volume, but then this slide will be displayed for a long time while all the music animation effects are fired. An alternative is to create a copy of the slide, remove the sounds and include this in your customised presentation in place of the loud version.

Right-click the **Our kind of music** slide in the list on the left-hand side of the PowerPoint window. Select **Copy** from the menu that appears.

Scroll the list of slides down and click below the bottom slide. A black horizontal line should appear, as shown in Figure 7.20, to show the new insertion point.

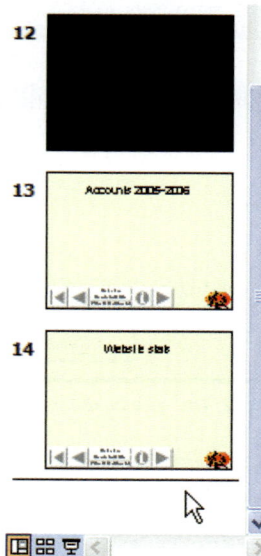

Figure 7.20: Inserting a new slide at the end of the presentation

From the main menu, select **Edit**, **Paste**. A copy of the **Our kind of music** slide appears at the end of the presentation.

Select each of the speaker icons in turn and press the **Delete** key to delete them. This will remove the sounds and their related animation effects from the slide. Use the **Bullets** button on the **Formatting** toolbar to add the original second-level bullet marks back in, as shown in Figure 7.21.

Bullets

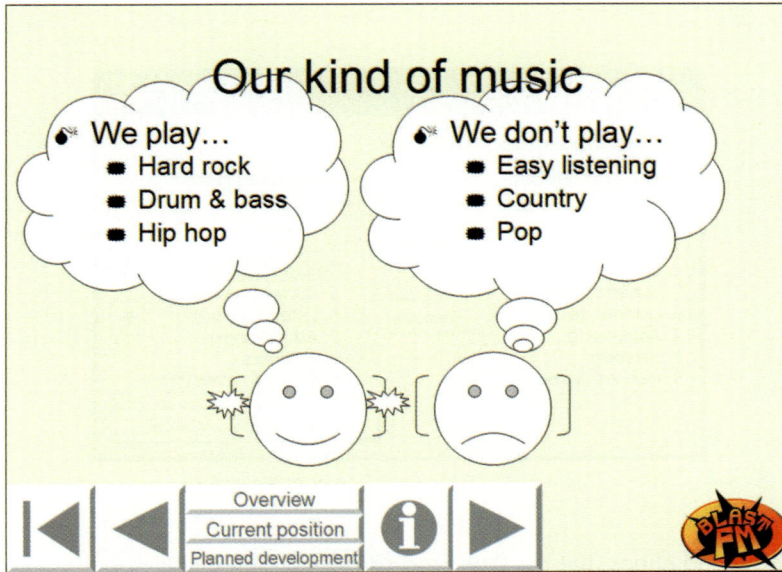

Figure 7.21: Silent copy of the Our kind of music slide

SYLLABUS

Ref: AM6.6.2.2
Edit a customised slide show.

From the main menu, select **Slide Show**, **Custom Shows** to display the **Custom Shows** dialogue box.

With **Blast FM Reception** highlighted, press the **Edit** button. The **Define Custom Show** dialogue box appears.

Select the **Our kind of music** slide from the right-hand list (**Slides in custom show**) and then press the **Remove** button.

Select the new **Our kind of music** slide from the bottom of the left-hand list (**Slides in presentation**) and then press the **Add >>** button.

When you add slides to a customised slide show, they always appear at the end. We need, therefore, to move the new slide up to the location of the old one.

Select the **Our kind of music** slide at the bottom of the right-hand list (**Slides in custom show**) and press the **Up** button repeatedly until the new slide becomes the fourth slide in the presentation. Press **OK**.

Up

Click here to move the selected slide u the list

Figure 7.22: Changing the order of the slides

Press **Show** and check that the **Our kind of music** slide displays without any sound.

Timed transitions

We also need to get the presentation to move automatically from one slide to the next. To do this, you can add timed transitions to the presentation.

SYLLABUS

Ref: AM6.6.1.3
Apply timings to, remove timings from slide transitions.

From the main menu, select **Slide Show**, **Slide Transition**. The **Slide Transition** task pane appears.

Make sure that the **AutoPreview** checkbox at the bottom of the task pane is ticked and then click on a few different transitions to see what they look like.

Select the bottom option (**Random Transition**) from the list of transition types. This will choose transitions randomly between each slide and the next, which will add a bit of variety to the slide show.

In the **Advance slide** section, set the **Automatically after** value to **00:10** (ten seconds). Leave **On mouse click** ticked – it won't do any harm and may be useful for testing. Your task pane should now look like Figure 7.23. Press **Apply to All Slides**.

Figure 7.23: Adding timed transitions

Use **Slide Show**, **Custom Shows** to run the **Blast FM Reception** show. Don't press any buttons – the slide show should play from beginning to end without any interaction. Each slide should be on display for ten seconds (or more in the case of the first slide).

It would be better if the content slides were on display for longer than the orange title slides. This is an easy change to make.

Select any of the title slides and change the **Automatically after** figure down to **00:03**. Press **Apply to Master** – this applies the change to all the slides that share the currently selected master, in this case the orange title master.

Test the **Blast FM Reception** customised show again. This time you should find that the title slides are displayed for only three seconds, but that the other slides remain at ten seconds.

Note!

If you make a change to the **Slide Transition** task pane without pressing either the **Apply to Master** button or the **Apply to All Slides** button, then the transition will apply only to the currently selected slides.

To remove the timings permanently, you can simply untick the **Automatically after** box and apply the change. The following section describes how to turn these timings on and off temporarily (so you can use the same slide show both to run unattended and to present to an audience, manually advancing the slides).

SYLLABUS

Ref: AM6.6.1.5
Apply settings so that slides advance manually, advance using timings if present, so that slide show is presented with animation, without animation.

➡ From the main menu, select **Slide Show**, **Set Up Show**. The **Set Up Show** dialogue box appears.

➡ In the **Advance slides** section, select the **Manually** option, as shown in Figure 7.24. Press **OK**.

Note!

You can use the **Show without animation** box to control whether animated effects occur.

Click here to ignore the slide transition timings

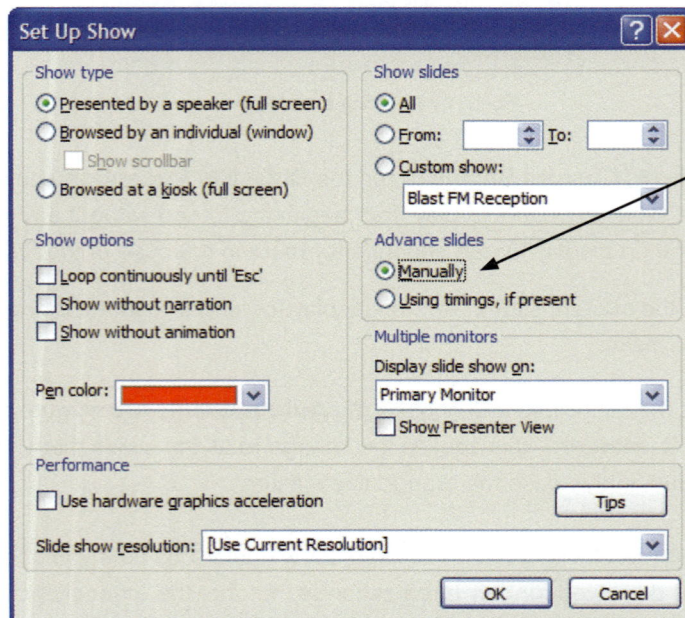

Figure 7.24: Changing the way that slides advance

Run the customised slide show again. This time, there will be no transition between slides until you click the mouse or press **Space**.

Continuous looping

At the moment, the slide show stops when it hits the last slide. We can, however, get PowerPoint to loop back round to the beginning, using the same dialogue box as we used to turn the timed transitions off.

SYLLABUS

Ref: AM6.6.1.4
Apply settings to a slide show so that it loops continuously when played, does not loop continuously when played.

From the main menu, select **Slide Show**, **Set Up Show**. The **Set Up Show** dialogue box appears again.

Tick the first of the **Show options**: **Loop continuously until 'Esc'**.

Change the **Advance slides** option back to **Using timings**, **if present**.

Press **OK** and run the custom show again. Leave it to run, and check that it loops back to the start after playing all the way through. Press the **Esc** key to exit the presentation.

TIP

For presentations that will be running unattended (for example, at a trade show), you can use the **Browsed at a kiosk (full screen)** option to protect against tampering.

Macros

A macro is a named batch of commands that you can play back later. You can program complicated macros from scratch, or create them by recording your actions in PowerPoint.

Here, we'll create a pair of macros that you can use to switch quickly between the manual presentation (a presenter standing in front of an audience and controlling the presentation manually) and the automatic presentation (running on the TV in reception and looping continuously).

First, check that PowerPoint is configured to run macros.

From the main menu, select **Tools**, **Options**. On the **Security** tab, press the **Macro Security** button. The **Security** dialogue box appears, as shown in Figure 7.25. Since you will not be signing your macros, the security level needs to be either **Medium** (recommended) or **Low**. Change the security level, if necessary, and then press **OK**.

Note!

If you use the **Low** setting, you will be more at risk from macro viruses – malicious macro code that replicates itself and infects your documents. These are becoming rarer, but do still exist. Using the **Medium** setting will at least warn you if you are opening a file that contains macros. If you didn't expect there to be any macros associated with the file, you can prevent them from running.

The **High** and **Very High** settings require that the person producing the macro has bought a security certificate and used it to prove that he or she wrote the macro. In practice, this doesn't happen very often, so these settings would, in effect, disallow macros.

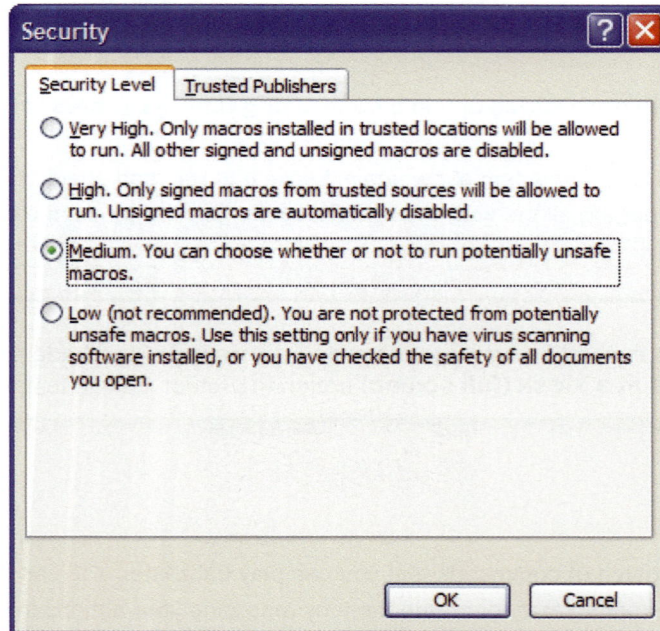

Figure 7.25: Changing the macro security level

Ref: AM6.8.1.1

Record a simple macro such as: animation effects on an image, rescale drawn object, formatting of text.

From the main menu, select **Tools**, **Macro**, **Record New Macro**. The **Record Macro** dialogue box appears. Set the **Macro name** to **ManualDelivery** (you're not allowed spaces in macro names), make sure that **Store macro in** is set to **Investment.ppt** and set a suitable description, as shown in Figure 7.26. Press **OK**.

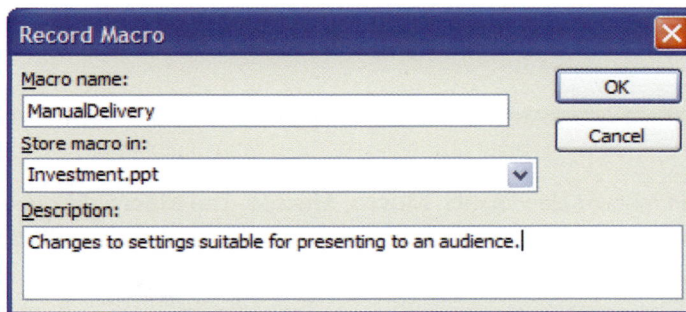

Figure 7.26: Starting to record a macro

From the main menu, select **Slide Show**, **Set Up Show**. Change **Advance slides** to **Manually** and make sure that **Loop continuously until 'Esc'** is not ticked. Press **OK**.

Click the **Stop Recording** button in the toolbar that appeared when you started recording the macro, as shown in Figure 7.27.

Figure 7.27: Stopping recording the macro

Before we test this macro, we'll create the other one.

Start to record a second macro. Call it **AutomaticDelivery** and give it a suitable **Description**, such as **Changes to settings for automatic looping**.

Change the slide show settings so that it loops continuously and uses the automatic timings. It would also be useful to click the **Custom show** option so that the **Blast FM Reception** show is the default (so you can start it by pressing **F5** instead of having to load the **Custom Show** dialogue box).

Stop recording the macro.

Press **F5** to launch the slide show, and confirm that it is currently in 'automatic' mode. Press **Esc** after you have seen the slides transition automatically.

SYLLABUS

Ref: AM6.8.1.2
Run a macro.

From the main menu, select **Tools**, **Macro**, **Macros**. The **Macro** dialogue box appears, containing the two macros, as shown in Figure 7.28. Select **ManualDelivery** and press the **Run** button. The dialogue box closes.

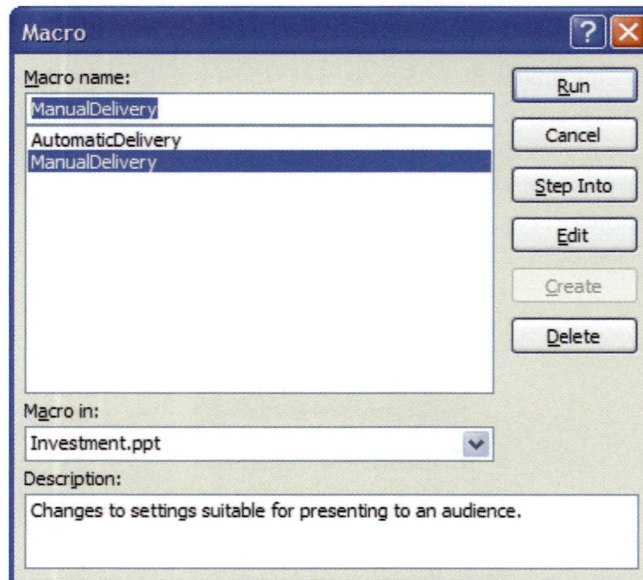

Figure 7.28: Running a macro

Run the presentation and confirm that it is now in 'Manual' mode (the slides do not advance by themselves).

Use the same technique to run the **AutomaticDelivery** macro, and test that the slides do now advance by themselves.

We can create a new toolbar to provide quick access to these macros.

SYLLABUS

Ref: AM6.8.1.3
Assign a macro to a custom button on a toolbar.

Right-click any of the toolbars and then select **Customize** from the menu. The **Customize** dialogue box appears, as shown in Figure 7.29.

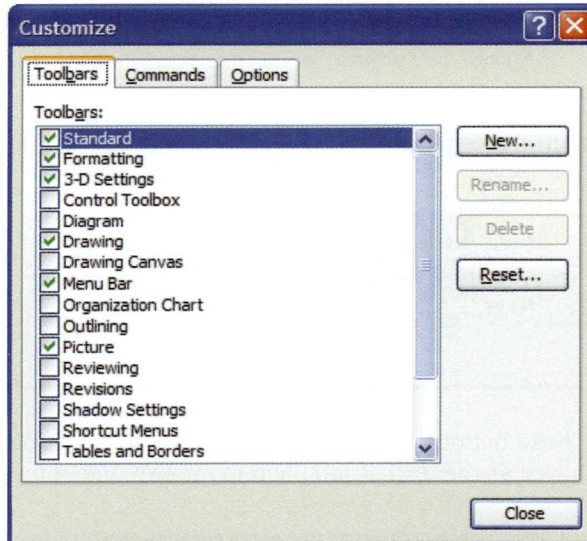

Figure 7.29: The first step in creating a new toolbar

With the **Toolbars** tab selected, click the **New** button on the right-hand side. In the dialogue box that pops up, type the name **Display Mode** and press **OK**. A new empty toolbar appears.

Change to the **Commands** tab and select **Macros** from the **Categories** list. The two recorded macros appear in the **Commands** list.

Drag the **ManualDelivery** macro with the mouse and drop it in the new toolbar, as shown in Figure 7.30.

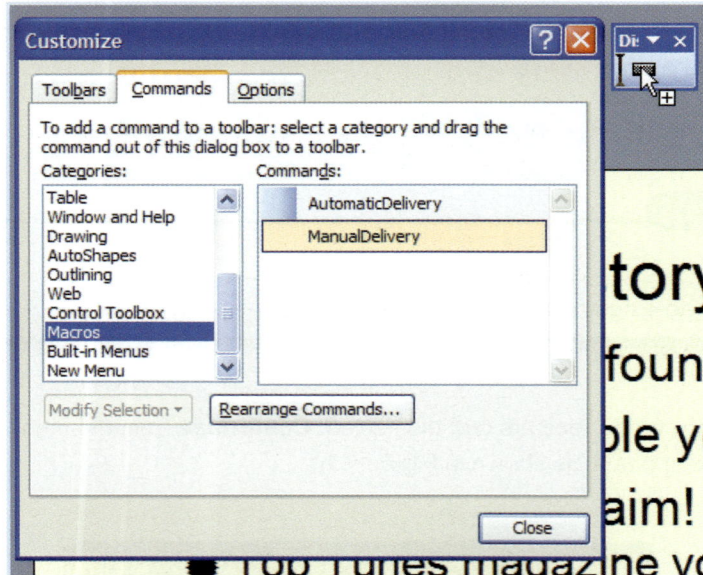

Figure 7.30: Adding a macro to the custom toolbar

Repeat this for the **AutomaticDelivery** macro. After this, your toolbar should look like Figure 7.31.

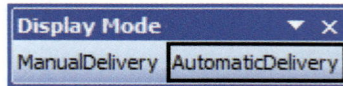

Figure 7.31: The Display Mode toolbar after adding the macros

TIP

You could right-click these buttons to reveal further options (for example, if you want to add icons instead of or as well as the text). If you need to remove one of the buttons, simply drag it off the toolbar.

Click **Close** on the **Customize** dialogue box. The new **Display Mode** toolbar should remain on display.

Test the **ManualDelivery** and **AutomaticDelivery** buttons to check that they do indeed run these macros.

Save your presentation.

Conclusions

This exercise has demonstrated the following points.

- You can press **F5** to view the current presentation from the beginning, or **Shift + F5** to view it from the current slide.

- The easiest way to add interactive buttons to a presentation is to use the **AutoShapes**, **Action Buttons** menu on the **Drawing** toolbar. However, you can right-click any drawing object and use the **Action Settings** option to add interactive content to that object or to change the existing behaviour.

- Select **Slide Show**, **Custom Shows** to access the **Custom Shows** dialogue box. From here, you can define, edit and run customised slide shows.

- Select **Slide Show**, **Slide Transition** to display the **Slide Transition** task pane. From here you can add and remove automatic timed transitions between slides. The **Apply to Master** button changes all slides sharing a master with the current selection; the **Apply to All** button changes all the slide transitions.

- Use **Slide Show**, **Set Up Show** to display the **Set Up Show** dialogue box. The **Advance slides** option controls whether PowerPoint uses any timings you have saved. The **Loop continuously until 'Esc'** option controls whether PowerPoint starts playing again from the beginning after it has displayed the last slide.

- To start recording a new macro, select **Tools**, **Macro**, **Record New Macro** from the main menu. Press the **Stop Recording** button when you have finished.

- To run a macro, select **Tools**, **Macro**, **Macros** from the main menu. Select the macro you wish to run and press the **Run** button.

- To edit a toolbar, right-click any existing toolbar and select **Customize** from the menu that appears. You can then create a new toolbar by switching to the **Toolbars** tab and pressing **New**. You can drag commands from the **Commands** tab to a toolbar – your macros are under the **Macros** category.

Test yourself

Run your **ManualDelivery** macro before starting these questions.

1. Create a customised slide show, called **Accounts**, containing just the **Accounts 2005–2006** slide.

2. Run the **Accounts** customised slide show to check that it works. Try both methods of running the customised slide show: from the **Custom Shows** dialogue box and from the **Menu** button of the playback controls when viewing the main presentation.

3. Change the **Funding Requirements** slide, as shown in Figure 7.32. Select the text **Strong financial growth** and add a link to the **Accounts** customised slide show. Make sure you tick the **Show and return** box, as shown in Figure 7.33.

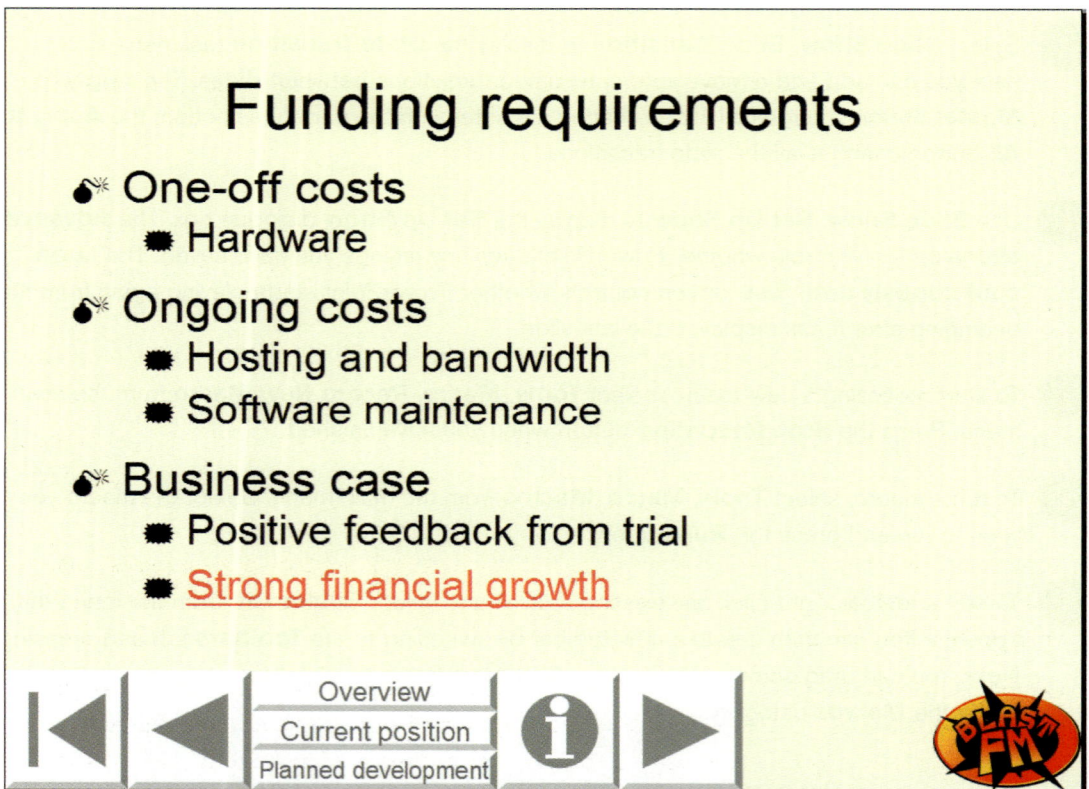

Figure 7.32: Changes to the Funding requirements slide

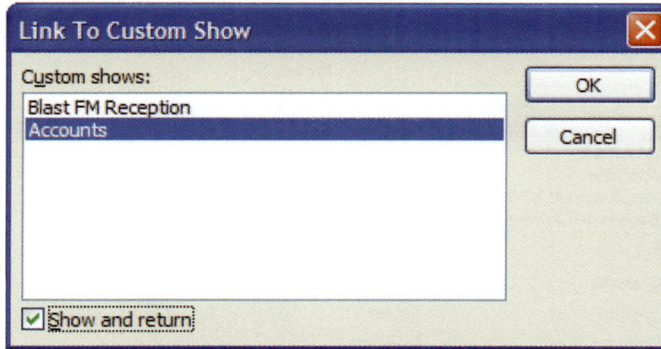

Figure 7.33: Linking to the customised show

> **Note!**
>
> If you didn't want to highlight the fact that there is a link, you could have used a transparent AutoShape placed over the text, as you did for the Blast FM logo link.

4. Edit the slide master and change the URL associated with the transparent oval that you drew over the Blast FM logo. Don't forget to test your change by running the presentation and clicking on the logo.

5. Edit the **Blast FM Reception** customised slide show. Remove the **Funding Requirements** slide. Run the customised slide show to check that this slide no longer appears.

6. Change the timing associated with the content slides down from **10** seconds to **8** seconds. Be careful to use the correct option to change only the content slides, not the title slides (which should remain at 3 seconds).

7. You should have already run your **ManualDelivery** macro before starting these questions. Manually change your presentation's settings so that it loops continuously and uses the timings. Test the result.

8. On the **History** slide, select the text **Blast FM**. Record a macro called **OrangeText** as you use **Format**, **Font** to make the selected text orange (see Figure 7.34). Add the macro to your **Display Mode** toolbar, and use it to change any instances of the text **Blast FM** in your presentation to be orange.

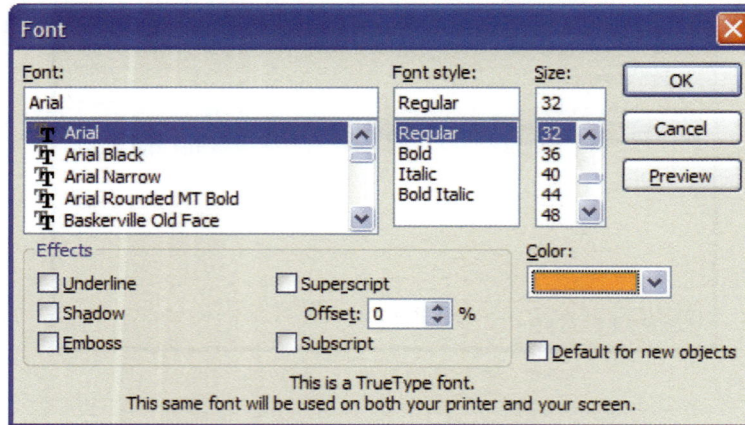

Figure 7.34: Setting the current text to be orange

9. Create a new slide and add any AutoShape to it. Record a macro, called **DoubleSize**, which doubles the selected AutoShape's size (drag the selection handles until it is approximately twice as wide and twice as tall). Add the macro to your **Display Mode** toolbar and test it on a variety of AutoShapes.

8 Linking

Introduction

In this chapter, we will explore the ways in which you can link information created outside PowerPoint into a presentation and have it automatically updated whenever the source information changes.

In this chapter, you will

- create a **link to text** in a Word document from PowerPoint

- create a **link to a range of cells** in an Excel spreadsheet from PowerPoint

- create a **link to a chart** in an Excel spreadsheet from PowerPoint

- **update** and **edit** linked data

- break the link to a linked object so that it becomes an **embedded** picture object

- insert a **linked image** and learn how to update it when the image changes.

Linking from Word to PowerPoint

One of the benefits of the Office suite is the interoperability of the applications. For example, you can create a chart in Excel and embed it in a Word document; and you can create a table in Word and embed it in a PowerPoint presentation.

Let's try this.

SYLLABUS

Ref: AM6.7.1.1
Link text from a document, a range from a worksheet, a spreadsheet generated chart into a slide and display as an object.

Load Microsoft Word. A new blank document should automatically open.

Type the title **Summary of accounts** and, with the cursor on the same line, press **Ctrl + Alt + 1** to change it into a **Heading 1** style.

Press **Enter** twice to create some blank space.

From Word's main menu, select **Table**, **Insert**, **Table**. The **Insert Table** dialogue box appears. Set **Number of columns** to **2** and **Number of rows** to **10**, as shown in Figure 8.1, and then press **OK**.

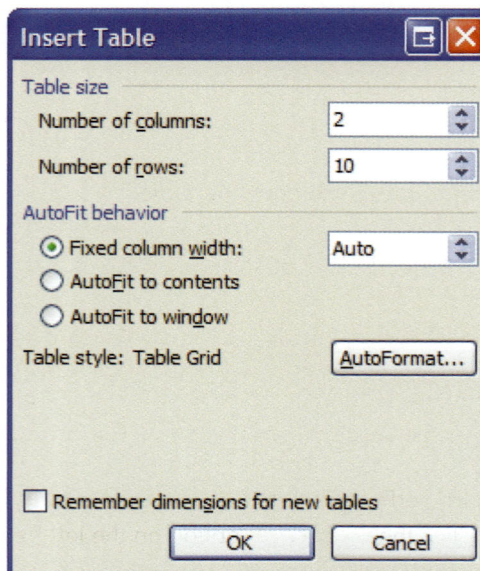

Figure 8.1: Inserting a table

Fill in the table as shown in Figure 8.2.

TIP

Press **Ctrl + Tab** at the start of each of the indented lines. This forces Word to insert a **Tab** character. Pressing just **Tab** on its own will jump to the next cell in the table.

Summary·of·accounts¶

¶

¤	2004–05·(£m)¤
Income¤	¤
→ Advertising·income¤	4.20¤
→ Other·income¤	0.25¤
Expenses¤	¤
→ Staff·costs¤	(1.75)¤
→ New·equipment¤	(0.18)¤
→ Operational·costs¤	(1.40)¤
→ Interest·on·loans¤	(0.05)¤
Gross·[net]·operating·profit¤	1.07·[0.82]¤

¶

Figure 8.2: Table of accounts in Word

Save this document as **Summary of accounts** in the same folder you have been using for your presentations.

Now we'll copy the table to the Windows clipboard.

Click anywhere in the table and use **Table**, **Select**, **Table** to select the table.

Use **Edit**, **Copy** (or press **Ctrl + C**) to copy the table.

Load **Investment.ppt** in PowerPoint if it isn't already open.

Change to the **Accounts 2005–2006** slide and click where it says **Click to add text**.

We could just paste the copied table into the presentation, but then the link with the original document would be broken. We can do better by creating a link.

From the main menu in PowerPoint, select **Edit**, **Paste Special**. The **Paste Special** dialogue box appears. Click the **Paste link** option on the left-hand side (see Figure 8.3), leave **Microsoft Office Word Document Object** selected and press **OK**.

Click here

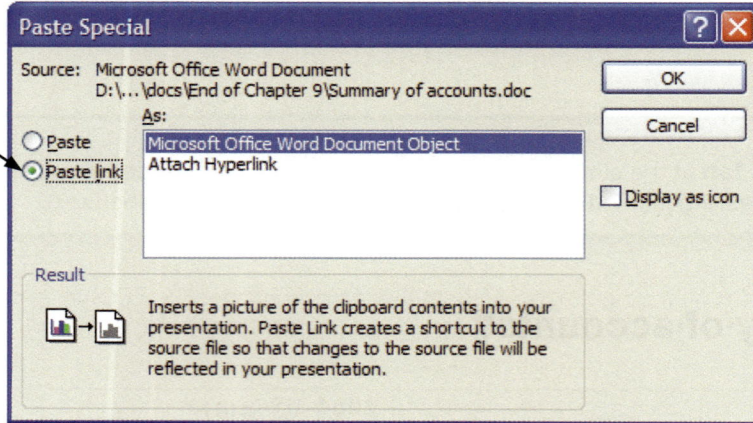

Figure 8.3: Pasting a link

The table should appear in your slide, as shown in Figure 8.4. (You may find that some of the gridlines don't appear because of the scaling – don't worry about this.)

Note!

These links are stored as absolute paths (e.g. **C:\My Documents\file.doc**), so if you move the files the links will break. PowerPoint will warn you when you open a presentation if there are any broken links in it. You can use **Edit**, **Links** to fix them.

Accounts 2005–2006

	2004–05 (£m)
Income	
Advertising income	4.20
Other income	0.25
Expenses	
Staff costs	(1.75)
New equipment	(0.18)
Operational costs	(1.40)
Interest on loans	(0.05)
Gross [net] operating profit	1.07 [0.82]

Overview
Current position
Planned development

Figure 8.4: The linked table in the slide

Use the handles to make the object as large as will fit on the slide, so that it is easier for people to read.

You may have spotted the deliberate mistake – we've inserted the account summary for 2004–05 instead of the one for 2005–06. We need to go back and change the table.

Switch back to Word.

Double-click on the right-hand edge of the table. This sizes the column to fit its contents.

Click anywhere in the right-hand column and then select **Table**, **Insert**, **Columns to the Left** from the menu. A new column appears between the original two.

Fill in the figures for 2005–06, as shown in Figure 8.5.

Summary·of·accounts¶

	2005–06·(£m)¤	2004–05·(£m)¤	¤
Income¤	¤	¤	¤
→ Advertising·income¤	4.85¤	4.20¤	¤
→ Other·income¤	0.60¤	0.25¤	¤
Expenses¤	¤	¤	¤
→ Staff·costs¤	(1.95)¤	(1.75)¤	¤
→ New·equipment¤	(0.55)¤	(0.18)¤	¤
→ Operational·costs¤	(1.70)¤	(1.40)¤	¤
→ Interest·on·loans¤	(0.12)¤	(0.05)¤	¤
Gross·[net]·operating·profit¤	1.13·[0.87]¤	1.07·[0.82]¤	¤

The two grey brackets show that a bookmark has been added around the table so that your link in PowerPoint has something to refer to

Figure 8.5: Updated table of accounts

Without even saving your changes in Word, switch back to PowerPoint. You should find that the linked table has automatically been updated to match, as shown in Figure 8.6. This is the benefit of linking!

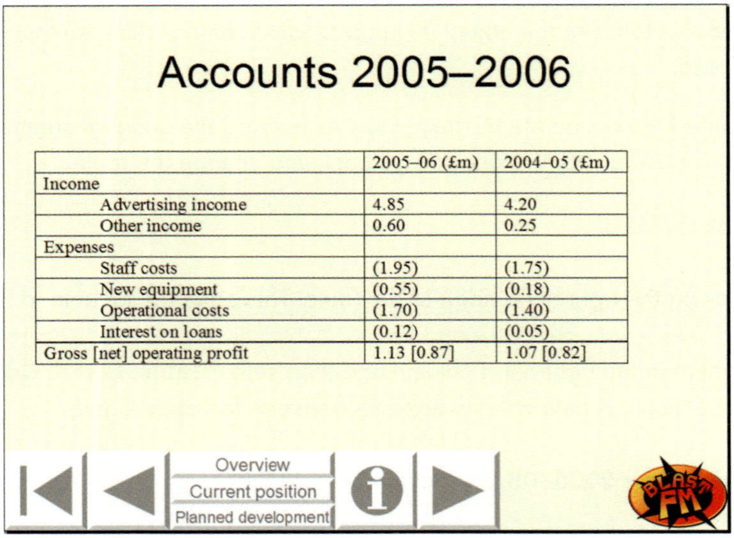

Figure 8.6: PowerPoint has updated the presentation automatically

Switch back to Word. Save and close your document.

Linking from Excel to PowerPoint

The same technique can be used to link Excel data and charts into PowerPoint presentations.

Load Microsoft Excel. A new blank workbook should be created automatically.

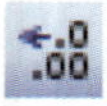

Increase Decimal 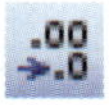   Decrease Decimal

Type in the data shown in Figure 8.7. (Press **Ctrl + B** to set the bold font for the headings; double-click the vertical line in the header between columns **B** and **C** to resize column **B** to fit. To get two decimal places, select **B2:B9** and then press **Increase Decimal** followed by **Decrease Decimal** on the **Formatting** toolbar.)

	A	B	C
1	**Quarter**	**Advertising income (£m)**	
2	Q1 2004	0.85	
3	Q2 2004	1.00	
4	Q3 2004	1.15	
5	Q4 2004	1.20	
6	Q1 2005	0.95	
7	Q2 2005	1.10	
8	Q3 2005	1.30	
9	Q4 2005	1.50	
10			

Figure 8.7: Excel data about advertising income

Click and drag across cells **A1:B9** to select them. Use **Edit**, **Copy** (or press **Ctrl + C**) to copy them.

Back in PowerPoint, change to the slide titled **Advertising**. From the menu, select **Edit**, **Paste Special**. Select the **Paste link** option, as shown in Figure 8.8, and then press **OK**. The worksheet data appears in the slide, much in the same way that the Word data did.

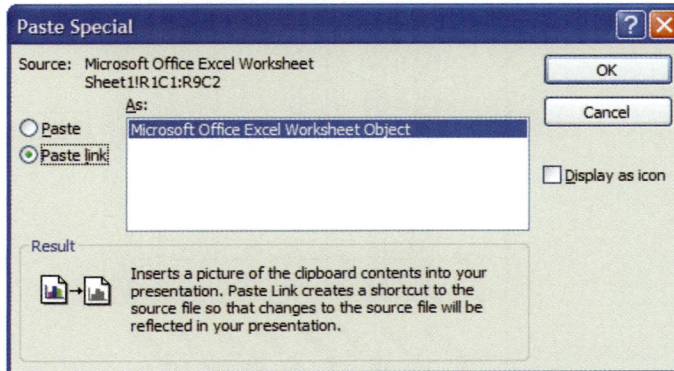

Figure 8.8: Pasting a link to data in Excel

Back in Excel, make sure that cells **A1:B9** are still selected. Use **Insert Chart** to load the **Chart Wizard**, as shown in Figure 8.9. The default column chart will be fine, so just press **Finish**.

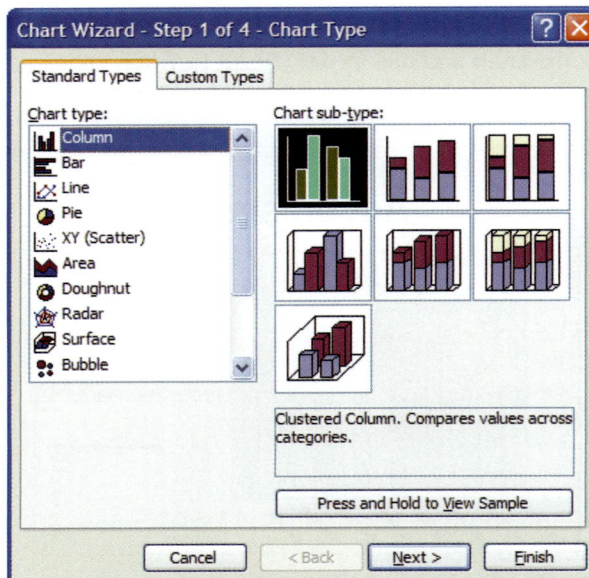

Figure 8.9: Inserting a chart

Your worksheet should now look something like Figure 8.10. Don't worry if the chart looks slightly different.

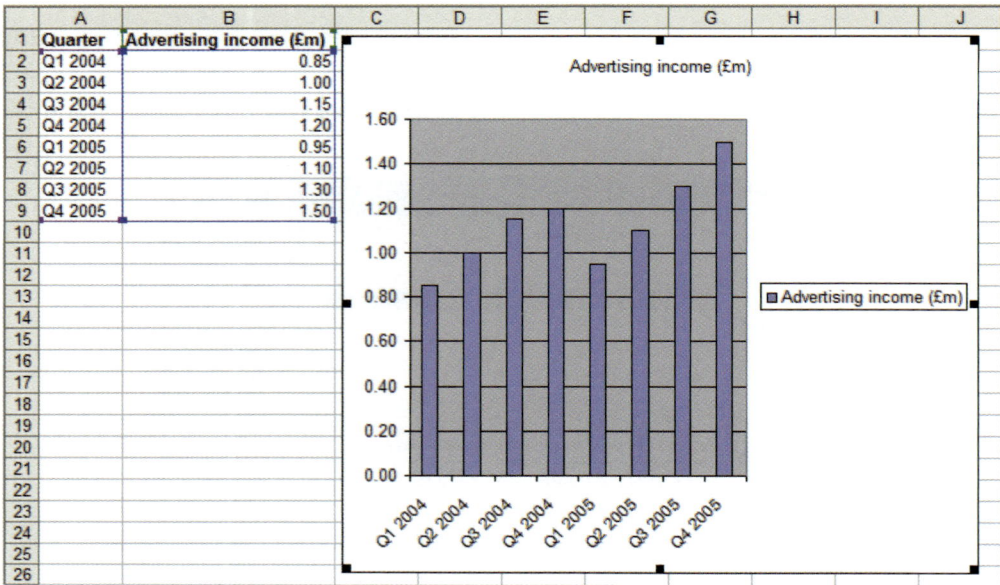

Figure 8.10: The new chart in Excel

Copy the chart from Excel and use **Paste Special** to paste a link to it into PowerPoint, just as you have been doing for the other objects.

Resize and rearrange the objects in PowerPoint so that they look like Figure 8.11. You will need to right-click the chart and use **Order**, **Send to Back**, otherwise it will obscure the other linked object.

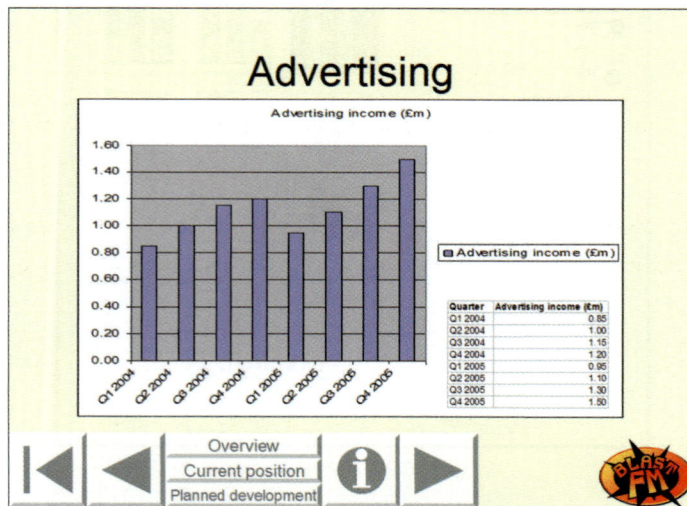

Figure 8.11: Excel objects in PowerPoint

→ Save your Excel worksheet as **Blast FM.xls** in the same folder as **Investment.ppt**.

→ Close Excel completely.

Note!

As with the information linked from Word, any updates made to the linked information will be automatically incorporated into the presentation.

Updating linked data

If you need to modify the underlying data in an object linked to from a presentation, you can simply double-click it to open the linked object. You can then make the necessary changes and they will be reflected in your presentation.

SYLLABUS

Ref: AM6.7.1.2
Update, modify data linked into a presentation.

→ Double-click the worksheet data grid (that is, the two columns of figures) in the bottom right of your slide. PowerPoint tells Excel to open the linked data: **Blast FM.xls**.

→ In Excel, change the first value from **0.85** to **2.0**. Notice that the linked grid in PowerPoint updates, as does the chart in Excel. However, the chart in PowerPoint does not update.

→ Save and close the spreadsheet in Excel.

Back in PowerPoint, the chart and data are out of sync. We need to tell the chart manually to update itself.

→ Right-click the chart object and select **Update Link** from the menu that appears. PowerPoint reads in the updated object from the Excel spreadsheet (Figure 8.12).

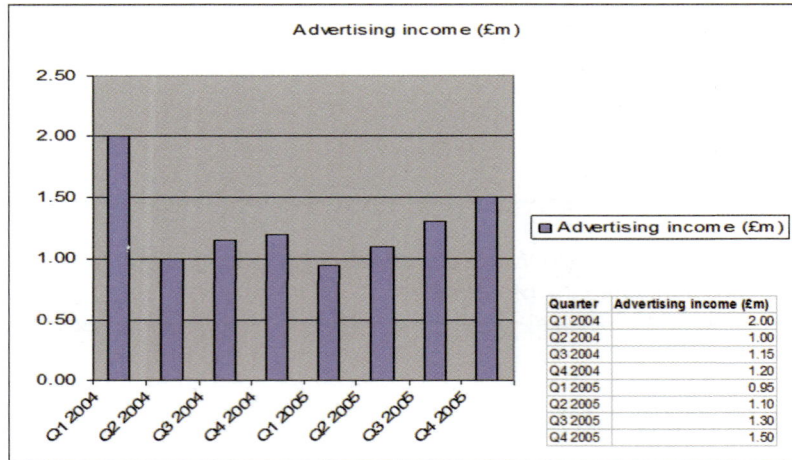

Figure 8.12: Updated chart and data grid

Try this technique again to set the Q1 2004 advertising income back to **0.85**. Don't forget to update the chart.

> **TIP**
>
> If you actually need to change a link so that it points to a different object (for example, if you have moved the target document), then use **Edit**, **Links** and click on the **Change Source** button. However, in the case of a spreadsheet, this will link to the whole of the first worksheet instead of the original object. To reconcile the links you would have to run a macro – see **http://support.microsoft.com/kb/222708/en-us**.

Embedding linked objects

Sometimes it can be useful to break the link so that the object in PowerPoint becomes totally independent. We'll demonstrate this by breaking the link you created on the **Accounts 2005–2006** slide.

> **SYLLABUS**
>
> **Ref: AM6.7.1.3**
> Change a linked object in a slide to an embedded object.

Change to the **Accounts 2005–2006** slide. Remember that the table on this slide is a link to the **Summary of accounts.doc** document.

From the main menu, select **Edit**, **Links**. The **Links** dialogue box appears, as shown in Figure 8.13(a). Highlight the link to **Summary of accounts.doc** and press the **Break Link** button. PowerPoint removes the link, as shown in Figure 8.13(b).

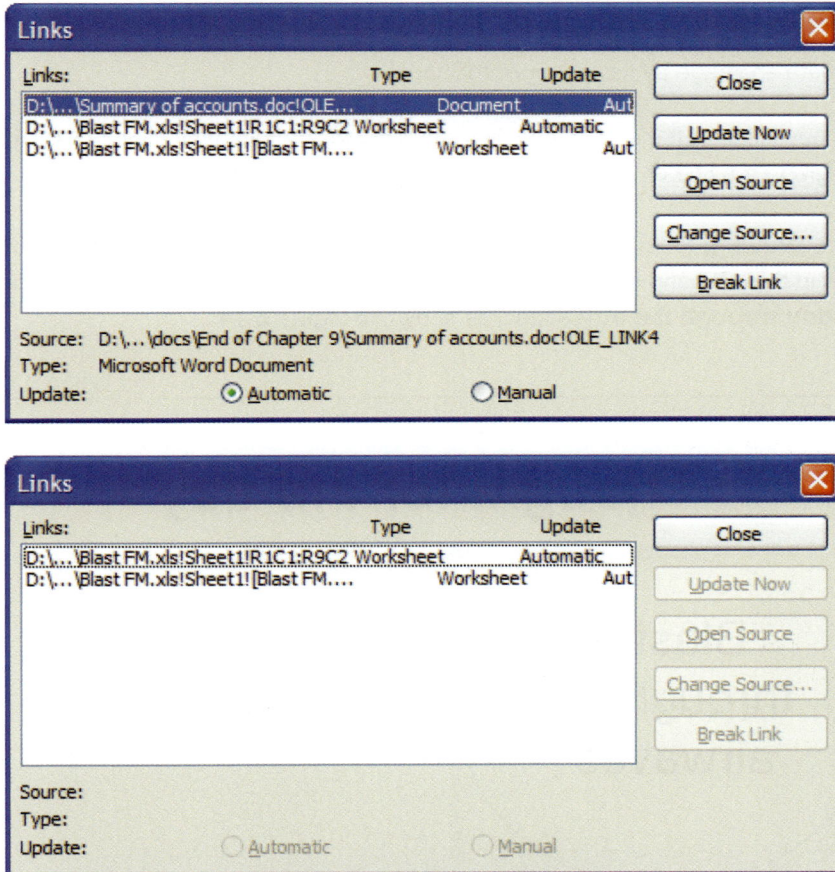

Figure 8.13: Before and after breaking the link

The table in the slide is now just a picture object. You can no longer edit the text. You could, however, edit **Summary of accounts.doc** in Word, changing it as you wish, and **Investment.ppt** would not be affected by the changes.

> **TIP**
>
> If you break the link to a linked object, you just end up with an embedded picture in your document. If you are likely to want to edit the underlying data, then delete the picture, go to the original application, copy the data and paste it into your presentation (just the normal **Paste** instead of **Paste Special**). You will end up with an editable copy of the original, not linked to it in any way. Note that, for spreadsheet data, a copy of the entire workbook will be embedded in your presentation, which may increase its size dramatically.

Linking images to their files

By default, when you insert an image into a presentation, you end up with an embedded copy of the original. Changes to the original image are not applied to the presentation's image unless you manually replace it. However, it's straightforward to link images to their files, although the approach is slightly different from what we have already seen for Word and Excel data.

First, we'll create an image by saving an AutoShape.

Add a new slide at the end of your **Investment.ppt** presentation. Set its **Layout** to **Title Only**, giving it a title of **Thought for the day**.

Use the **Drawing** toolbar's **AutoShapes**, **Callouts** menu to draw a large speech bubble in the left-hand half of the slide. Increase the text size to **36** and then add the text **"Blasting through the airwaves"**, as shown in Figure 8.14.

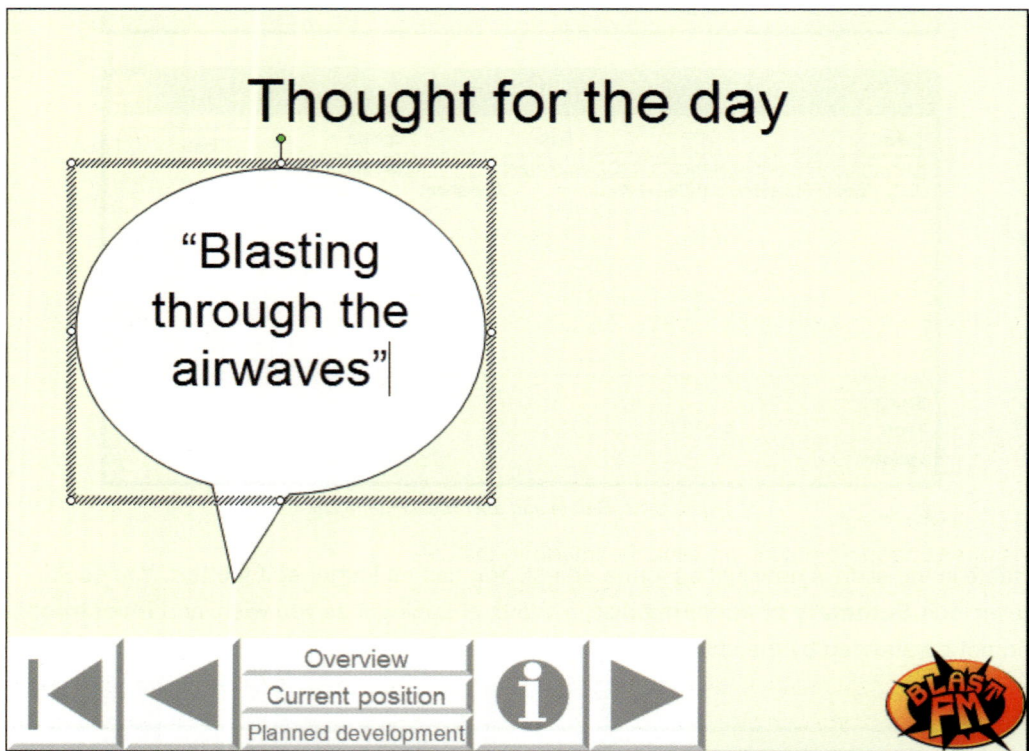

Figure 8.14: Adding text to the thought for the day

Right-click on the border of the speech bubble and choose **Save as Picture** from the menu. The **Save As Picture** dialogue box appears. Change the **Save as type** to **PNG Portable Network Graphics (*.png)**. Navigate to the same file as your presentations and type the **File name** as **Thought for the day.png**, as shown in Figure 8.15. Press **Save**.

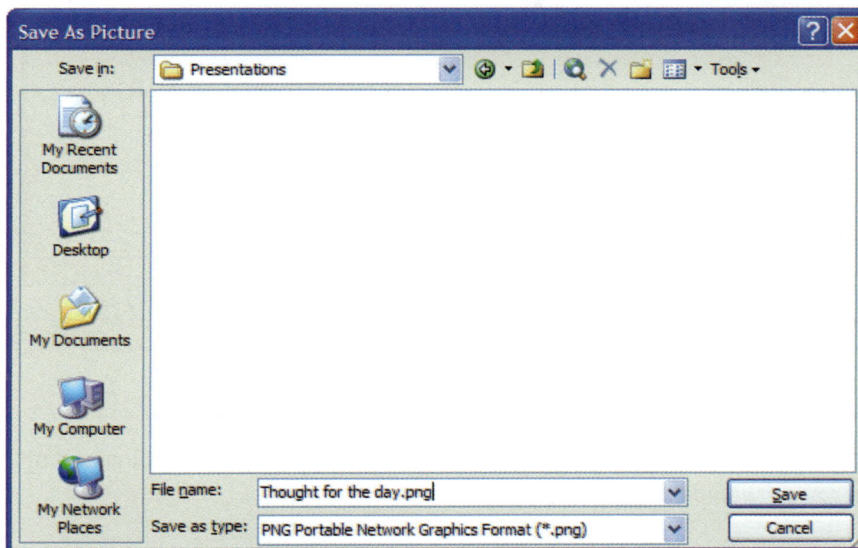

Figure 8.15: Saving the AutoShape as an image

We now have a file called **Thought for the day.png** that you can insert into your presentation as a link.

SYLLABUS

Ref: AM6.7.1.4
Insert an image from a file and link the image to the file.

From the main menu, select **Insert**, **Picture**, **From File**. The **Insert Picture** dialogue box appears. Navigate to your saved **Thought for the day.png** and click on it once to select it. Click on the arrow to the right of **Insert** to reveal another option – **Link to File** – as shown in Figure 8.16. Click on **Link to File**.

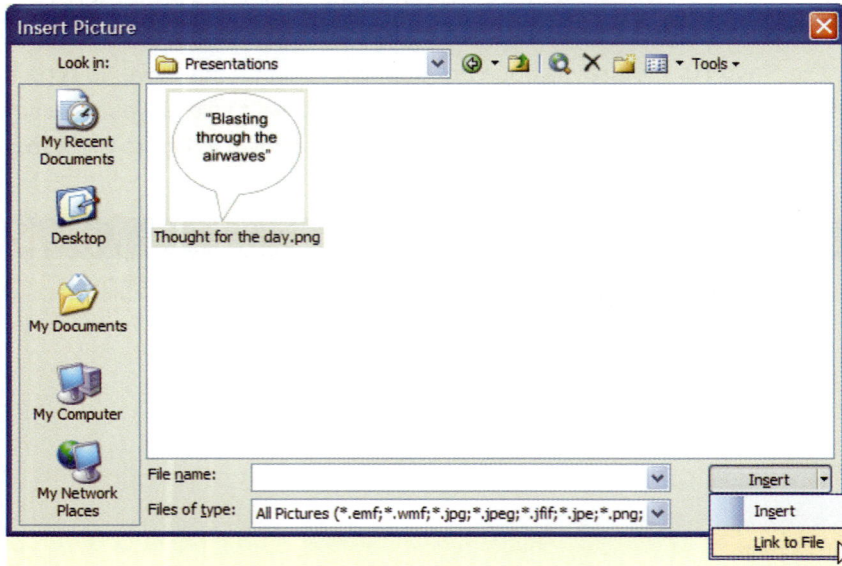

Figure 8.16: Linking to an image file

A linked copy of the image file appears in your slide. If you had used **Insert** instead of **Link to File** then the image would have been embedded.

Note!

It's not at all obvious that the image has actually been linked. It doesn't appear in the list of links you can get to via **Edit**, **Links**. If you right-click on the image, there are no options for updating the image from the linked file.

Change the text in the original AutoShape to be **"Blasting through your ears"**. Save the AutoShape again, using exactly the same format, name and location as before. PowerPoint should warn you about this: press **Yes**, since this is deliberate.

Nothing happens! The linked image on the right-hand side of your slide is unchanged, as shown in Figure 8.17. To update it, you must close and reopen the presentation.

Figure 8.17: Before reloading the presentation

Save and close **Investment.ppt**.

Open **Investment.ppt** again. Depending on your macro security settings, you may get a warning about macros – if so, OK it. You should then get the dialogue box shown in Figure 8.18. Press **Update Links**.

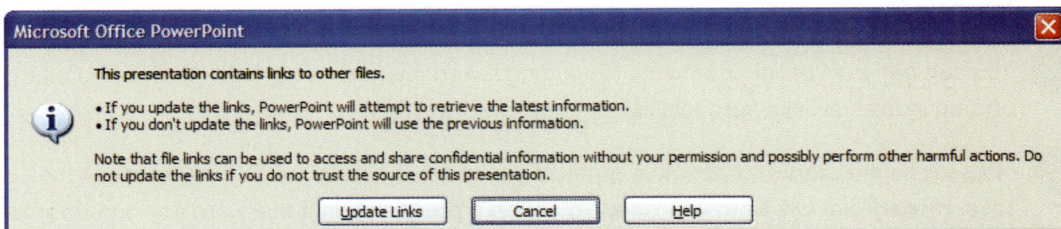

Figure 8.18: Dialogue box from which you can update the links

All the linked items should now have been updated. In particular, your **Thought for the day** slide should now look like Figure 8.19.

Figure 8.19: Proving that the image is indeed linked

Save your presentation again.

Congratulations. That's everything you need to know about linking.

Conclusions

This exercise has demonstrated the following points.

You can copy objects from Word or Excel and then use **Edit**, **Paste Special** in PowerPoint to create links.

You can get a list of linked objects (excluding linked images) using **Edit**, **Links**. You can update individual links from this list.

These links are stored as absolute paths: if you move the files, you're likely to break the links. PowerPoint will warn you when you open a presentation if there are any broken links in it. You can use **Edit**, **Links** to fix them.

Double-click on a linked object to open it for editing.

🛈 Right-click on a linked object and choose **Update Link** to force an update.

🛈 You can use **Edit**, **Links** and press the **Break Link** button to convert a link to an embedded picture object. If you need an editable (non-picture) object, delete the linked object and use **Edit**, **Paste** from the original source.

🛈 To insert a linked image, use **Insert**, **Picture**, **From File** and use the arrow to the right of the **Insert** button to reveal the **Link to File** button. The only way to force these linked images to update is to close the presentation and then open it again.

Test yourself

1. Open your **Blast FM.xls** spreadsheet and create the graph shown in Figure 8.20 on one of the empty worksheets. Link to the chart from the **Listeners** slide in **Investment.ppt**, as shown in Figure 8.21. Save and close **Blast FM.xls**.

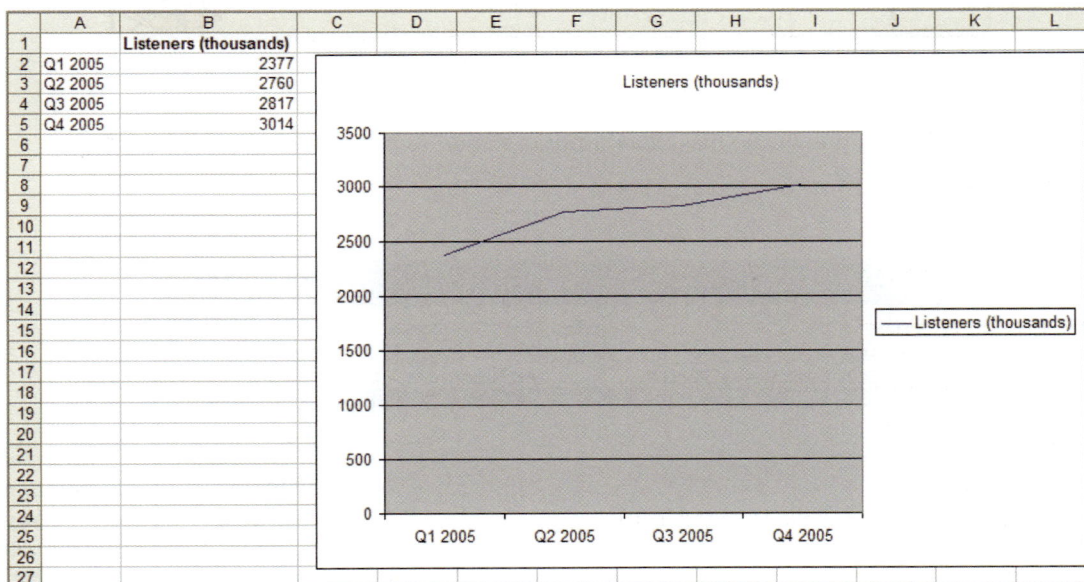

Figure 8.20: Listener numbers spreadsheet

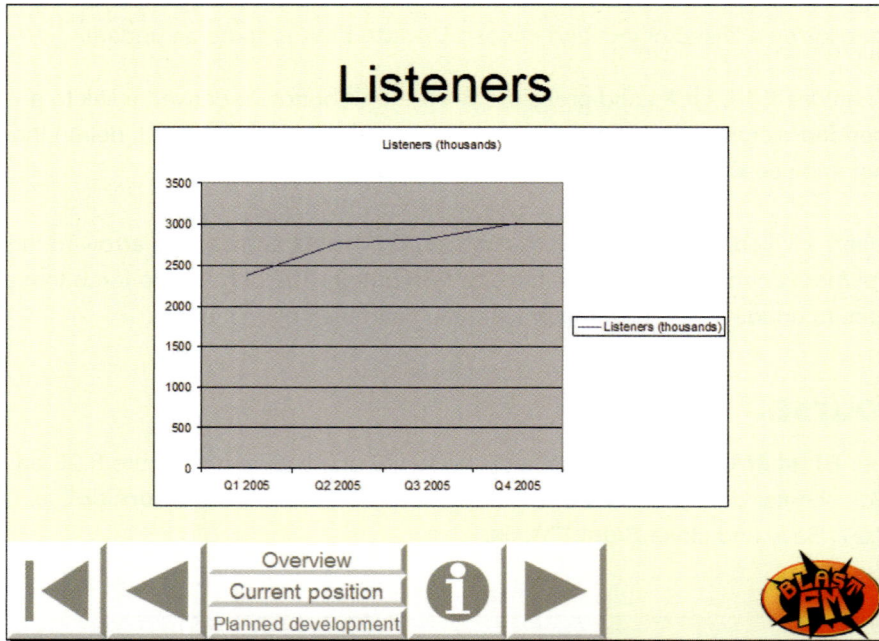

Figure 8.21: The linked chart in PowerPoint

2. Use the **Links** dialogue box to make the **Listeners** chart (on **Sheet 2**) update manually, as shown in Figure 8.22.

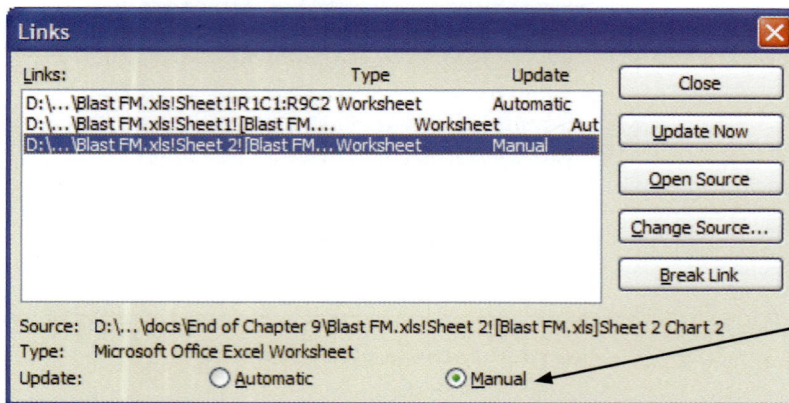

With the chart selected, click here to change it to update manually

Figure 8.22: Setting the Listeners chart to update manually

3. Use the chart in the presentation to open Excel and edit the spreadsheet. Change the **Q2 2005** listener number to **2500**. Save and close **Blast FM.xls**. Manually update the link for the chart in PowerPoint (can you think of two different ways to do this?).

4. Break the link between the new chart and the spreadsheet.

5. Delete the new chart object. Copy the chart again from **Blast FM.xls** and paste it normally into **Investment.ppt**. Double-click the chart to edit it in place, as shown in Figure 8.23. You can click on the tabs at the bottom to edit the worksheet data. Click outside the chart to complete the edit. Save and close **Blast FM.xls**.

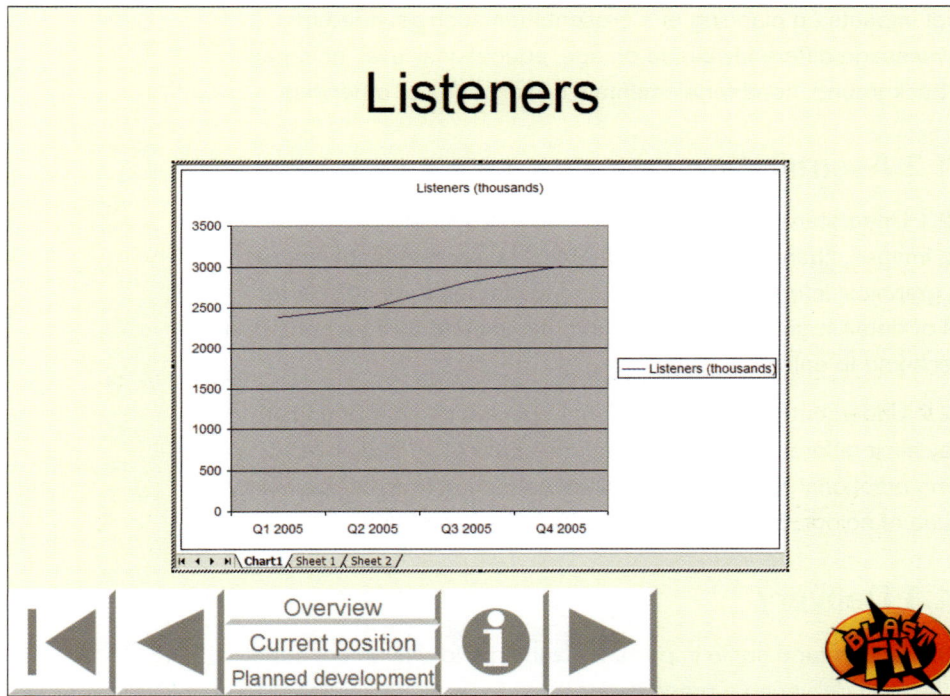

Figure 8.23: Editing a pasted (not linked) chart in place

6. Save your embedded chart as a picture (**Listeners.png**), using its right-click menu. Delete the embedded chart and replace it with a **link** to **Listeners.png**.

Index of syllabus topics

AM6.6.2 Customised Shows

AM6.7.1 Linking

AM6.8.1 Record, Assign [Macros]

Index